REDUCING
GLOBAL
POVERTY

REDUCING GLOBAL POVERTY

The Case for Asset Accumulation

CAROLINE MOSER

Editor

BROOKINGS INSTITUTION PRESS
Washington, D.C.

Library of Congress Cataloging-in-Publication data
Reducing global poverty : the case for asset accumulation / Caroline O. N. Moser, editor.
   p.   cm.
  This volume grew out of the Brookings Institution–Ford Foundation Workshop on
Asset-Based Approaches to Poverty Reduction in a Globalized Context, held in
Washington, D.C., on June 27–28, 2006, led by Caroline Moser and co-hosted by the
Ford Foundation.
  Summary: "Provides a set of case studies of asset-building projects around the globe
aimed at designing and implementing public policies that will increase the capital assets
of the poor. Highlights the ways in which poor households and communities can move
out of poverty through longer-term accumulation of capital assets"—Provided by
publisher.
  Includes bibliographical references and index.
  ISBN-13: 978-0-8157-5857-0 (pbk. : alk. paper)
  ISBN-10: 0-8157-5857-X (pbk. : alk. paper)
  1. Poverty—Developing countries—Congresses. 2. Poverty—Government policy—
Developing countries—Congresses. 3. Poor—Developing countries—Finance,
Personal—Congresses. 4. Developing countries—Social policy—Congresses.
  5. Microfinance—Developing countries—Congresses. I. Moser, Caroline O. N. II. Title.
  HC59.72.P6R427 2007
  339.4'6091724—dc22   2007007720

9 8 7 6 5 4 3 2 1

The paper used in this publication meets minimum requirements of the
American National Standard for Information Sciences—Permanence of Paper for
Printed Library Materials: ANSI Z39.48-1992.

Typeset in Adobe Garamond

Composition by Peter Lindeman
Arlington, Virginia

Printed by R. R. Donnelley
Harrisonburg, Virginia

Contents

v

Foreword

Asset-based approaches in development focus on how the poor use their resource base to develop strategies for acquiring, mobilizing, expanding, and preserving their assets. The asset accumulation approach addresses important shortcomings in income- or consumption-focused poverty reduction strategies by emphasizing the way the poor themselves establish a base of resources under their control. Over time they can mobilize this base to generate income, produce additional resources, and transfer resources across generations to broaden opportunities for their children. Ownership and effective mobilization of assets help establish personal and family security and encourage risk taking and diversification of productive and social activities. By focusing on the resources and capacities of those living in poverty, asset-based approaches address inequality in resource endowments and access to opportunity, providing a concrete way to measure empowerment and ultimately sustainable reduction of poverty.

This volume surveys emerging research projects, policies, and programs from around the world on the topic of asset-based approaches to poverty reduction, and explores efforts and impacts. The volume grew out of a workshop held at the Brookings Institution in the summer of 2006, led by Visiting Fellow Caroline Moser, and includes papers from the key contributors to the field.

In preparation for the workshop at Brookings, Moser developed an updated conceptual review of asset-based approaches that led to participant reflections on the role of assets in a broad set of development strategies and socioeconomic settings. The result is this volume, which goes beyond traditional analysis to explore an expanded agenda for the asset accumulation field, including identifying areas of collaboration with rights-based approaches; linkages with work in settings of entrenched poverty, such as postdisaster and fragile state contexts; and the relation of asset accumulation to key development processes of market expansion and migration.

The Ford Foundation cohosted the conference with Brookings, bringing its expertise from more than a decade of work with poverty reduction programs in the United States and internationally that focuses on asset building and community development. For example, in the United States, the Ford Foundation has shown how building lifelong savings and expanding access to home ownership can reduce poverty. Similarly, work in diverse countries such as India, Indonesia, China, South Africa, Kenya, Mexico, and Guatemala demonstrates how implementing new systems of community forest management can expand the asset base of natural resource–dependent communities and generate sustainable livelihoods. Furthermore, Ford's support of microfinance models in these types of settings and others underscores the importance of access to financial services as another key component of successful asset accumulation and poverty reduction strategies. In sum, these efforts demonstrate the critical role social and economic asset building plays in advancing equity and sustainability as part of poverty reduction.

At Brookings the Global Economy and Development Program explores the asset-based approach to poverty reduction as part of a spectrum of globalization issues. From international trade to global pandemics and environmental challenges, this program examines how the new inputs, outputs, and pressure points of globalization can affect the world's poor and how policymakers should respond based on independent research results, like those detailed in this volume.

Overall, this volume fuses these perspectives and represents an opportunity to stimulate dialogue on poverty reduction and to highlight the importance of a dynamic focus on the participation, resource mobilization, and access to opportunity of those living in poverty.

LAEL BRAINARD
Vice President and Director
Global Economy and Development
Program
Brookings Institution

PABLO FARIAS
Vice President
Asset Building and Community
Development Program
Ford Foundation

Acknowledgments

This book, and the associated research and workshop on which it is based, was undertaken with support from a grant from the Asset Building and Community Development Program of the Ford Foundation. I would like to gratefully acknowledge vice president Pablo Farias for his sustained commitment to and support of the development of this work on asset-based approaches to poverty reduction.

Lael Brainard, Brookings vice president and director of the Global Economy and Development program, gave me the opportunity to undertake this work as a visiting fellow. At the Ford Foundation, Carl Anthony, Frank de Giovanni, Miguel Garcia, and Suzanne Siskell provided invaluable assistance in identifying workshop participants. In addition, I would like to thank Monique Cohen, Michael Carter, Anis Dani, Andrew Felton, Clare Ferguson, Estanislao Gacitua-Mario, Andrew Norton, Alison Scott, Michael Sherraden, and Peter Sollis for their generous support at different stages of this endeavor.

Kathryn Lankester kindly offered essential assistance in organizing the workshop and a complementary one undertaken in Quito, Ecuador. The editorial work of Yvonne Byron Smith, Diane Hammond, and Starr Belsky is gratefully recognized. In the Brookings Institution Press, Janet Walker has been invaluable in negotiating this book through the production process. The dedicated editorial and management assistance of James Pickett throughout the entire process made the completion of this book possible.

Finally, I would like to express my deep gratitude to all of the participants who attended the Brookings Institution–Ford Foundation Workshop on Asset-based Approaches to Poverty Reduction in a Globalized Context, held in Washington, D.C., on June 27–28, 2006. Without their intellectual curiosity, enthusiasm, and operationally focused commitment to address this new concept of asset accumulation policy, it would not have been possible to compile this edited volume.

REDUCING
GLOBAL
POVERTY

1

Introduction

CAROLINE MOSER

As poor communities, policymakers, and politicians all seek to identify new, innovative, and more appropriate policies and strategies for confronting poverty, it is clear that successful reduction solutions are not easily found. This book addresses this challenge by introducing asset accumulation, both as a conceptual framework and as an operational policy to address poverty reduction in a globalized context. In the United States, asset building is already well established as an antipoverty strategy (see Sherraden 1991; Oliver and Shapiro 1990). The Ford Foundation, in particular, has actively supported grantees focusing on community asset building through its Asset Building and Community Development Program (Ford 2004). However, the importance of asset accumulation is far less recognized internationally, particularly in regions of the south such as Africa, Asia, and Latin America.

The objective of this volume, therefore, is to demonstrate the value added by asset-based approaches, for both better understanding poverty and developing appropriate long-term poverty reduction solutions. Since this is a new field, particularly in terms of operational practice, the work presented here does not provide definitive answers; rather, it shares new research conclusions, explores potentially useful operational frameworks, and identifies sectors where asset accumulation strategies resonate, in terms of providing robust solutions to problems of persistent poverty.

Background

This volume draws on two recent initiatives. The first was the completion of a longitudinal research project on intergenerational asset accumulation and poverty reduction in Guayaquil, Ecuador, from 1978 to 2004, which includes the development of an econometric methodology to measure asset accumulation. Linked to this was research focused on asset accumulation policy.[1] The second was the Brookings Institution–Ford Foundation Workshop on Asset-Based Approaches to Poverty Reduction in a Globalized Context, held in Washington, D.C., on June 27–28, 2006.

The workshop employed a methodology developed by Ravi Kanbur (2002) that invites participants to write short, reflective papers in place of the longer, in-depth academic papers more commonly associated with conferences. In the Washington workshop, participants were asked to consider how an asset accumulation policy perspective influenced or affected their work on poverty reduction in terms of research, policy, or operational practice. To assist this process and create a unified framework, a background briefing document was distributed before the workshop.[2] Due to the extensive interest in the topic and liveliness of the debate, sixteen of the papers were selected for publication, all of which have since undergone extensive revision.[3] Nevertheless, they remain true to the original workshop objectives and are therefore short, reflective chapters.

Definitional Issues

It is useful to begin with two brief clarifications. First is the definition of an asset. Generally, an asset is identified as a "stock of financial, human, natural or social resources that can be acquired, developed, improved and transferred across generations. It generates flows or consumption, as well as additional stock" (Ford 2004). In the current poverty-related development debates, the concept of assets or capital endowments is closely linked to the concept of capabilities. Therefore, assets "are not simply resources that people use to build livelihoods: they give them the capability to be and act" (Bebbington 1999). The assets of the poor are commonly identified as natural, physical, social, financial, and human capital.[4]

The second clarification is the distinction between asset building and asset accumulation. In both academic and operational literature, there is widespread confusion and conflation of terminology relating to terms such as assets, livelihoods, and social protection; equally, the distinction between asset building and asset accumulation is not always clear. However, "asset building" is closely associated with the U.S. debate about increasing the state's institutional support for assisting the poor to build assets (Boshara and Sherraden 2004). For this reason this book, and the policy-focused research underlying it, adopts the phrase "asset accumulation" as more appropriate in the development context, where the state's role is much more limited, and the process of acquiring and consolidating assets is not only lengthy but also primarily achieved from the "bottom up" by individuals, households, and communities themselves.

Making the Case for Asset Accumulation Policy

In making the case for asset accumulation policy, this volume addresses the issue through three distinct entry points: first, specific asset accumulation research using an asset index conceptual framework as an analytical and diagnostic tool to understand poverty dynamics and mobility; second, the elaboration of an asset accumulation policy as an operational approach to design and implement sustainable asset accumulation interventions; third, the practice of poverty reduction strategies in a range of specific sector and cross-sector contexts informed by the asset accumulation framework. This introduction outlines some of the salient issues relating to each of these areas, before concluding with a brief discussion of priority themes for further work.

Asset Accumulation Research

The diagnosis of poor communities based on the measurement of their assets, rather than their income or consumption, is not new, but to date such research has not been widely recognized. Equally, the econometric methodology for constructing an asset index is still at an innovative stage. Three chapters in the book describe research that focuses on the accumulation of assets.

The longitudinal research project on intergenerational asset accumulation and poverty reduction in Guayaquil, Ecuador (1978–2004), which formed the background to the project associated with this book, is described by Caroline Moser and Andrew Felton in chapter 2. It uses a fourfold asset index as a diagnostic tool to understand poverty dynamics and mobility. Data come from a twenty-six-year panel data set and associated anthropological fieldwork examining how different capital assets are accumulated or eroded at different times.[5] The project also identifies sequencing in the acquisition of assets; households first invested in housing capital, even though it was not a significant factor in getting them out of poverty, followed by other types of capital, particularly human capital (education) and financial capital. Finally, while community social capital actually fell between 1992 and 2004, household social capital rose.

Today, the adult sons and daughters of the original study participants are better educated but also have higher expectations and face different challenges in a globalized context. Nearly half still live on the family plot and benefit from the assets accumulated by their parents. Others have acquired homes of their own, squatting on the hills that form the city's new periphery. A third group has migrated, primarily to Barcelona, Spain, where the employment opportunities, labor rights, and access to financial capital such as mortgages all contribute to more rapid asset accumulation than that of their peers in Guayaquil. There, increasing alienation, associated with a lack of wage employment opportunities, has resulted in a dramatic rise in violent robbery, theft, and drug dealing. Insecurity and fear predominate in all households. For the current generation, the acquisition of assets may not be enough. Inequality and exclusion are also important issues to address.

In chapter 3 Michael R. Carter complements this research by providing an econometric model to measure a "poverty threshold," defined as the amount of a given bundle of assets a household must have in order to accumulate more assets. Households with assets in quantities below this threshold stand little chance of climbing out of poverty, while households maintaining enough assets to rest just above the threshold risk falling below it in the event of a significant shock, such as a natural disaster or illness. Carter argues that this group should be kept out of poverty through "safety nets." For households already well below the poverty threshold, he proposes "cargo nets" to equip them with enough assets to push themselves above the threshold. Failure to implement either or both policies can result in a self-perpetuating cycle of increasing poverty.

Poverty-focused research focuses almost entirely on how people stay in poverty or on how they get out of it. However, populations include people simultaneously moving into poverty and escaping it. The reasons for the two are different. In chapter 4 Anirudh Krishna uses water running into a bathtub as a metaphor to illustrate this process: just as water is constantly draining out of the tub, it is also filling it up; thus research on poverty should examine not just how people escape poverty but also how they descend into it. Using a participatory "stages of poverty methodology," he highlights the fact that erosion of human capital (relating to ill health and health-related expenses) is the primary cause for households descending into poverty.

Asset Accumulation Policy

The next section of this volume makes the case at the policy level through the elaboration of an asset accumulation policy as an operational approach. Over the past decade, alongside the range of poverty-focused frameworks using similar concepts, such as capabilities, assets, and vulnerabilities, has been the parallel design of new antipoverty programs. Foremost among these in the late 1990s were sustainable livelihoods programs, and more recently, social protection policies, widely adopted due to the influence of the World Bank's *World Development Report* on poverty (World Bank 2000). This then makes it important to clarify how asset accumulation policy differs from or complements other poverty-reduction approaches.

In chapter 5 Caroline Moser provides a detailed introduction to asset accumulation policy. She starts by distinguishing among the primary objectives of three operational approaches. While a sustainable livelihood approach concentrates on sustaining activities required for a means of living, social protection is concerned with providing protection for the poor and vulnerable against negative risks and shocks that erode their assets. Asset accumulation policy differs from both of these approaches since it focuses directly on creating opportunities for the poor to accumulate and consolidate assets in a sustainable way. Important differences in relation to risk can be identified. For social protection, risk is a danger, with risk management strategies designed to defensively reduce or overcome the associated shocks, stresses, and vulnerabilities. By contrast, for asset accumulation policy, risk is an opportunity. Managing such risk is about proactively identifying and investing in opportunities, so the biggest risk is not taking a risk.

The chapter then outlines the components of asset accumulation policy, in terms of an iterative asset-institutions-opportunities nexus, while noting that assets are not static but constantly changing and being revalorized. For this reason it is useful to distinguish between first- and second-generation asset accumulation policy. While first-generation policy provides social and economic infrastructure essential for assets such as human capital, physical capital (housing), and financial capital (durable goods), it does not necessarily provide the precondition for further accumulation. In contrast, second-generation policy is designed to consolidate accumulated assets and prevent erosion though strategies that, for instance, address citizen rights and security, governance, and the accountability of institutions.

In practice, social protection and asset accumulation policies sit at different ends of the same continuum, often complementing one another. In chapter 6 Sarah Cook describes the Ford Foundation–funded social protection program in Asia that seeks to be welfare enhancing while also contributing to growth and efficiency objectives. Although the program does not explicitly adopt an asset-based approach, its initial analysis and framework had a strong focus on various forms of asset accumulation as the underpinning of sustainable development and social protection. The premise of the program argues that assets reduce dependence on social protection, but social protection will remain the dominant and essential element of social policies for poor countries. Social protection needs to be seen as developmental and not just as relief assistance.

Finally, in chapter 7 Andrés Solimano also emphasizes the significance of a "continuum" from social protection to asset accumulation policies in Latin America. Citing the increasing inequality in the region, he identifies the importance of building a stronger middle class through better access to assets, such as education and housing, as well as through financial capital linked to small and medium-sized enterprises. Such interventions are essential to democratize traditionally elitist Latin American societies and ensure political stability in the region.

Asset Accumulation in Specific Contexts and Sectors

The practice of asset accumulation strategies in a number of "sector" and "cross-sector" contexts is informed by the underlying research and policy framework briefly outlined above. Several chapters specifically illustrate the usefulness of the framework in different fields and explore the links between them.

Communal assets constitute a broad sector that includes housing, human settlements, and natural resource management in both rural and urban contexts. These sectors are clearly distinct from one another but nevertheless share a common theme: the increasing importance of communal or collective—as opposed to individual—agency. For example, housing is clearly of great importance to poor families. The Guayaquil study found that while accumulating housing itself as an asset does not pull families out of poverty, it is a prerequisite for the assets that do.[6] Cook reaches similar conclusions in Asia while Solimano concludes more broadly that although Latin Americans place great importance on housing, the lack of land titling impedes the use of housing as collateral.[7]

Like housing, natural resources represent an asset that has the potential to generate income and pull households out of poverty, but it is one that is found predominantly in the rural context. In chapter 8 Paula Nimpuno-Parente illustrates the ways in which communities can assert ownership of tourist enterprises, thereby not only leveraging their natural assets to pull themselves out of poverty but protecting the environment as well.

Postdisaster and fragile states expose households to extreme risks and vulnerability, often leading to large-scale erosion of assets. In contexts such as these, an asset framework is useful not only to evaluate different strategies to protect assets but also for asset reconstruction. For instance, in chapter 9 Lilianne Fan describes asset rebuilding in Aceh, Indonesia. Thirty years of armed conflict had left the region's population destitute, and after the tsunami in late 2004, their plight only worsened. However, because an extensive area of land, with its associated housing, was permanently submerged, opportunities arose for the redistribution of certain assets, such as land rights, in a manner more equitable than before the disaster.

Amy Liu examines an equally severe catastrophe in chapter 10. As in Aceh, before Hurricane Katrina the situation in New Orleans was abysmal, and the disaster eroded the few assets that the poor, especially the African American community, already possessed. Elderly homeowners—asset rich and cash poor—were particularly hard hit. Social capital, as well as capital invested in transportation, was devastated. Nevertheless, as in Aceh, reconstruction provided an opportunity to fix many of the inequalities that predated the storm.

In fragile or failing states, personal insecurity can have important implications for asset accumulation. Nicaragua, for instance, epitomizes a postconflict context where many assets have been eroded. In chapter 11 Dennis Rodgers describes how violence has become a strategy for accumulating different types of assets. Initially, gangs accumulated "positive" social capital, bringing a form of stability to the local community in a highly unstable society. However, over time, they have shifted toward accumulating the "negative" financial capital associated with the drug trade. In this context asset accumulation is not necessarily a positive sum gain.

Financial assets are crucial both in themselves and for the accumulation of other assets, contends Vijay Mahajan in chapter 12. He identifies savings as crucial for asset accumulation, perhaps even more so than microcredit. Because the poor view microcredit as a liability, not an asset, they are often reluctant to take advantage of services provided by microfinance practitioners. He also advocates microinsurance as protection for the poor against shocks and argues that microfinance packages should be customized to the needs of poor communities, based on these trends as well as local factors.

In chapter 13 Monique Cohen and Pamela Young support Mahajan's contention that microinsurance is vital to effective development. She identifies health shocks as one of the single most prevalent causes of descent into poverty. Mahajan mentions that in India nongovernmental organizations are already taking these findings into account by providing comprehensive strategies in which microcredit is only one component, and savings and insurance products figure prominently.

The impact of international migration on asset accumulation is discussed in three chapters. In chapter 14 Manuel Orozco argues that migration is one of the most successful strategies the poor employ for accumulating assets. Migrants increase direct involvement in economic and social activities in their home communities by, for example, capital investment, remittance transfers, and charitable donations. Héctor Cordero-Guzmán and Victoria Quiroz-Becerra elaborate these points further in chapter 15, stressing that migration is a two-way process. For instance, migrants often set up travel agencies and money transfer businesses that facilitate asset building, both in the destination country and country of origin.

In chapter 16 Sarah Gammage argues that there are also negative aspects associated with migration. Sending people to the United States from Central America, for instance, often involves taking out large loans or the promise of labor as payment (essentially amounting to indentured servitude). In such cases migration is a high-risk investment whereby families jeopardize their very well-being to send a few family members abroad in pursuit of a better life.

Although to date the relationship between human rights and assets has not been widely addressed, a rights framework provides the basis for analyzing the links between power relations and asset accumulation. In chapter 17 Clare Ferguson, Caroline Moser, and Andy Norton argue that political capital can be considered an asset in its own right—one that encapsulates agency and the political capability to pursue rights. Furthermore, they argue that human rights can be classified according to the types of assets they represent. Thus rights protecting property are tied to physical capital, the right to education is tied to human capital, and citizenship rights are tied to social capital. Similar to Amartya Sen's concept of entitlements (Sen 1981), rights are essentially resources that can be accumulated and used to get out of poverty by empowering citizens to struggle for improvements in their circumstances.

Themes for Future Work

As emphasized earlier, this volume is intended to open up a dialogue on the applicability and usefulness of an asset accumulation framework. As such, it is intended to raise questions rather than provide definitive solutions. This introduction concludes by identifying issues requiring further research and policy elaboration to enhance the asset accumulation framework, both in theory and practice.

An important debate concerns the appropriateness of generic "one size fits all" accumulation policies, as opposed to context-specific tailoring of interventions. For instance, it is not clear whether the importance of housing as the first-priority asset accumulated by the poor (and a prerequisite for the accumulation of other assets) is context specific or widespread. Therefore, while broadly applicable "universal" principles are important, the context-specific determinant of specific interventions requires additional identification.

Prioritization or triage in interventions among different poor groups is another critical policy issue. For example, if there is a "poverty threshold," as Carter contends in chapter 3, does it make more sense to help the most destitute or those who are close enough to the threshold that they are able to better use assistance to pull themselves out of poverty and continue to accumulate assets? The fact that programs need to target populations raises a "moral question": should assistance be given to the most desperate or to those who will be most helped by aid? Policymakers often face important ethical decisions relating to the difference between "triage" (assisting those more able to help themselves through "productive safety nets"), or supporting the "worst" cases first through social protection safety nets for the poorest. Here, additional asset-focused research can assist in identifying which of the policies available works best.

Often, increasing returns to assets are yielded by structures and institutions that go beyond households and are based on collective or group agency, as well as "new" capital assets. In chapter 5 Moser identifies the importance of thinking "outside the box" and moving beyond the five well-established capital assets. In chapter 17 Ferguson and colleagues discuss the links between human rights and political assets. As the value of additional assets is recognized, their grounding in empirically measured research becomes even more important.

Asset accumulation is a dynamic process and one that changes substantially over time.[8] It requires distinguishing between different generations of asset accumulation strategies, as well as constantly revalorizing the assets acquired. In addition, because of the interconnections between different assets in the portfolios of the poor, the effect of a program targeted to one asset may be misleading in terms of its poverty-reduction impact. All these issues call for further research on asset accumulation strategies, including the examination of time, generations, and the interconnectedness between different assets.

One noted limitation is the lack of specific identification of the gendered nature of asset accumulation. Yet it is recognized that men and women, starting with similar asset portfolios, appear to utilize them differently. For instance, imbalances between women's and men's political capital mean that their power to accumulate assets differs. This means asset accumulation-related interventions specifically targeted to women are needed. These include safety from physical abuse and access to divorce, alimony, family planning materials, education, and inheritance.

These suggestions for further research represent a few of the many important questions facing those working in this area. The chapters presented in this volume are intended to provide an introduction for those who are interested in this new cutting-edge focus on poverty reduction—at the research and policy level—and who will undoubtedly identify further issues of importance.

Notes

1. This includes a review of Assets, Livelihoods and Social Policy (see Moser 2007), commissioned by the World Bank's Social Development Department for their conference on New Frontiers of Social Policy: Development in a Globalizing World, held at Arusha, Tanzania, December 12–15, 2005.

2. See chapter 5 for a more recent version of this paper.

3. Before the workshop, some papers—for instance, by Augusta Molnar and David Satterthwaite—were already committed to a forthcoming publication based on the World Bank's Arusha conference (see note 1), and therefore they could not be included here. However, all of the original twenty-two conference papers are available on the public website, along with PowerPoints and the workshop agenda. See www.brookings.edu/global/assets06/conference.htm (December 2006).

4. For a more detailed explanation of these categories, see Moser, chapter 5 in this volume.

5. This combined research methodology is called "narrative econometrics" (see Moser and Felton 2006).

6. See Moser and Felton, chapter 2.

7. See chapters 6 and 7, respectively.

8. See chapter 5.

References

Bebbington, Anthony. 1999. "Capitals and Capabilities: A Framework for Analyzing Peasant Viability, Rural Livelihoods and Poverty." *World Development* 27, no. 12: 2021–44.

Boshara, Ray, and Michael Sherraden. 2004. *Status of Asset Building Worldwide*. Washington: New America Foundation Asset Building Program.

Ford Foundation. 2004. *Building Assets to Reduce Poverty and Injustice*. New York.

Kanbur, Ravi, ed. 2002. *Qual-Quant: Qualitative and Quantitative Methods of Poverty Appraisal*. Delhi: Permanent Black.

Moser, Caroline. 2007 (forthcoming). "Assets and Livelihoods: A Framework for Asset-Based Social Policy." In *Assets, Livelihoods and Social Policy*, edited by Caroline Moser and Anis Dani. Washington: World Bank.

Moser, Caroline, and Andrew Felton. 2006. "The Construction of an Asset Index: Measuring Asset Accumulation in Ecuador." Paper presented at workshop on Concepts and Methods for Analyzing Poverty Dynamics and Chronic Poverty. University of Manchester, October.

Oliver, Melvin, and Thomas Shapiro. 1990. "Wealth of a Nation: A Reassessment of Asset Inequality in America Shows at Least One Third of Households Are Asset-Poor." *American Journal of Economics and Sociology* 49, no. 2: 129–51.

Sen, Amartya. 1981. *Poverty and Famines: An Essay on Entitlement and Deprivation*. Oxford: Clarendon Press.

Sherraden, Michael. 1991. *Assets and the Poor: A New American Welfare Policy*. Armonk, N.Y.: M. E. Sharpe.

World Bank. 2000. *World Development Report 2000/2001: Attacking Poverty*. Washington: World Bank.

PART I

Lessons from Research

2

Intergenerational Asset Accumulation and Poverty Reduction in Guayaquil, Ecuador, 1978–2004

CAROLINE MOSER AND ANDREW FELTON

This chapter focuses on the relationship between long-term changes in income poverty and asset accumulation. The use of longitudinal data here varies from the usual short-term, "snapshot" approach to collecting data on poverty, while the focus on asset accumulation complements the more common income and consumption measures of changing poverty levels. The chapter draws on the results of a research project that analyzes how, over the past twenty-six years, poor households in a low-income community in Guayaquil, Ecuador, have struggled to accumulate assets and get out of poverty.

A "narrative econometric" methodology, combining econometric measurements of change with anthropological narratives, is used to identify the social relations and associated causality underpinning economic mobility. First, changes in household income poverty are measured over the twenty-six-year

Caroline Moser would like to acknowledge Emma Torres and all the families in the Guayaquil community, whose trust and support over the past twenty-six years have been invaluable and without which this study could not have been undertaken. The latest phase of this project has been supported by the Ford Foundation, New York. Particular thanks go to Pablo Farias. Thanks also go to Michael Carter as adviser to the project and to Carol Graham, Caren Grown, Jesko Hentschel, John Hoddinnott, Deepa Narayan, and Michael Woolcock for their guidance during this phase. Finally, sincere thanks go to Peter Sollis, whose constant support is gratefully recognized.

period. Then an asset index is used to track the accumulation of capital assets—human, social, financial-productive, and physical—over the same period. This is followed by an examination of the relationship between income poverty and asset accumulation, and the link between household assets and income mobility is explored. While identifying how the asset accumulation choices of the first generation have affected the second generation, the analysis also shows how asset accumulation patterns differ between generations.

This research shows that for the majority of households, the most common route out of poverty is a gradual accumulation of a range of assets as opposed to a dramatic change based on one asset. Moreover, trade-offs between investments in different assets can influence poverty outcomes.

Analytical Framework: Asset Accumulation and Poverty

Longitudinal analysis of changing household income poverty levels identifies who remains stuck in poverty, who gets out of poverty, and who falls back into poverty. It can also identify why some households are more economically mobile than others. However, one aspect, often neglected in such studies, is the role of asset accumulation over time. Can an understanding of this issue provide a better insight into how households escape poverty? To what extent is asset accumulation associated with income mobility? What are the implications for asset-based poverty reduction strategies? Answering these questions requires a framework that can examine how stocks of assets change over time, the contribution of different assets to household mobility, and their relationship to income poverty.

As a result of Amartya Sen's work (1981) on famines and entitlements, concepts such as capital assets, capabilities, and livelihood security are increasingly used to analyze the risks and vulnerabilities of the poor (see World Bank 2000). Identifying how the poor cope with short-term shocks, as well as with longer-term exigencies, through mobilizing their entitlements or assets helps in understanding well-being. The more assets people have, the less vulnerability and insecurity they experience in the face of risks, insecurity, and violence; the more their assets are eroded, the greater their vulnerability (Moser 1998). To achieve positive livelihood outcomes, no single category of assets is sufficient on its own (Department for International Development 2000). This is particularly true in the case of poor people who are challenged with managing complex asset portfolios. The five most important capital assets of the poor are physical, financial, human, social, and natural capital (Carney 1998; Chambers and Conway 1992; World Bank 2000).[1] In this study four of these five essential elements are combined to form an asset index that is used to examine changes in asset ownership over time.

Narrative Econometrics and Natural Experiments

The research methodology combines anthropological and sociological fieldwork undertaken over the past twenty-six years in Indio Guayas, a poor urban community in Guayaquil, Ecuador. Along with anthropological participant observations, the sociological surveys include a panel data set of fifty-one households revisited and interviewed (with the same questionnaires) in 1978, 1992, and 2004 (see appendix table 2A-1).[2] While these households, comprising more than 600 individuals, are the primary unit of analysis, they are not necessarily representative of the dynamics of individual members, whose personal narratives are often unique.

According to the data, half the second generation (the children of the original settlers) still live on the family plot while the rest live in other areas of Guayaquil, other cities in Ecuador, or abroad (see appendix table 2A-2). The panel data were enhanced by an additional survey of forty-six adult sons and daughters who had left the family plot by 2004 but were still living in Guayaquil in 2005 (representing a 24 percent attrition rate). Finally, a survey was conducted of sons and daughters who had migrated to Barcelona, Spain; this survey was extended to include other migrants from Indio Guayas and nearby barrios.[3]

The data analysis builds on earlier cross-disciplinary combined methodologies (Sollis and Moser 1991a; Kanbur 2002; Hulme and Toye 2006) and introduces a methodology called "narrative econometrics."[4] This combines statistical analysis with both in-depth anthropological, fieldwork-based narrative and associated analysis of the socioeconomic power relationships within households and communities that influence well-being.[5] The near-identical circumstances of the households at the beginning of the study provided the conditions for a "natural experiment."[6] More than 80 percent of households fell below the income poverty line; two-thirds of households were nuclear families; the average household size was 5.96; the average age of children was seven years; and the average number of working members per household was 1.59. Adults had little education, few assets, and the same amount of land provided by the government. Over time, however, this population became more differentiated in terms of poverty levels and asset ownership. This made it possible to analyze patterns of income mobility and asset accumulation and the relationship between them.

The neighborhood of Indio Guayas, named after its community committee, is an eleven-block area (*manzana*) in Cisne Dos, one of a number of neighborhoods (*barrios*) in the parish (*parroquia*) of Febres Cordero, a working class suburb (*suburbio de clase popular*) in Guayaquil. Cisne Dos is located in the south-west edge of the city, about seven kilometers from the central business district, with Indio Guayas at the far end of the parish, running up to one of the estuaries (or *estero*) of the River Guayas. The area is bounded by two wide "artery" roads, *Calle* (street) 25 and Calle 26, and stretches from Calle F to Calle Ñ. In the early 1970s, when the first "homeowners" arrived in the area, it was a water-logged mangrove swamp, which professional squatters sold off as 10- by 30-meter plots (*solars*) to settlers anxious to escape high rents in the inner city. The young population survived living on the water and lacked not only land but all basic services such as electricity, running water, and plumbing, as well as social services such as health and education.

Many of the families that settled on Calle K, in the middle of Indio Guayas, were remarkably similar. Susana, a dressmaker, and her husband Julio, a tailor, were among the first to arrive with their two young daughters. Susana became president of the local self-help committee. Josefina and her husband Victor, a builder, and their three children soon settled beside her. On the other side of the wooden walkway (*puente*) were three other young families. Maria and her husband Francisco, another tailor (but also an informal dental "mechanic" [technician]), and their two young children moved in directly opposite Susana. To the left of Maria lived Anna, a laundrywoman, and Darwin, a skilled builder, and their three daughters. Margarita and Hector and their four children lived on the other side. Among others settling nearby was Cristina, another washerwoman, who lived four doors down from Susana. A thirty-six-year-old single mother with seven children, she was somewhat atypical. A few doors away in the other direction from Susana were two brothers, Manuel and Pedro, both tailors. Manuel and his wife Lorena had two sons; two doors down from them was the bachelor household of Pedro. He would later marry Carolina and have three children.

Despite minor differences between households in terms of family size and marital status, these neighbors were surprisingly similar in age, life cycle, household structure, and professions. The men were craftsmen—tailors or builders—and the women were domestic servants, washerwomen, or dressmakers. Both men and women were also involved in informal sector retail selling. In these early days, they had to make their own way economically. They lived in bamboo houses, connected by perilous walkways, without land, roads, running water, lighting, or sewerage. However, over time, the community mobilized national and local government authorities, as well as political parties, and acquired basic infrastructure.

By 2004 Cisne Dos (within which Indio Guayas is located) was a stable urban settlement with an estimated 75,364 established inhabitants.[7] It had

Table 2-1. *Distribution of Household Poverty Status in Indio Guayas, 1978–2004*
Percent

Poverty category	1978	1992	2004
Very poor	51.0	56.8	31.4
Poor	33.3	31.4	29.4
Nonpoor	15.7	11.8	39.2
Total	100.0	100.0	100.0

Source: Authors' calculations.

physical and social infrastructure, and due to the city's rapid expansion, it was no longer on the periphery. Children of the original settlers had formed families of their own, either in the community or elsewhere.

In terms of income poverty reduction, it has been a relative success story, but at the same time, there have been winners and losers. Households moved in different directions; some moved steadily upwards, some downwards, while others remained stuck in poverty. The following sections explore these different outcomes from the perspectives of both income poverty and asset accumulation.

Changes in Income Poverty, Inequality, and Mobility

This section examines the extent to which households have become poorer or richer, in terms of income data from the three time periods covered by the panel data set: 1978, 1992, and 2004. It then shows how this relates to inequality and mobility.

Income poverty provides an important measurement of poverty trends.[8] Building on earlier research using the Ecuadorian poverty line (see Moser 1996, 1997), the analysis divides households into three categories: nonpoor, poor, and very poor.[9] In the medium term, from 1978 to 1992, income poverty levels increased. However, by 2004 they had declined, with the number of nonpoor households more than doubling during this twenty-six-year period (see table 2-1). But given how few households were nonpoor in 1978, the majority were still below the poverty line in 2004. Nevertheless, the result from Indio Guayas reflects national trends for coastal areas, which show a slow decline in poverty levels despite increasing poverty levels at the national level.[10]

While poverty declined over time, inequality increased over the same period (see appendix table 2A-3). Low levels of inequality did not change greatly from 1978–92 but increased dramatically by 2004. The percentage of households categorized as poor over the twenty-six-year period was fairly consistent. However,

Table 2-2. *Definition of Household Income Mobility Categories*

1978 status	2004 status		
	Not poor	*Poor*	*Very poor*
Not poor	Stable not poor	Downward	Downward
Poor	Upward	Stuck in poverty	Stuck in poverty
Very poor	Upward	Stuck in poverty	Stuck in poverty

Source: Constructed from Carter and May (2001).

between 1992 and 2004, households shifted considerably from the very poor to the poor category and from the poor to the nonpoor category. The increased inequality was driven by households at the top of the income distribution rising faster than those at the bottom. The Gini coefficient increased during each time period, rising from 0.322 in 1978 to 0.375 in 1992 and 0.416 in 2004. The 2004 measure was close to that for all of Ecuador (0.437), reflecting the gradual process of differentiation among households in this "natural experiment," such that it had become more representative of the entire country (United Nations Development Program 2004).

Rising levels of income and inequality were accompanied by a great deal of income mobility. This study utilizes Carter and May's distinction (2001) among four mobility categories: stable not poor (those remaining above the poverty line in both 1978 and 2004), stuck in poverty (below the poverty line in 1978 and 2004), and upward and downward mobility (moving into or out of poverty between 1978 and 2004). These categories are illustrated in table 2-2.

Between 1978 and 1992, most households were stuck in poverty, with the mean per capita income staying roughly the same. However, during at least one of the two intersurvey periods, twenty-three households (45 percent) experienced upward mobility and eleven (22 percent) experienced downward mobility; four households were upwardly mobile in both periods; and only one household was downwardly mobile in both periods (see table 2-3). Therefore the aggregate trends mask the fact that there was considerable household income mobility.

Most families impoverished in 1978 remained so in 2004, with less than half able to rise above the poverty line. Overall, however, conditions in the community improved because more families climbed out of poverty than sank into it.

Long-term poverty trends are influenced by internal life cycle factors as well as external contextual factors. The latter include the broader structural macroeconomic and political context during different phases of Ecuador's and

Table 2-3. *Frequencies in Household Income Mobility Categories in Indio Guayas, 1978–2004*
Units as indicated

	Households					
	1978–92		1992–2004		1978–2004	
Mobility categories	Number	Percent of total	Number	Percent of total	Number	Percent of total
Stable not poor	2	4	1	2	3	6
Upward	4	8	19	37	17	33
Downward	6	12	5	10	5	10
Stuck in poverty	39	76	26	51	26	51
Total	51	100	51	100	51	100

Source: Authors' calculations.

Guayaquil's history, which can be summarized in three periods. First, there was the 1975–85 democratization process during which Ecuador emerged from military rule and established new democratic parties such as Izquierdo Democrática. This resulted in the municipal reforms that gave mangrove land to the poor in Guayaquil (Moser 1981) and in the community-driven processes for the acquisition of infrastructure. The second period, from 1985 to 1995, was marked by macroeconomic structural adjustment policies associated with a decline in state social sector provision and the increasing presence of international antipoverty agencies, such as UNICEF and Plan International (Moser 1997). The third period, from 1995 to 2005, was one of globalization and dollarization associated with financial crisis, increased penetration of private social sector delivery systems, and rapid expansion of international migration as an alternative "safety net" for many households.

The inhabitants of one street (Calle K) provide a microcosm of the mobility trends and differentiation that occur over time as a result of changing external circumstances and internal household dynamics. Susana, the community leader, and her tailor husband Julio were income poor in 1978 when they first arrived with their two young daughters. By 1992, despite the worsening macroenvironment, they had moved out of poverty and maintained this upward mobility through 2004. By contrast, Margarita and Hector remained stuck in poverty throughout the same period, staying in the very poor category from 1978 to 2004. Both households suffered serious negative shocks. Hector left Margarita and had a relationship with another woman for most of the 1990s, reducing her status to that of female household head. Susana's husband became ill, and after eight years of expensive treatment, he died in 2002, leaving her a widow.

Although household characteristics, such as the number of children, may be significant, it is nevertheless important to understand differences in poverty dynamics and look beyond income to asset accumulation. For example, Susana and Julio invested heavily in human capital through the education of their daughters and son. By 2004 all three children had achieved some level of tertiary education, still lived on the family plot, and were contributing to the family income. Julio had left tailoring and become a waged state employee. Parental income was used to expand the house, accumulating financial capital through rental income and the establishment of a microbusiness. By contrast, none of Margarita's children finished high school, so the income from their unskilled jobs contributed far less than that from Susana's children. Equally, Hector was not a successful earner. When the building boom collapsed in Guayaquil in the 1990s, he became a street seller. Most recently, he became unemployed when new municipal legislation pushed sellers off the streets into fixed markets. Margarita fared no better, with a series of low-paid cooking jobs while, at the same time, trying to raise five children.

Patterns of Asset Accumulation

While longitudinal analysis of changing poverty levels based on income provides one measure of well-being and demonstrates movement between poverty levels, understanding household accumulation of assets complements income data. It helps identify why some households are more income mobile than others and how some households successfully pull themselves out of poverty when others fail.

By using narrative econometrics, this study aims to advance the methods for measuring asset accumulation. It offers a quantitative complement to the anthropological analysis and use of statistical methods to identify which types of assets are particularly important for poverty reduction.

To quantitatively measure the accumulation or erosion of different assets, it is necessary to create an asset index. The study built on the asset index methodology of Carter and May (2001) and Filmer and Pritchett (2001), earlier research on asset vulnerability (Moser 1996, 1997, 1998), and the empirical data derived from the panel data set.[11] The asset index identified four types of capital and their associated asset index categories, each of which contains a number of index components.[12] Quantitatively measurable composite asset indexes associated with each capital asset were then constructed (see table 2-4).[13]

Figure 2-1 uses the asset index methodology to illustrate how, between 1978 and 2004, households in Indio Guayas accumulated different types of assets at

Table 2-4. *Asset Types, by Index Categories and Components*

Capital type	Asset index categories	Index components
Physical	Housing	Roof material
		Walls material
		Floor material
		Lighting source
		Toilet type
	Consumer durables	Television (none, black and white, color, or both)
		Radio
		Washing machine
		Bike
		Motorcycle
		VCR
		DVD player
		Record player
		Computer
Financial-productive	Employment security	State employee
		Private sector permanent worker
		Self-employed
		Contract or temporary worker
	Productive durables	Refrigerator
		Car
		Sewing machine
	Transfer-rental income	Remittances
		Rental income
Human	Education	Level of education:
		Illiterate
		Some primary school
		Completed primary school
		Secondary school or technical degree
		Some tertiary education
Social	Household	Jointly headed household
		Other households on plot
		"Hidden" female-headed households
	Community	Whether someone on the plot:
		Attends church
		Plays in sports groups
		Participates in community groups

varying rates. It shows that households invested heavily in housing capital when they first arrived in Indio Guayas. This was the first priority for households when invading swampland and living under very basic conditions. As basic housing needs were met, however, households accumulated other types of capi-

Figure 2-1. *Household Asset Accumulation, Indio Guayas, 1978–2004*

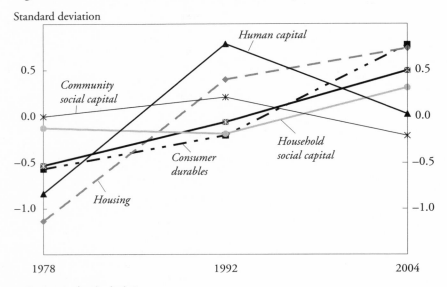

Standard deviation

Source: Authors' calculations.
a. 0 = mean across the time periods.

tal, both for production and consumption purposes. As a result housing capital accumulation leveled off and was replaced by the accumulation of consumption capital. Education and financial-productive capital increased fairly steadily between 1978 and 1992. The human capital available to households declined between 1992 and 2004, reflecting the fact that many of the fifty-one households' children, having completed their education, had moved off the plot. Financial-productive capital, by contrast, continued to rise. Finally, while community social capital actually fell between 1992 and 2004, household social capital rose.

This summary of asset accumulation provides the background for a more detailed description of individual assets. Here, the econometric measures of the rate of accumulation from the panel data set are complemented by narrative descriptions from the anthropological research that identify the causalities behind the differences among households.

Physical Capital

Physical capital generally comprises the stock of plant equipment, infrastructure, and other productive resources owned by individuals, businesses, and public sectors. In this study it is more narrowly defined and includes housing, defined as the land as well as the physical structure, and the range of consumer durables households acquire.

Housing is the most important component of physical capital. In Indio Guayas households that informally purchased their 10- by 30-meter plots from professional invaders squatted on a plot of mangrove swamp, often under severe conditions. While their rights were guaranteed by a 1974 municipal ordinance, their lack of legal deed (*escritura*) meant that ownership was ultimately determined by physical possession.[14] Plots left unoccupied were randomly invaded overnight. This led households to erect wooden stilts and gradually build basic houses with bamboo walls, wooden floors, and corrugated iron roofs. However, houses were unstable—bamboo walls could easily be split by knives, and the building materials rapidly deteriorated.[15] Consequently, as soon as resources were available, households upgraded their houses. They started by filling in their plots to provide land, followed by reconstruction with more permanent materials such as cement blocks and floors. Thus gradual incremental upgrading occurred over time.

This process is reflected in the econometric findings on housing based on four indicators: type of toilet, light, floor, and walls.[16] They are ordered in terms of increasing quality (for instance, "incomplete" walls are those in the process of being upgraded from bamboo to wood, brick, or concrete), with the data showing a high degree of interhousehold correlation. The rarest type of housing asset to own was a flush toilet, and it was only in 2004 that most households acquired one, although many people had connected to the main electrical grid and upgraded their floors and walls to brick or concrete by 1992.

The number of households that had achieved the maximum measured level of housing, in terms of the asset index, increased from 0 percent in 1978 to 24 percent in 1992 and 47 percent in 2004. Thus there was a slightly greater shift upward in the average level of housing stock and in equality of housing stock between 1978 and 1992 than between 1992 and 2004. These increases demonstrate the importance households placed on increasing their housing stock. Shelter and security were by far the most important early priorities for newly established residents in Indio Guayas, as in other invasion settlements.[17]

Nevertheless, housing investment varied among neighbors on Calle K. For instance, a high demand for builders meant Darwin, a skilled builder, earned well in 1978. With his wife Anna's earnings as a washerwoman, they were income nonpoor. Yet their house was extremely basic, lacking side and back walls and a proper roof. By 1992, when the building boom had ended and the household had more mouths to feed and educate, the household income had hardly improved, and the family had sunk into poverty. By 2002 Anna had decided to migrate to Spain, leaving her elder daughters to look after the family. In 2004 the household had moved out of both asset and income poverty as a result of Anna's remittances from abroad. Her $20,000 earnings remitted over four years were a "positive" shock, providing family income support and the funds to upgrade and expand the family home, resulting in separate sleeping quarters for four of her five children and their families.

Consumer durables are the second type of physical capital. The majority of families arrived with few durable assets; a radio and record player were the most common, and a black-and-white TV was a sign of real affluence. Ownership was limited by their high cost and lack of reliability, since electricity, while free, was pirated off the main supply. Over the years households accumulated a range of household items, influenced not only by income availability but also by increased access to cheap goods, credit, and regular electricity and water connections.

The asset index was constructed using nine consumer durables utilized purely for consumption purposes.[18] The best indicators of wealth are electronic items, such as computers, VCRs, or DVD players. These were only available in 2004 and even then only to rich households. A key sign of poverty was not having a television, as this was one of the first items many households acquired once they had the means. Consequently, if a household did not have a television, it was unlikely to have other consumer durables. In contrast to housing, consumer durables declined between 1978 and 1992. Only after households improved their housing did they invest in consumer durables.

The lack of consumer durables among poor households often led to theft and illegal earnings, particularly if the next generation desired these goods. Josefina and Victor, Susana's neighbors, remained stuck in poverty throughout the twenty-six-year period. With a background in rural agricultural work, Victor had trouble keeping jobs, while Josefina earned little as a dressmaker and washerwoman. They sought to improve their home and educate their six children, but only one finished high school. In 2004 those still remaining at home tried to contribute with casual work. Yet the household had a DVD player, an "aspirational good" illegally acquired by one of the sons.

Financial-Productive Capital

Financial-productive capital comprises the monetary resources available to households. The asset index distinguishes three categories: employment security, which measures how much security individuals have in the use of their labor potential as an asset; transfer-rental income as nonearned monetary resources; and productive durables, which are goods with an income-generating capability.

Employment security is undoubtedly the most challenging category in the index.[19] It represents an effort to include labor as an asset (omitted so far in the work on asset indexes) and to focus on employment vulnerability as linked to stability of job status. This category is a composite of two widely used employment survey categories on employer type and work status, and its components are ranked in terms of vulnerability, from the most secure state employee to private sector permanent worker to self-employed to the least secure contract or temporary worker.

In terms of transfer-rental income, the main sources of unearned income are remittances, government transfers, and rent. The first two are transfers of income within society and the latter is a return on capital—similar to income from physical goods, as analyzed above. Nonwage income has increasingly played an important role in household income. Remittance income has risen the most dramatically, resulting from the explosion of Ecuadorian emigrants in the late 1990s after dollarization and the banking crisis.[20] The fact that remittances accounted for more than 50 percent of nonwage income in 2004 illustrates that having someone abroad is a significant household asset. In 2004, for example, remittance income constituted more than half of total income for some households. Rental income, on the other hand, is a much smaller and more recent source of money. Households have only just started to build extra rooms to accommodate renters, either at the back of their plots or on additional floors to their houses.

With respect to productive durables in the specific context of Guayaquil, three durable goods with an income-generating capability were identified: sewing machines, refrigerators, and cars, each predominating during different time periods. Numerous families acquired sewing machines in the 1970s. Men used them in their work as tailors, while fewer women used them to generate income as dressmakers and for family use. Refrigerators, until recently a costly consumer item, were mainly used for small enterprise (such as selling ice, frozen lollies, and cold drinks). In the 1970s the lack of reliable electricity meant few took on the costs and risks associated with refrigerator ownership. Even now, the cost and unreliability of electricity make refrigerator ownership viable only for small enterprises. Car ownership is also a recent phenomenon and one that requires far more capital (usually based on credit). Most local men who own cars use them as taxis to generate income. While for some this is a full-time occupation, for others it supplements other jobs, particularly on weekends when there is high demand. Empirical evidence shows that these assets differ from those used purely for consumption.[21]

Financial-productive capital increased between both 1978 and 1992, and 1992 and 2004. By 1992, when Ecuador was undergoing major macroeco-

Table 2-5. *Average Financial-Productive Capital, by Poverty Category, 1978–2004*[a]
Standard deviations of the asset index

Households	1978	1992	2004
Very poor	−0.60	−0.31	0.05
Poor	−0.50	−0.01	0.92
Not poor	−0.38	0.77	0.85

Source: Authors' calculations.
a. Average for all groups over all time periods is 0.

nomic turmoil, financial-productive capital remained low for households below the poverty line but increased dramatically (by more than one standard deviation) on average for nonpoor households. This reflects the increasing inequality of the community. By contrast with poorer households, nonpoor households were able to diversify their sources of income and obtain jobs. By 2004 poor households had obtained financial-productive capital at a level essentially equal with nonpoor households, although very poor households remained far behind. Much of this growth can be attributed to increased income from renters and remittances; households across the income spectrum also steadily accumulated productive durables (see table 2-5).

The comparative experiences of the Marquez brothers, Manuel and Pedro, both living on Calle K, demonstrate the impact of different types of financial-productive assets on household well-being. Both self-employed tailors by profession, in 1978 they lived in poor households. By 1992 their income levels had changed. Manuel, the more skilled of the two, was making jackets and trousers and succeeded in moving out of poverty. Supported by Lorena, he invested in housing and in his two sons' education. By contrast, his younger brother Pedro, who only made trousers, was severely affected by the arrival of cheap mass-produced trousers into the local Guayaquil market and moved further into poverty. With three young children to support, he made ends meet with help from the evangelical church and Plan International. Yet twelve years on, even Manuel's best made plans had failed; his skills had not proved a buffer, and he had fallen back into poverty. Pedro, on the other hand, was no longer poor. Both households had been affected by the declining demand for hand tailoring. However, Manuel's productivity was further reduced by ill health, and the minimum wages earned by his two sons as temporary contract workers in local factories did not provide sufficient security to keep the family out of poverty. Pedro had benefited from the fact that one of his sons had migrated to Palma, Majorca, and was remitting $700 every two months from his wages as a beach attendant.

Human Capital

Human capital assets refer to individual investments in education, health, and nutrition—investments that determine people's capacity to work and the returns from their labor. Education is the only category in this index and therefore provides only a partial picture of human capital.[22]

Over twenty-six years the quantity and quality of schooling has changed in Indio Guayas along with an increase in the proportion of private to state schools. In the late 1970s, free community preschools were introduced through UNICEF's Urban Basic Services Program, but by the late 1990s, these had been replaced by private, fee-based nurseries. The number of state primary and secondary schools grew along with the expanding young population, and their quality improved during the 1980s with support from Plan International. By 2000, when nongovernmental support was withdrawn, a growing number of parents put their children in private schools, particularly at the primary level. Education became a bigger household cost, due not only to tuition and private transportation—associated with increased insecurity on public transport—but also to the increased number of years spent at school.

Human capital is measured by estimating its value in income terms. It differs from physical capital because it measures the accumulation of one item—education—rather than different items. Furthermore, educational human capital is an intermediate asset rather than an end in itself that can help households escape poverty. This contrasts with physical assets that act as indicators of whether a household has risen out of poverty. With that in mind, educational capital is calculated in terms of the labor market value associated with attaining each extra qualification.

Income earned from wages is measured on the level of education, age and age squared to proxy for experience, and a gender dummy variable.[23] The regression is estimated separately for each year because the value of each type of degree changes every year as the job market changes. Therefore the value of the educational capital of a household can change even though the composition of the household does not. Results show that in 1978 there was very little difference in the value of being illiterate, having some primary education, or having completed primary school. Almost 90 percent of the young settlers in Indio Guayas fell into these three categories. The few that had higher education earned considerably more in the labor market. Over time, however, being illiterate or incomplete primary schooling became more disadvantageous, with those people earning lower wages.

The data show that households make choices between investing in consumer durables or education for their children. A regression of the amount of education that a household's children had completed by 2004 against the level of consumer durables acquired in 1992 reveals a negative, statistically significant relationship. In other words, households that invested more in their children's education purchased fewer consumer durables. This negative relationship is even stronger when the income level of the household is considered because poorer households have less ability to invest in both simultaneously and therefore have to make more difficult choices.

On Calle K it was not just the wealthier households that invested in human capital. Cristina, for instance, went to considerable lengths to give her nine children some education, despite her single-parent status, meager earnings as a washerwoman, and the fact that, in income and asset terms, she was always very poor. While two of her nine children completed high school, a further two completed fifth grade, one of whom went on to do a nursing course, qualifying her to work in the local clinic.

Social Capital

Social capital, the most commonly cited intangible asset, is generally defined as the rules, norms, obligations, reciprocity, and trust embedded in social relations, social structures, and societies' institutional arrangements that enable that society's members to achieve their individual and community objectives.[24] Social capital is generated and provides benefits through membership in social networks or structures at different levels, ranging from the household to the marketplace and political system. The index differentiates between community level social capital and household social capital. The latter is based on detailed panel data on changing intrahousehold structure and composition (see Moser 1997, 1998).

In Indio Guayas the trust and cohesion that constitutes community social capital developed out of the common experience of living in an insecure physical environment in the initial stages of settlement. Reciprocal relationships based on survival commodities such as food, water, and child care were vital. This cooperation provided the basis for establishment of Committee Indio Guayas, the local self-help committee (Moser 1987, 1996). The strength of this social capital, though never statistically measured, was demonstrated by the extensive range of physical and social infrastructure the committee acquired for the community. Here, the commitment and role played by Susana, her neighbor Maria, and other committee members were crucial. Comparisons of relative infrastructure provision as a result of collective contestation by the local committees in Cisne Dos showed dramatic differences between highly cohesive communities, such as Indio Guayas, and those that were not (Moser 1987). Infrastructure consolidation occurred not through top-down state provision but as a consequence of lobbying and negotiation with vote-seeking populist political parties and later with international organizations such as UNICEF and Plan International (see Sollis and Moser 1991b). Once the infrastructure had been obtained, and the international organizations had moved on to other "poorer" communities, the importance of community collaboration was considerably reduced.

Three indicator variables were used to measure community-level social capital: whether someone in the household takes part in community groups, attends church, or participates in a sports clubs.[25] Although these are far from comprehensive, and quantitative data are only available for 1992 and 2004, analysis based on these components nevertheless supports the findings from the anthropological narrative that this is the only asset that unambiguously declined between those years. While the number of people who participated in community activities and attended church declined, the number playing sports rose slightly. Informal football games held on the streets during weekends provided important male networking and socializing opportunities, often accompanied by alcohol and, more recently, drug consumption.

Household social capital as an asset is complex because it is both positive and negative in terms of accumulation strategies.[26] Households act as important safety nets, protecting members during times of vulnerability, but they can also create opportunities for greater income generation through effective balancing of daily reproductive and productive tasks (see Moser 1993). Over time, households restructure their headship, composition, and size to reduce vulnerability related to life cycle and wider external factors. These characteristics provide the components for the asset index.

The first component, jointly headed households, indicates trust and cohesion within the family between partners and applies to both nuclear and couple-headed extended households. In 1978, when the community comprised young families, nearly two-thirds were nuclear in structure (see appendix table 2A-4).[27] By 1992 this proportion had dropped to a third, and in 2004 only one in ten households was nuclear in structure. By contrast the reverse was true for couple-headed extended households, which grew from one-fifth in 1978 to two-fifths by 1992 and was slightly more by 2004.

The second component is the presence of "hidden" female household heads within extended households, that is, unmarried female relatives with at least one child living on the family plot, sharing resources and responsibilities with others. This arrangement has increased from less than one in ten households in 1978 to more than one in four in 2004.

The third component relates to other households on the plot. These are second-generation children who remain on their parents' plot with families of their own. In 1992 about two-thirds of households had between four and nine people living on one plot, although that proportion dropped to approximately half by 2004.

Based on these three variables, household social capital remained at basically the same level from 1978 to 1992, but it had increased by 2004.[28]

Two examples from Indio Guayas illustrate these household types. In 1978 Cristina's household was headed by a single female with seven children, although later she had two more children by the same man. Three daughters repeated this cycle. Doris had four children by two different fathers and remained living at home until she finally settled around the corner with Hugo, Don Guillermo's younger son. Jessica had four sons, lived with their father for a while, but soon moved home again. Monica, the youngest, had three children by different fathers while still living at home. At one point Cristina had fifteen people living in her house, although by 2004 it was down to ten, of which two were "hidden" heads of households.

In 2004 one of the households with the largest household social capital (with all three components) was headed by Fernando and Blanca, who lived on the *estero* periphery. This three-generation household had twenty-six members, comprising five of their children and their spouses and children, loosely separated into four "families" occupying overlapping space within a two-floor house. The household was stuck in poverty, moving from very poor to poor to very poor over the twenty-six-year period. They coped through a clear division of labor, with the men involved in income-generating activities and the women in domestic tasks relating to child care and the care of their now-elderly parents.

Income and Assets: How Assets Help Households Move Out of Poverty

This section uses the insights derived from the separate discussions of income and assets to explore the relationship between the two and to identify whether there are particular assets that are more helpful than others for moving and keeping households out of poverty and thus affecting longer-term income mobility. It also describes how households accumulate assets in a sequenced process.

First and foremost, households accumulated housing. Virtually all households improved this type of physical capital, although it was not in itself significant for getting out them of poverty. Investment occurred especially during the 1978–92 period and then tailed off from 1992 to 2004. Because Indio Guayas squatters started under such basic conditions, there were enormous incentives to incrementally upgrade. Bamboo walls, for instance, degraded and had to be changed after seven years, so it made economic sense to replace them with concrete blocks.[29]

Although financial-productive capital grew steadily over time, there were important differences by poverty category. In 1992 a considerable gap in financial-productive capital existed between the poor and nonpoor, reflecting the devastating economic conditions in that year. However, by 2004 the poor (not counting the very poor) actually achieved greater levels of financial-productive capital than the nonpoor. This was because poor people were more likely to rent out part of their houses to lodgers and received higher levels of remittances, compensating for the fact that they had less secure jobs and fewer productive durables.

Differences among households regarding consumer durables were more apparent, illustrating diversity in priorities over time. While all households made sacrifices to reach a certain standard of housing, after they had achieved that, some cut back to invest in consumption items. The purchase of consumer durables did not lead to poverty reduction; rather it was an indicator of household priorities after escaping poverty. Between 1992 and 2004, nonpoor households shifted their spending to consumer durables, while poor and very poor households restrained their consumption in favor of housing.[30] Indeed, very poor households invested more in housing between 1992 and 2004 than did the nonpoor.

Figure 2-2 shows the different patterns of investment over time in housing and consumer durables by income levels and highlights that wealthier households had higher levels of total physical capital. However, the gap was wider for consumer durables than for housing, especially by 2004 when all income groups converged in terms of acquiring housing.

In terms of the relationship between assets and income mobility, it is useful to identify whether those poor who moved out of poverty started out with better assets. Examination of the average starting level of each household experiencing mobility between 1978 and 2004 shows that households that experienced upward mobility did not necessarily start out with higher levels of capital than households that remained stuck in poverty (see appendix table 2A-5). However, households that remained nonpoor between 1978 and 2004 started out with significantly higher levels of financial-productive capital and smaller households than those that started out nonpoor but sank into poverty. Households that experienced upward mobility acquired significantly higher levels of human capital and financial-productive capital than households that remained stuck in poverty. Moreover, households that were nonpoor in 2004—both those that

Figure 2-2. *Investment in Housing and Consumer Durables, by Income Group, 1978–2004*

Standard deviations from average

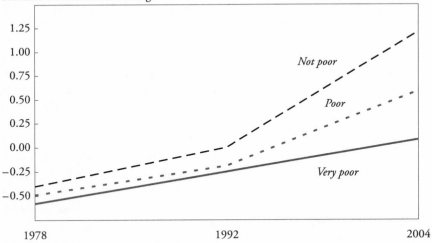

Source: Authors' calculations.

were stable and those that were upwardly mobile—acquired far fewer additional household members than households that ended up in poverty (see appendix table 2A-6). Ultimately, for many households, it is the slow appreciation of the entire asset portfolio rather than one asset in particular that ensures long-term upward mobility. Household size and dependency ratios are important but are not a determinant of mobility alone.

Asset Poverty Lines: Structural versus Stochastic Poverty

How can asset ownership complement consumption, or income data be a predictor of long-term welfare? To measure asset poverty requires using levels of assets to estimate either income directly or using a binary poverty status variable. Carter and May (2001), for instance, use an asset poverty line to complement income poverty lines and distinguish between structural and stochastic poverty. The structurally poor (or nonpoor) are those whose income and asset poverty levels match whereas the stochastically poor (or nonpoor) are those whose income and asset poverty levels do not match (if poor, their income is below their assets; if nonpoor, their income is above their assets). Income is more subject to stochastic shocks than assets are. A household may have low income because of temporary factors such as job loss or illness. A household that is structurally poor, on the other hand, has income below the poverty line and lacks the assets to lift itself above that level.

In this study an asset poverty line was estimated by regressing income on the levels of assets for each time period.[31] This made it possible to calculate for each household whether it was expected to be above or below the income poverty line based on the assets each household owned. This was called its "expected" poverty level. If a household was poor according to its income and assets, then it was categorized as being in structural poverty; however, if a household was below the income poverty line, but its assets indicated that it should have been above the income poverty line, it was considered to be in stochastic poverty. Table 2-6 shows the number of instances of each type of poverty, structural or stochastic, in Indio Guayas throughout the entire time period. It indicates that most poverty was indeed structural; however, many of the households that were above the poverty line appeared to be stochastically nonpoor.

The stochastically nonpoor are vulnerable to falling back into poverty: of the eleven households that were stochastically nonpoor in 1978 or 1992, only three of them were above the poverty line during the next sample period. Although this sample is too small for drawing statistical inferences, the generally negative outcomes of the stochastically nonpoor complement our anthropological insight that low levels of assets do not lead to sustainable income.

Table 2-6. *Categorization of Actual and Expected Household Poverty Levels, Indio Guayas, 1978–2004*

	Expected poverty level		
Actual poverty level	Not poor	Poor	Total
Not poor	13	21	34
	(structurally not poor)	(stochastically not poor)	
Poor	4	115	119
	(stochastically poor)	(structurally poor)	
Total	17	136	153

Source: Authors' calculations.

In 2004 most of the stochastically poor were elderly people who had remained in the family home unable to earn sufficient income themselves but having some financial capital from family income support. For instance, Andres, a clothing seller, and Norma, a domestic servant, arrived in 1971 and raised six children, all of whom completed some secondary education. By 2004 all the children had left home except Lydia, who was in her first year of university studies. Although their other five children lived in other areas of Guayaquil, they did not support their parents, so the couple lived off Andres's meager earnings. By contrast stochastically nonpoor households tended to be populated by people with poor job prospects but who were propped up by a large number of working children. All of them had low levels of consumer durables, which is usually a good indicator of poverty status, as well as low levels of financial capital. These were households with a lot of people working but few prospects.

Intergenerational Income Poverty and Asset Accumulation

The intergenerational focus of the study makes it possible to identify the extent to which households are locked into intergenerational poverty cycles (popularly identified as the culture of poverty by Oscar Lewis [1961]), or whether upward mobility occurs from one generation to the next. Identifying intergenerational outcomes is complicated by the level of diversity among the children, above all in terms of location. The second generation has pursued distinct strategies to improve their well-being. While some remained on the family plots, others moved to other parts of Guayaquil, and the most ambitious migrated primarily to Barcelona, Spain (see appendix table 2A-1).

Income poverty comparisons of the households of adult sons and daughters that have moved off the family plot but are still in Guayaquil in 2004 show levels of poverty comparable to that of their parents. Two-fifths of the children's households are nonpoor, and a slightly larger proportion are poor as opposed to very poor. This means that generally the next generation is better off than their parents were at a similar stage in their lives. The external context together with internal socioeconomic characteristics contribute to the fact that the next generation is starting with more. For instance, households settling on the periphery of the city do not have to mobilize through a local community committee to get electricity and basic services, as their parents did.

When the incomes of all three sets of children—living on the plot, living off the plot in Ecuador, and living abroad—are compared, those living at home earn the least while those taking the greatest risk and initiative are the most successful. For the latter group of young people, Barcelona appears to provide much more opportunity than Ecuador: the average income for those that migrated abroad is $820.66 a month, compared with $67.97 for those that moved out of the plot but remained in Ecuador and $60.24 for those that remained living with their parents. The parents made less than the children ($58.48) on average in 2004, but their incomes were more stable, with significantly lower standard deviations.

Hugo and Alberto, the two sons of Don Guillermo and Gloria, chose career paths in different cities and illustrate the diverse opportunities in Guayaquil and Barcelona. The family arrived in 1973 with three children, living two doors down from Cristina on Calle K. Don Guillermo, with three years of primary education, was a shop assistant, and Gloria, with no formal schooling, was a domestic worker. Their son Alberto completed four years of secondary education and worked as a shop delivery driver for ten years before immigrating to Europe. He worked in Italy as a domestic worker before going to Barcelona, where he now has a permanent job as an industrial night cleaner earning nearly $1,200 per month. Over the years his wife and four children have joined him. His younger brother Hugo completed high school and became a driver of oil tankers. When, after ten years, he lost his job, he became a chauffeur taking local children to school. He earns approximately $120 a month and lives with Doris, Cristina's eldest daughter, and their five children. Alberto recently loaned him $2,000 while still remitting $150 monthly to his father.

In terms of assets, the second generation has benefited greatly from the investments of their parents. Children are better educated than their parents, with girls better educated than boys. Only 6 percent of parents have completed high school compared with 45 percent of children, while 4 percent of parents have some college education compared with 12 percent of children (see appendix table 2A-7). Furthermore, the children living off the plot tend to have better education than those still living on the plot, although this difference is not statistically significant.

Consequently, children are more selective about the jobs they will and will not take. Better educated, they aspire to better work than their parents had. In addition, the second generation often lives in better housing—half are assisted by their parents' accumulation of housing as a physical asset by still living on the family plot.[32] Those choosing to set up their own homes have not been as fortunate since they have not acquired low-cost "invaded" land. Nevertheless, some 12 percent have chosen to repeat their parents' experience in order to acquire their own plot. Now it is the hills and agricultural land on the city's periphery, sold off by land entrepreneurs, that provide the only opportunities for the children. In terms of household structure, these next-generation children are repeating the struggle experienced by their parents—living in muddy streets rather than over water, without running water, plumbing, or state-provided social infrastructure. In 2004 two-thirds of the children off the plot lived in nuclear households headed by couples, a quarter lived in extended families, and a very low proportion lived in female-headed households.

The second generation accumulates different types of capital than their parents. In particular, they have a much higher level of consumption capital goods relative to their housing stock and other assets (see figures 2-3 and 2-4). This represents raised levels of expectations. Growing up in a more connected, media-saturated world, they reverse the asset accumulation pattern of the earlier generation, first acquiring consumer goods and then improving their housing. They are also willing to borrow to finance their consumption. Some 68 percent of the children are engaged in borrowing, compared with 58 percent of parents. Indeed, their financial capital in 2004 was less than that of their parents in 1978. Since few can afford to buy such consumer goods, local community members attribute the desire for easy money as one of the main reasons for the rise in street gangs, theft, and violence in the community.

As noted above, many parents have made "sacrifices" to pay for their children's education. An indicator of increasing intergenerational well-being might relate to the second generation's capacity or willingness to support their parents, especially once they are no longer able to generate an income. In a context where very few households receive state social security or pension support, this is particularly important given the number of elderly households that slip into poverty when the income earners are no longer able to work as before.

The story of Francisco and Maria is particularly poignant. Francisco always wanted to be a dentist and went to enormous lengths to "get on." In 1978, with three years of primary schooling, he returned to night school to complete his

Figure 2-3. *Accumulation of Assets, Parents in 1978 versus Children in 2004*

Standard deviation

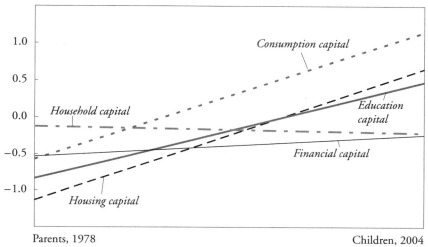

Source: Authors' calculations.

Figure 2-4. *Accumulation of Assets, Parents versus Children, 2004*

Standard deviation

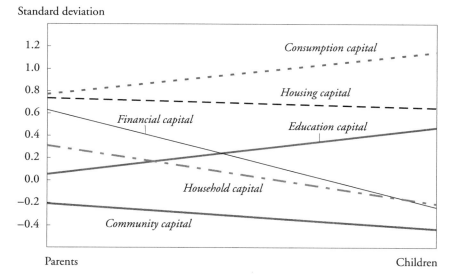

Source: Authors' calculations.

education. In 1980 he left tailoring and became a dental "mechanic" and in 1984 he got his high school diploma. In 1987 he started studying dentistry at university, combining his studies with paid work, but that same year he was forced to quit due to financial constraints. He then transferred his aspirations to his son Ricardo, who successfully graduated from Guayaquil University as a dentist. While doing his rural dental service, he married a local woman, and both migrated to Madrid, Spain. Ricardo soon returned to Guayaquil "to work in his chosen profession" since the only work he found in Spain was in agriculture and the postal services. He moved back to his wife's rural area and established his own practice. He gives his parents $30 a month, which is all he can afford while undertaking further part-time graduate training in orthodontics. While very proud of their son, the now-poor parents would welcome a greater return on their human capital investment.

Those living in Barcelona are most likely to support their families back in Guayaquil, with average remittances of $143 a month (with more than three out of four remitting) compared with an average of $7.75 for children in Guayaquil. Nevertheless, such remittances are often context specific and time bound. In the sample, women were often more reliable remitters because they had left children behind in Guayaquil. Over time men were far more likely to bring their families to Barcelona and, once residing legally, buy a flat with very low interest. To pay the mortgage, as many rooms as possible are rented out. So as in Indio Guayas, lots of people live in a small space, sharing a communal kitchen and sitting-dining room. The difference is that in Barcelona they are buying apartments while in Guayaquil they are squatting in self-help housing on the city's periphery.

In twenty-six years Indio Guayas has changed from a marginal squatter settlement without services and infrastructure, but with little youth violence or street gangs, to a consolidated well-serviced neighborhood, with second generation families with children completing high school education. But with better services, education, and jobs has come a devastating acceleration in the levels of daily violence. A recent event on Calle K illustrates this. In early 2005 a "sane" (the local description) university student killed the leader of the rival gang after repeated taunts. The perpetrator's mother, a local schoolteacher and secretary of the community committee, and her extended family fled for their lives when their houses were torched in retribution. Thus it is not just the violence but the impact on immediate families that influences asset accumulation. At a time when levels of community social capital have already seriously declined (because of the acquisition of physical and social infrastructure and the withdrawal of community-based services), the combination of increased violence and declining trust and cohesion has led to extreme fear and impotence on the part of local barrio community leaders. They feel increasingly unable to deal with the new drug dealer elites and the gun-related violence. Yet there are both perpetrators and victims in the same communities, and ultimately community members know they must deal with the problem.

Conclusion

This chapter has briefly summarized the complexities associated with household asset accumulation in Indio Guayas, Guayaquil, and its relationship to poverty reduction. The narrative econometrics methodology combines narratives of people's lives with econometric asset indexes. Together, they show how a highly homogeneous community, which provides a natural experiment, has changed over time into a "normal" heterogeneous lower-income area. For some this has meant increased prosperity while for others, who have remained poor or descended further into poverty, it has resulted in greater inequality and insecurity.

Focusing on the relationship between asset accumulation and income poverty, the study shows that households make crucial choices in managing complex asset portfolios at different stages of their life cycles. Housing is the first-priority asset, and while it does not necessarily get households out of poverty, adequate housing is generally a necessary precondition for the accumulation of other assets.

There are no magic solutions in terms of specific assets contributing to poverty reduction. Both income and assets matter. Moreover, a longitudinal study such as this shows that poor people also consider it important to accumulate assets. Over time those who do best consolidate slowly—first human capital, followed by financial-productive capital. They often make trade-offs in the process, investing in their children's education before acquiring consumer durables. Important differences among households exist; those that do best make their assets work for them. They purchase assets with their income and then generate more income from those assets (see appendix table 2A-6). In this complex process of getting out of poverty, some succeed while others who start as poor or nonpoor fall further into poverty.

At the intergenerational level, children benefit considerably from their parent's investments, both in terms of housing and human capital. Those that still live on the family plot do not experience the housing problems of their parents while those setting up homes on the city's periphery tend to be poor and are more typical of other young families. The outliers help identify the different levels of reciprocity between the second and first generation. Income-poor but asset-rich households tend to comprise elderly parents no longer supported by their children. By contrast, income-rich households with few assets are often those where the children still live at home and contribute to the household's income.

Finally, better education has changed the work preferences of many children; they are no longer prepared to do the onerous manual and semiskilled work their parents did. At the same time, they have higher expectations in terms of consumer durables. For some the solution is to resort to petty theft and drug selling. Thus increasing well-being and associated inequality brings its own constraints. The study shows that twenty-six years ago Indio Guayas was a poorer but far safer community than it is today. The world has changed fundamentally since the 1970s when that community began, and policy solutions appropriate then are not necessarily suitable now.

Appendix 2A: Supplementary Data Tables

Table 2A-1. *Database of Households for Intergenerational Asset Transfer and Poverty Reduction Study*
Units as indicated

Survey data for longitudinal study	Survey date	Panel size	Size and nature of source	Percent attrition rates
Household panel data sets	1978	56	244 (universe)	0
	1992	56	263 (random sample survey)	0
	2004	51	56 (panel data set)	9
Households of sons and daughters living outside family plot and in Guayaquil in 2004	2005	46	61 (universe of sons and daughters)	24
Households of sons and daughters living in Barcelona	2005	3	23 interviews from 3 different data sources	. . .[a]

a. Not appropriate as not a universe or random survey.

Table 2A-2. *Location of All Sons and Daughters over Sixteen Years Old from 2004 Panel Data Set*
Units as indicated

Category	Location	Number per location	Number per category	Percent of total
Still on family plot	In parents' house on plot	94	120	50.0
	Living "apart" on parents' plot[a] (secondary households)	26		
Same barrio	Same barrio with other family members (in-laws)	20	33	13.5
	Same barrio rent	8		
	Same barrio own plot	5		
Other areas, Guayaquil	Another barrio, Guayaquil, own plot	29	29	12.0
Other city, Ecuador	Another city or town in Ecuador	23	23	9.5
Abroad	Spain	9	17	7.0
	Italy	1		
	United States	4		
	Germany	1		
	Venezuela	2		
No information (parents have lost touch)		19	19	8.0
Total		241	241	100.0

a. Although, in some respects, these form separate households, the level of collaboration in cooking, food acquisition, and sharing of space means that overall they constitute members of the same household plot.

Table 2A-3. *Real Income Summary Statistics*

	1978	1992	2004
Mean	150.74	202.79	332.62
Median	145.45	157.72	232.92
Standard deviation	89.69	147.9	271.29
Minimum	14.54	0	563.71
Maximum	407.27	34.94	1,327.67

Table 2A-4. *Household Structure from the Three Panel Data Sets, 1978–2004*
Percent

Year	Headed by couple		Female-headed, single or married	Male-headed, single	Single or multiple adults only
	Nuclear family	Extended family			
1978	62.8	19.6	9.8	0.0	7.8
1992	33.3	39.2	25.5	2.0	0.0
2004	11.8	41.2	35.3	9.8	2.0

Table 2A-5. *Household Asset Portfolios, by Mobility Categories, 1978*[a]

1978 level of capital	Housing	Consumer durables	Per capita human capital	Per capita financial capital	Number of household members
Stuck in poverty	−1.692	−0.581	3.157	−0.083	6.115
Upward	−1.556	−0.498	3.155	−0.137	6.824
Downward	−1.232	−0.197	3.160	−0.091	4.400
Stable not poor	−1.534	−0.725	3.251	−0.497	2.333
Total	−1.592	−0.524	3.162	−0.126	5.961

a. Values refer to level of assets in standard deviations, calculated using polychoric principal components analysis as described in the text, relative to the entire 1978–2004 sample.

Table 2A-6. *Household Asset Accumulation, by Mobility Categories, 1978–2004*[a]

Change, 1978–2004	Housing	Consumer durables	Per capita human capital	Per capita financial capital	Number of household members
Stuck in poverty	2.597	0.858	0.418	0.162	2.962
Upward	2.555	1.752	1.088	0.253	0.176
Downward	2.688	0.775	−0.126	0.360	4.000
Stable not poor	2.725	1.655	−0.403	0.599	2.000
Total	2.599	1.195	0.542	0.226	2.078

a. Values refer to number of standard deviations increase of assets measured, calculated using polychoric principal components analysis as described in the text, relative to the entire 1978–2004 sample.

Table 2A-7. *Comparative Education Levels between Generations, 2004*
Percent

Education level	Parents	Children	Total
Illiterate	16	1	6
Some primary school	19	7	11
Completed primary school	55	34	41
Completed secondary school or technical degree	6	46	33
Tertiary (college) education	4	12	9
Total	100	100	100

Notes

1. This list can be extended to include the capacity to aspire (Appadurai 2004) and other psychological assets (Alsop, Bertelsen, and Holland 2006). However, the assets in this study are grounded in quantitatively measured research.

2. In 1978 a universe survey of 244 households was undertaken over the eleven-block area; in 1992 a random sample survey of 263 households, undertaken in exactly the same spatial area, picked up fifty-six households that had also been in the 1978 universe survey. In 2004 these same fifty-six households were tracked, and fifty-one were reinterviewed (indicating a 9 percent attrition rate). Sociological questionnaire surveys were undertaken by Caroline Moser, together with other researchers at different stages, including Brian Moser, Peter Sollis and Alicia Herbert, as well as a trained team of community members including Lucy Zavalla, Rosa Vera, Carmita Naboa, and Angela Vinueza.

3. The Barcelona survey comprised twenty-three questionnaires and semistructured interviews, using five adult members from three households from the panel data set, boosted by households from Calle K (located in the middle of the survey area), as well as a network of other local ex-schoolmates of the community leader's daughter.

4. The cross-disciplinary combined methodologies research that Ravi Kanbur began at Cornell University has since become a research program at the Centre for International Studies at the University of Toronto. See "Q-Squared: Combining Qualitative and Quantitative Approaches in Poverty Analysis" (www.q-squared.ca. [November 2006]).

5. Since traditional econometrics only incorporates variables that can be measured, this means that it is often vulnerable to misspecification and endogeneity. The latter occurs when the independent (explanatory) and dependent (outcome) variables are linked in a way that is not specified in the model. For example, an explanatory or "treatment" variable such as migration may be itself directly caused by unobservable household characteristics (entrepreneurial spirit) that affect the dependent or outcome variable (household income). The model is misspecified because it should include immeasurable variable x but instead contains a measurable variable y.

Because the discipline of anthropology includes the identification and analysis of intangible factors, it can enhance econometric analysis in several ways. One of the most useful is its ability to help explain outliers. When small, detailed data sets (the kinds of data sets for which an anthropological perspective is most effective) are used, outliers (or, more generally, a limited number of observations) can make a big difference to the results. Anthropologists can provide insight into whether these should or should not be included, and why outliers are dissimilar to the other observations.

6. A natural experiment is a naturally occurring event or situation that can be exploited by a researcher to help answer a research question. These types of experiments are quasi-experiments in that the experimenter has little or no control over the situation that is being observed. See University of Salford, "Natural Experiments" (www.chssc.salford.ac.uk/health-Sci/resmeth2000/resmeth/natural.htm [November 2006]).

7. Personal communication from Department of Social Development, Municipality of Guayas, 2005.

8. Although consumption data are more widely used, this study uses income data. The anthropological research revealed that even people's short-term recall of consumption expenditures was often inaccurate or underestimated. Data from expenditure diaries, for instance, were widely inconsistent with expenditure data from anthropological participant observation. In contrast, given the trust that had been established from working with the community, income panel data about formal and informal sector earnings showed a high level of compatibility across the fifty-one households.

9. A household was considered nonpoor if its income was at or above the poverty line; it was poor if its income was below the poverty line but at or above half of the poverty line; and it was very poor if its income was below half of the poverty line. A monthly per capita income of 84,243 sucres was defined as the World Bank's 1992 poverty line for urban Guayaquil, Ecuador (Moser 1996, p. 87). In year 2000 dollars, this translates into a real per capita poverty line of $50.52 a month, based on International Financial Statistics data on consumer price index and exchange rates (International Monetary Fund 2004).

10. Comparisons of poverty line data are highly contentious given the incompatibility of data sources. The 1978–1992 Indio Guayas study went to great lengths to assess how representative the study was and concluded that in 1992, "poverty levels are higher than in the country as a whole or in Ecuador's urban areas generally" (Moser 1997, p. 28). The World Bank Ecuador Poverty Assessment (2004) states that the poverty headcount for Guayaquil declined from 38 percent in 1990 to 34 percent in 2001, with the national poverty level increasing from 40 to 45 percent. Absolute numbers of poor increased by about 54 percent in Guayaquil during that period, but the percent of the total number of poor who live in Guayaquil remains stable at about 14.5 percent, whereas it increased from 10 to 26 percent for the urban coastal region in general.

11. Limitations in the longitudinal panel data set mean that the capital assets evaluated do not cover all those included in the extensive academic definitions of assets in the literature (see Moser and Felton 2006).

12. Natural capital includes the stocks of environmentally provided assets such as soil, atmosphere, forests, water, and wetlands. This capital is more generally used in rural research. In urban areas, where land is linked to housing, this is more frequently classified as productive capital, as is the case in this study. However, since all households lived on similar plots, this was not tracked in the data set.

13. See Moser and Felton (2006) for an econometric description of the construction of an asset index.

14. The 1974 ordinance required the municipality to give existing squatters titles to plots (solars), provided that the person had been there at least a year and owned no other land in the city, and that the plot was no larger than 300 square meters. It also established the Office for the Distribution of Solars to allocate and administer titles to the land (Moser 1982).

After more than twenty-five years, some of the original squatters had still not completed the process of transaction (*en tramite*) to acquire their title documentation, despite living on the same plot for two or three generations. This seems inexplicable until one appreciates the complexity and associated time needed to acquire this documentation (see Moser 2005).

15. Bamboo as a building material has a "shelf life" of approximately seven years.

16. Polychoric principal component analysis (PCA) (Kolenikov and Angeles 2004) was used to construct the weights for housing as a physical asset. This is an optimization of principal components analysis for ordinal variables, like the variables that we use to measure housing stock. See Moser and Felton (2006) for a more detailed explanation.

17. It is important to note that by 2004 some of the wealthier households were expanding the size of their buildings to accommodate the second generation, or indeed to rent out rooms. At this stage of analysis, for methodological and other reasons, such data have not been coded as indicators of physical capital. However, these changes are reflected in indicators of financial capital (rental income) and household social capital (numbers of families still living on the plot).

18. Polychoric PCA was used to construct their weights. The term *consumer durable* is used to distinguish these items from assets that can be used for business purposes, which are called *financial durables*.

19. Further analysis of the labor market is still needed for a complete understanding of changing income sources.

20. By 2004 two million Ecuadorians were working overseas (15 percent of the total population). Some 550,000 have left the country since 1999, one-fifth of the labor force. Emigration peaked in 2000 but subsequently dropped due to controls introduced by the European Union, especially Spain (Hall 2006).

21. To measure ownership of these assets, the marginal extra income from obtaining one of these items was calculated. Polychoric PCA was used to construct the weights of financial-productive capital.

22. The study contains detailed information on health status, particularly in terms of shocks arising from serious illnesses or accidents, as well as the use and cost of health services. However, lack of an adequate methodology to translate these into a health asset index means that the information remains at the narrative level.

23. Levels of education are defined as illiterate, some primary school, completed primary school, secondary-technical degree, and some college or more (see appendix table 2A-7).

24. Social capital is the most contested form of capital (Bebbington 1999). The development of the concept is based on the theoretical work of Putnam (1993) and Portes (1998), among others.

25. Polychoric PCA was used to construct this index.

26. Household social capital is defined as the sum of three indicator variables: whether the household is headed by a couple (as opposed to a single female or male); whether multiple households are living on the plot; and whether the main household contains "hidden" household heads, defined as a single woman and her children living in the same household as her parents.

27. A nuclear household comprises a couple living with their children. An extended household comprises a single adult or couple living with their own children and other related adults or children. A female-headed household comprises a single-parent nuclear or extended household headed by a woman—if married, she identifies herself as the head usually because her husband is not the main income earner.

28. The difference between 1978 and 1992 is not statistically significant; however, the 1992–2004 difference is statistically significant at the 1 percent level.

29. As mentioned earlier, further analysis of the 2004 data is needed regarding the increased size of houses. This may assist in further disaggregating consolidated housing as an asset.

30. Because income in developing countries is particularly volatile, consumer durables may in fact provide a better measure of the household's long-term income potential than any one year's income. According to the permanent income hypothesis, households make purchases based on expected future income as opposed to income during any one year.

31. To implement a simple version of the Carter and May approach, we estimated the probability of a household being below the poverty line using a logistic regression of the four assets—physical, financial-productive, human, and social—that have been measured in the three panel data sets.

32. Of the half that still live on their parents' plots, one in five (21 percent) live "apart" in a separate physical structure on the plot, while a further 14 percent still live in the same area—mainly with parents-in-law (see appendix table 2A-2).

References

Alsop, Ruth, Mette Bertelsen, and Jeremy Holland. 2006. *Empowerment in Practice: From Analysis to Implementation.* Washington: World Bank.

Appadurai, Arjun. 2004. "The Capacity to Aspire: Culture and the Terms of Recognition." In *Culture and Public Action,* edited by Vijayendra Rao and Michael Walton, pp. 59–85. Stanford University Press.

Bebbington, Anthony. 1999. "Capitals and Capabilities: A Framework for Analyzing Peasant Viability, Rural Livelihoods and Poverty." *World Development* 27 (12): 2021–44.

Carney, Diana. 1998. "Implementing the Sustainable Livelihoods Approach." In *Sustainable Rural Livelihoods. What Contribution Can We Make?* edited by Diana Carney, pp. 3–23. London: Department for International Development.

Carter, Michael, and Julian May. 2001. "One Kind of Freedom: Poverty Dynamics in Post-Apartheid South Africa." *World Development* 29, no. 12: 1987–2006.

Chambers, Robert, and Gordon Conway. 1992. "Sustainable Rural Livelihoods: Practical Concepts for the 21st Century." Discussion Paper 296. Brighton: Institute of Development Studies.

Department for International Development. 2000. *Sustainable Livelihoods—Current Thinking and Practice.* London.

Filmer, Deon, and Lant Pritchett. 2001. "Estimating Wealth Effects without Expenditure Data—or Tears: An Application to Educational Enrollments in States of India." *Demography* 38, no. 1: 115–32.

Hall, Anthony. 2007 (forthcoming). "International Migration and the Challenges for Social Policy: The Case of Ecuador." In *Assets, Livelihoods and Social Policy*, edited by Caroline Moser and Anis Dani. Washington D.C.: World Bank.

Hulme, David, and John Toye. 2006. "The Case for Cross-Disciplinary Social Science Research on Poverty, Inequality and Well-Being." Q-Squared Working Paper 19. University of Toronto.

International Monetary Fund. 2004. *International Financial Statistics*. Washington D.C.

Kanbur, Ravi, ed. 2002. *Qual-Quant: Qualitative and Quantitative Methods of Poverty Appraisal*. Delhi: Permanent Black.

Kolenikov, Stas, and Gustavo Angeles. 2004. "The Use of Discrete Data in Principal Component Analysis: Theory, Simulations, and Applications to Socioeconomic Indices." Working Paper WP-04-85. MEASURE/Evaluation Project, Carolina Population Center, University of North Carolina.

Lewis, Oscar. 1961. *The Children of Sanchez: Autobiography of a Mexican Family*. New York: Random House.

Moser, Caroline. 1981. "Surviving in the Suburbios." *Institute of Development Studies Bulletin* 12, no. 3: 19–29.

———. 1982. "A Home of One's Own: Squatter Housing Strategies in Guayaquil, Ecuador." In *Urbanization in Contemporary Latin America*, edited by A. Gilbert and others, pp. 159–90. London: Wiley.

———. 1987. "Mobilization Is Women's Work: Struggles for Infrastructure in Guayaquil, Ecuador." In *Women, Human Settlements and Housing*, edited by Caroline Moser and Linda Peake, pp. 166–94. London: Tavistock.

———. 1993. *Gender Planning and Development: Theory, Practice and Training*. London: Routledge.

———. 1996. "Confronting Crisis: A Comparative Study of Household Responses to Poverty and Vulnerability in Four Poor Urban Communities." Environmentally Sustainable Development Studies and Monograph Series 8. Washington: World Bank.

———. 1997. "Household Responses to Poverty and Vulnerability, Volume 1: Confronting Crisis in Cisne Dos, Guayaquil, Ecuador." Urban Management Policy Paper 21. Washington: World Bank.

———. 1998. "The Asset Vulnerability Framework: Reassessing Urban Poverty Reduction Strategies." *World Development* 26, no. 1: 1–19.

———. 2002. "'Apt Illustration' or 'Anecdotal Information.' Can Qualitative Data Be Representative or Robust?" In *Qual-Quant: Qualitative and Quantitative Methods of Poverty Appraisal*, edited by Ravi Kanbur, pp. 79–89. Delhi: Permanent Black.

———. 2005. "Rights, Power and Poverty Reduction." In *Power, Rights and Poverty: Concepts and Connections*, edited by Ruth Alsop, pp. 29–50. Washington and London: World Bank and Department for International Development.

———. 2007 (forthcoming). "Assets and Livelihoods: A Framework for Asset-Based Social Policy." In *Assets, Livelihoods and Social Policy*, edited by Caroline Moser and Anis Dani. Washington: World Bank.

Moser, Caroline, and Andrew Felton. 2006. "The Construction of an Asset Index: Measuring Asset Accumulation in Ecuador." Paper presented at workshop on Concepts and Methods for Analyzing Poverty Dynamics and Chronic Poverty. University of Manchester, October.

Portes, Alejandro. 1998. "Social Capital: Its Origins and Applications in Modern Sociology." *American Review of Sociology* 24, no. 1: 1–24.

Putnam, Robert. 1993. *Making Democracy Work: Civic Traditions in Modern Italy.* Princeton University Press.

Sen, Amartya. 1981. *Poverty and Famines: An Essay on Entitlement and Deprivation.* Oxford: Clarendon Press.

Sollis, Peter, and Caroline Moser. 1991a. "A Methodological Framework for Analyzing the Social Costs of Adjustment at the Micro Level: The Case of Guayaquil, Ecuador." *Bulletin of the Institute of Development Studies* 22, no. 1. 23–30.

———. 1991b. "Did the Project Fail? A Community Perspective on a Participatory Health Care Project in Ecuador." *Development in Practice* 1, no. 1: 19–33.

United Nations Development Program. 2004. "Human Development Index." In *Human Development Report 2004.* New York.

World Bank. 2000. *World Development Report 2000/2001: Attacking Poverty.* Washington.

———. 2004. *Ecuador Poverty Assessment.* Washington.

3

Learning from Asset-Based Approaches to Poverty

MICHAEL R. CARTER

P overty is most frequently measured and analyzed in terms of income flows or the stream of consumption expenditures financed by those income flows. While these flow measures permit calculation of a suite of indicators that variously count the number of people whose standard of living falls short of a predetermined poverty line, they do not reveal much about who the poor are, why they are poor, or whether their material situation is likely change over time.

Information on the asset stocks that underlie and generate income and consumption flows can be used to help answer these questions.[1] At a descriptive level, information on assets can provide a more comprehensive picture of who the poor are. Asset pentagons are one example of this descriptive use of asset data, permitting insight into the dimensions along which the poor and the nonpoor differ. The work by Attanasio and Székely (2000) is another example. A complementary approach is taken by Moser and Felton (2006) in a dynamic setting that enables them to describe how the asset positions of households evolve over time, which provides important insights into the nature of the pathways from poverty.

The topic of this chapter was suggested by questions raised at the Brookings Institution–Ford Foundation Workshop on Asset-Based Approaches to Poverty in a Globalized Context, held in Washington, D.C., on June 27–28, 2006. It is a deliberative reflection on a body of collaborative work undertaken over the years with a number of people, especially Christopher Barrett, Menobu Ikegami, Julian May, and Fred Zimmerman. While it draws liberally on the work of these individuals, none of them should be held responsible for the interpretations here.

While these uses of assets are instructive, they do not explicitly take advantage of the fact that there are well-developed bodies of economic theory that relate to the constraints that shape how people are able to use the assets they have and how they accumulate assets over time. And yet these are precisely the *structural* determinants of why people are poor and whether they stay poor.

This chapter concentrates on approaches that use asset information in conjunction with insights from economic theory to gain additional insight into why the poor are poor and whether their material situation is likely to change over time. Drawing on recent work and work in progress, it considers three specific domains where an asset-based approach—armed with theory—can offer insights into the nature and persistence of poverty.

The first part of the chapter considers a problem that appears in longitudinal or panel data when significant numbers of households are observed to transition from poor to nonpoor status (and vice versa) over time. Information on asset stocks (in conjunction with theory-guided insights on the relationship between assets and income) can be used to decompose observed transitions into structural poverty change (for example, a household has successfully built up productive business assets and moved to a higher standard of living) versus a "churning" around that is being driven by short-term shocks and recovery from them. Such a decomposition allows a much deeper analysis of why and how poverty levels change over time.

The second part of the discussion describes how insights from the economics of asset accumulation and poverty traps can be used with panel data on household living standards to identify asset dynamics and create forward-looking measures of chronic poverty. While subject to a number of methodological challenges, an asset-based approach to poverty provides insights into one of the most important questions about poverty, namely whether it persists over time.

The final section of the chapter explores how the same analytical devices that permit insight into these questions can be used to design durable and cost-effective antipoverty policies that place and maintain families in positions from which they can be expected to accumulate assets and move ahead. Much remains to be done to realize the full potential of asset-based approaches, and it is hoped that this discussion will help motivate the needed investigation.

Using Asset Stocks to Distinguish "Churning" from Structural Changes in Poverty

Longitudinal or panel living standards surveys that repeatedly interview the same respondent households over time offer important insights in comparison to consecutive cross-sectional surveys that interview different respondents with each survey. While both types of surveys can indicate, for example, that the aggregate poverty rate has held constant at 35 percent, panel surveys permit us to know whether it is the same 35 percent of the population that is persistently poor or whether there is large movement into and out of poverty. Clearly a society where the same households are poor year after year would be very different, economically and politically, from a society with more mobility. In permitting us to distinguish between these two very different situations, panel studies of poverty have made an important contribution.[2]

While the use of panel data to characterize persistent versus transitory poverty is highly informative, it is subject to several limitations. First, as a number of authors have noted, data measurement error will lead to an overstatement of the amount of mobility and transitory poverty. In a recent paper, Glewwe (2005) proposes a way to determine the degree to which measurement error leads to an overstatement of mobility.

While the significance of measurement error should not be underplayed, there is a second difficulty with standard mobility analysis. As stressed by Carter and May (2001), this second-generation analysis does not distinguish between mobility that is driven by temporary shocks and setbacks (and recovery from them) and mobility that has a more structural foundation (for example, accumulation of new productive assets that predict a continuing nonpoor standard of living into the future). Note that shocks, and recovery from them, are not the same thing as measurement error. A household in which a key earner is beset by a temporary illness could indeed slip into poverty when its expenditures (or income) are measured without error. A subsequent survey round could again accurately find that this household had transitioned to nonpoor status. Transitions driven by these kinds of events are what Carter and May call "stochastic mobility." In contrast, Carter and May label as structural mobility instances where (accurately measured) changes in poverty status are driven by changes in asset holdings or in the general set of prices that reflect the economic returns to assets.

Building on their 1999 work, Carter and May suggest that structural mobility can be distinguished from stochastic mobility by referring to the asset poverty line (APL). As illustrated in figure 3-1, the APL is the level of assets (denoted $\underline{A}$) that predicts a level of well-being equal to the poverty line, $\underline{u}$. To identify the APL, it is necessary to estimate the expected relationship between assets and income—the function $\hat{u}(A)$ in figure 3-1—or what Carter and May call the livelihood mapping from asset stocks to expenditure flows.

While there are a number of challenges to estimating the APL, economic theory provides some very useful insights on the nature of livelihood mapping. As

Figure 3-1. *Decomposing Transitions with an Asset Poverty Line*

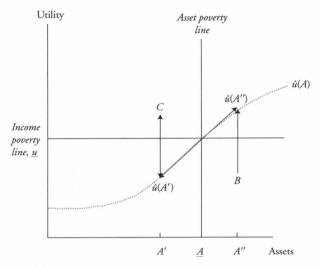

Source: Carter and May (2001).

discussed by Carter and May (1999), in the economist's mythical world of full and complete markets, the livelihood map will simply be linear in all dimensions. However, as was long ago noted by Chayanov (1965) in his analysis of pre-Soviet Russian agriculture (and as has been subsequently amplified by models of multiple market imperfections), missing markets add curvature and nonlinearities to the livelihood map.[3] That is, households of different wealth levels will use their assets differently and attain different returns to their factors of production. For example, the livelihood function will be flat—indicating low marginal returns— for poorer households without access to the finance needed to adequately capitalize a production process. It will be steeper for wealthier households or for households with better access to financial markets. Estimation of the livelihood map and identification of the APL require attention to these nonlinearities.

For illustrative purposes, figure 3-1 assumes that there is only one asset (for ease of drawing) and that the nonlinearities suggested by economic theory have been captured. Purely for expositional purposes, assume for the moment that the livelihood function does not change over time.[4] Then in any time period, a household is stochastically poor if it holds assets worth at least $\underline{A}$ yet its realized income or expenditure falls stochastically below $\underline{u}$. Conversely, a household is structurally poor if its stock of assets is less than $\underline{A}$ and its realized income or expenditure level falls, as expected, below $\underline{u}$.

A household that moved over time from above to below the standard expenditure-based poverty line could be said to have made a stochastic transition back to its expected status if the household's assets still mapped into an expected standard of living below the poverty line. In figure 3-1, this transition is illustrated as the movement from point C back to the point $\hat{u}(A')$. Alternatively, a household that moves from $\hat{u}(A'')$ to $\hat{u}(A')$ would have made a structural transition below the poverty line due to a loss of assets from A'' to A'. A similar decomposition of upward mobility into its stochastic and structural components can be made for households that are observed over time to move above the standard poverty line.

This asset-based approach thus opens the door to a much deeper understanding of the nature of poverty and how and why it is changing over time.[5] Carter and May (2001), for example, estimate that less than half of the observed transitions out of poverty in South Africa over the 1993 to 1998 period are structural, as 60 percent of the households that made the transition had initial period assets that strongly predicted well-being in excess of the standard poverty line. In terms of downward mobility, Carter and May find that only a small fraction (15 percent) clearly fell into poverty for stochastic reasons whereas fully 51 percent of those who fell behind suffered asset losses that left them structurally poor in the latter survey period. While there is ample room for improvement in estimation and other methods needed to use the APL to decompose poverty transitions, it does illustrate the possibilities attached to asset-based approaches to poverty.

Using Asset Dynamics to Measure Chronic Poverty

Asset-based approaches to poverty have the potential to contribute to our understanding of chronic poverty and poverty traps. Conventional quantitative poverty analysis invariably looks backward to the most recent living standards survey to enumerate (the past) extent and nature of poverty. By its very construction such approaches are ill-equipped to answer questions about the future persistence of observed poverty status: are the observed poor chronically poor or are they in a transitory status? Note that this question applies even to those identified as structurally poor using an approach based on the APL.

Others have struggled with this question. One approach is empirical and relies on panel data. With numerous repeated observations of the same households, the chronically poor can be identified as those who have been "frequently" poor in the observed past.[6] While this approach has much to recommend it, it is expensive and has an ad hoc element.[7] It is also backward looking.

However, some recent work has taken a rather different approach to the definition and measurement of chronic poverty. Guided by the increasingly sophisticated microeconomic theory of poverty traps, Carter and Barrett (2006) use the past to identify structural patterns of change—asset dynamics—rather than past levels of poverty. The statistical identification of these patterns then permits the creation of forward-looking poverty measures that can be used to predict where the poor will be in the future, not where they have been in the past. These new measures do not obviate other approaches. Indeed, when combined with standard approaches, they promise a more complete poverty diagnostic for a particular economy.

Building on the theoretical work of Buera (2005), Barrett, Carter, and Ikegami (forthcoming) construct a dynamic model of asset accumulation where individuals are heterogeneous in the sense that they have distinct innate skills or abilities. Individuals have access to two livelihood strategies: a low-potential and a high-potential strategy. The low-potential strategy can be run with very little accumulated capital assets, whereas the high-potential strategy requires a minimum level of capital before it is effective. Higher skill levels boost the returns to both strategies. The key question asked by the model is whether individuals who begin with low asset levels will be willing and able to accumulate assets over time so that they can eventually switch to the high-potential strategy and reach a nonpoor standard of living.

Analysis of this model shows that the answer to this question depends on the individual's ability level and how far he or she is from having the assets required to switch to the high-return strategy. More precisely, the model shows that the structurally poor—even those who are observed to be frequently poor over a short-term time horizon—are potentially of three types with distinct future prospects and possibilities:

—The *economically disabled* are those of relatively low skill and possibilities who are inevitably in a poor, low-level equilibrium trap.

—The *multiple equilibrium poor* are a middle-ability group that will move to the high-potential strategy if they are not too far away from the needed minimum capital; otherwise they remain with the low-potential strategy.

—The *upwardly mobile* are those of relatively high ability who will always try to steadily accumulate the capital needed to switch strategies and are expected to surmount a poor standard of living given a sufficiently long period of time.

Figure 3-2, which was created through numerical analysis of the dynamic model, illustrates these three classes. Along the horizontal axis are skill levels (α), ranging from least to most able. The vertical axis measures the stock of productive assets (k). The dashed line labeled $\hat{k}(\alpha)$ denotes the asset levels needed to

Figure 3-2. *The Micawber Threshold and Asset Accumulation*

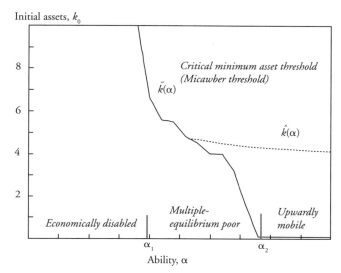

Source: Barrett, Carter, and Ikegami (forthcoming).

switch to the high-potential strategy. The key question of the model, then, is whether individuals located below $\hat{k}(\alpha)$ will be willing to sacrifice consumption over time, accumulating assets until they cross over $\hat{k}(\alpha)$ and can adopt the high-potential livelihood strategy. The individual's choice is further complicated by risk, meaning that there is no guarantee that consumption sacrifice will pay off since negative shocks can destroy accumulated assets.

Analysis of this choice problem identifies the solid curve, $\bar{k}(\alpha)$, shown in figure 3-2. An individual who begins life with a skill-asset combination right on the curve is indifferent between staying with the low-potential strategy and trying to build up stocks of assets so that a transition to the high-potential strategy eventually becomes feasible. An individual i with initial assets in excess of that amount $[k_0 > \bar{k}(\alpha_i)]$ will attempt to accumulate assets and move out of poverty. Otherwise, the individual will stay with the low-potential strategy, accumulating only the modest levels of capital that it requires. Note that the curve $\bar{k}(\alpha)$ is a generalization of what Carter and Barrett (2006) call the Micawber threshold (MT) as it divides those who have the wealth needed to accumulate from those who do not.[8]

As figure 3-2 shows, highly skilled individuals with $\alpha > \alpha_2$ will always move toward the high equilibrium as $\bar{k}(\alpha) = 0$ for all $\alpha > \alpha_2$, even if they find themselves with a zero stock of initial assets. These are the *upwardly mobile*—perhaps poor over some extended period as they move toward their steady state value but eventually nonpoor. In contrast, those with ability below the critical level α_1 will never move toward the high-potential livelihood strategy. These are the *economically disabled* individuals who suffer a fundamental disability and lack the ability to achieve a nonpoor standard of living in their existing economic context.[9]

Finally, and most interesting, the intermediate group with skills between α_1 and α_2 have positive but finite values for $\tilde{k}(\alpha)$. If sufficiently well endowed with initial assets $[k_0 > \tilde{k}(\alpha_i)]$, these individuals—the *multiple-equilibrium poor*—will accumulate additional assets over time and eventually adopt the high-potential strategy and reach a nonpoor standard of living. If they begin with assets below $\tilde{k}(\alpha_i)$, these individuals will no longer find the high equilibrium attainable and will settle into a low standard of living. Like the economically disabled, this subset of the multiple-equilibrium poor will be chronically poor.

This theoretical perspective on asset accumulation suggests that an asset-based approach potentially can be used to sort the poor into those who are expected to escape poverty and those who are not. However, practically this first requires estimation of the MT. Under the strong assumption that $\tilde{k}(\alpha)$ is the same for everyone, several recent studies have used panel data to estimate patterns of asset dynamics and thereby identify the MT (Barrett and others, 2006; Adato, Carter, and May, 2006). With this threshold empirically identified, the analyst can count the number of people who are below the threshold, giving a forward-looking headcount of the chronically poor. As discussed by Carter and Barrett (2006), a fuller suite of poverty measures can also be constructed based on the distance between individuals' asset positions and the MT. Asset dynamics, used in conjunction with standard poverty measures and those based on the aforementioned APL, offer a longer-term perspective on the likely evolution of well-being and thereby flesh out the dynamics of well-being at the lower tail of the wealth distribution.

Using Asset Thresholds to Design Social Protection Policy

It has been shown that asset-based approaches can generate new insights into the nature and persistence of poverty. This section explores the idea that these same approaches can be used to design and structure antipoverty policy interventions.

The theory outlined in the prior section has two very powerful implications for individuals in the middle-skill category:

—Individuals below the MT will need a discrete asset transfer to lift them to a position from which they have a feasible accumulation strategy to eventually reach a nonpoor standard of living. Barrett, Carter, and Little (2006) refer to these transfers as "cargo net" policies.

—Individuals who are above the MT, but are in danger of falling below it because of random shocks, can be assisted by a productive safety net that keeps them from falling below the critical threshold.

The social returns to both cargo and safety nets are potentially quite high because they place and keep individuals in positions where they can help themselves. Failure to do so can mean an ever-increasing number of chronically poor people. To the extent that these individuals become claimants on conventional forms of relief and disaster assistance, failure to design proper policies to keep individuals out of poverty traps can itself place aid and public expenditures into a relief trap where ever larger budget shares are soaked up by assistance. Using simulation analysis of the model outlined in the preceding section, Barrett, Carter, and Ikegami (forthcoming) demonstrate the high returns to modest investment in productive safety nets. While such work illustrates the potential of an asset-based approach, much still needs to be done to move these ideas to the stage of policy implementation.

Conclusion

This chapter has laid out a case for asset-based approaches to poverty. While a number of studies have used asset indicators to provide a more detailed characterization of the poor, the focus here has been on approaches that use asset information in conjunction with insights from economic theory to decompose poverty into its stochastic versus structural components in the short term, and its transitory versus chronic components in the long term. Each of these approaches can be used to create new classes of poverty measures that in conjunction with conventional flow-based poverty measures promise a fuller characterization of an economy, its income distribution, and for whom it is working. Finally, these same analytical devices that can be used to create more complete poverty measures offer themselves as key components for the design of durable and cost-effective antipoverty policies.

Notes

1. *Assets* is used here to denote the general class of factors that can be used to generate livelihood, including human capital, land, machinery, and social capital.

2. See, for example, the study by Grootaert and Kanbur (1995), as well as the various studies reported in the volume edited by Baulch and Hoddinott (2000).

3. For examples of models of multiple market imperfections, see Eswaran and Kotwal (1986), Carter and Zimmerman (2000), and Finan, Sadoulet, and Janvry (2005).

4. In general, one would expect the livelihood function, and therefore the asset poverty line, to move as rates of return change due, for example, to price changes or to technological change that affects productivity.

5. As discussed in greater detail by Carter and May (2001), using the APL to decompose transitions requires attention to the fact that there are only (imprecise) estimates available for a household's level of well-being.

6. See, for example, Chronic Poverty Research Centre (2004) and Hulme and Shepherd 2003).

7. For example, how frequently must an individual be observed to be poor in order to be classified as "chronically poor"?

8. As discussed by Carter and Barrett, the phrase *Micawber threshold* was first used by Michael Lipton (1993) and was subsequently adopted by Zimmerman and Carter (2003), who give it a meaning similar to that used here.

9. For examples of individuals who suffer such fundamental disabilities, see Chronic Poverty Research Centre (2004).

References

Adato, Michelle, Michael R. Carter, and Julian May. 2006. "Exploring Poverty Traps and Social Exclusion in South Africa Using Qualitative and Quantitative Data." *Journal of Development Studies* 42, no. 2: 226–47.

Attanasio, Orazio P., and Miguel Székely. 2000. *An Asset-Based Approach to the Analysis of Poverty in Latin America*. Washington: Inter-American Development Bank.

Barrett, Christopher B., Michael R. Carter, and Menubu Ikegami. Forthcoming. "Social Protection Policy to Overcome Poverty Traps and Aid Traps: An Asset-Based Approach." Working Paper. University of Wisconsin.

Barrett, Christopher B., Michael R. Carter, and Peter D. Little. 2006. "Understanding and Reducing Persistent Poverty in Africa: Introduction to a Special Issue." *Journal of Development Studies* 42, no. 2: 167–77.

Barrett, Christopher B., and others. 2006. "Welfare Dynamics in Rural Kenya and Madagascar." *Journal of Development Studies* 42, no. 2: 248–77.

Baulch, Bob, and John Hoddinott. 2000. *Economic Mobility and Poverty Dynamics in Developing Countries*. London: Frank Cass.

Buera, Francisco. 2005. "A Dynamic Model of Entrepreneurship with Borrowing Constraints." Working Paper. Northwestern University.

Carter, Michael R., and Christopher B. Barrett. 2006. "The Economics of Poverty Traps and Persistent Poverty: An Asset-Based Approach." *Journal of Development Studies* 42, no. 2: 178–99.

Carter, Michael R., and Julian May. 1999. "Poverty, Livelihood and Class in Rural South Africa." *World Development* 27, no. 1: 1–20.

———. 2001. "One Kind of Freedom: The Dynamics of Poverty in Post-Apartheid South Africa." *World Development* 29, no. 12: 1987–2006.

Carter, Michael R., and Frederick J. Zimmerman. 2000. "The Dynamic Cost and Persistence of Asset Inequality in an Agrarian Economy." *Journal of Development Economics* 63, no. 2:265–302.

Chayanov, Alexander V. 1965. *Peasant Farm Organization.* Homewood, Ill.: Richard Irwin Press.

Chronic Poverty Research Centre (CPRC). 2004. *The Chronic Poverty Report 2004–05.* Manchester, U.K.

Eswaran, Mukesh, and Ashok Kotwal. 1986. "Access to Capital and Agrarian Production Organization." *Economic Journal* 96, no. 382: 482–98.

Finan, Frederico, Elisabeth Sadoulet, and Alain de Janvry. 2005. "Measuring the Poverty Reduction Potential of Land in Mexico." *Journal of Development Economics* 77, no.1: 27–51.

Glewwe, Paul. 2005. "How Much of Observed Economic Mobility Is Measurement Error? A Method to Remove Measurement Error Bias, with an Application to Vietnam." Mimeo. University of Minnesota.

Grootaert, Christiaan, and Ravi Kanbur. 1995. "The Lucky Few amidst Economic Decline: Distributional Change in Côte d'Ivoire as Seen through Panel Datasets, 1985–1988." *Journal of Development Studies* 31, no.4: 603–19.

Hulme, David, and Andrew Shepherd. 2003. "Conceptualizing Chronic Poverty." *World Development* 31, no. 3: 403–23.

Lipton, Michael. 1993. "Growing Points in Poverty Research: Labour Issues." Paper presented at the International Labour Organization symposium "Poverty: New Approaches to Analysis and Policy." Geneva, November.

Moser, Caroline, and Andrew Felton. 2006. "Intergenerational Asset Accumulation and Poverty Reduction in Guayaquil, Ecuador, 1978 to 2004." Paper presented at the Brookings Institution–Ford Foundation Workshop on Asset-Based Approaches to Poverty in a Globalized Context. Washington, June 27–28.

Zimmerman, Frederick J., and Michael R. Carter. 2003. "Asset Smoothing, Consumption Smoothing and the Reproduction of Inequality under Risk and Subsistence Constraints." *Journal of Development Economics* 71, no. 2: 233–60.

4

The Stages-of-Progress Methodology and Results from Five Countries

ANIRUDH KRISHNA

A new participatory method, the Stages of Progress, was developed in 2002 to assess and explain households' movements out of poverty. It was found in the first investigation (conducted within thirty-six rural communities in Rajasthan, India) that almost as many households fell into poverty over the past generation as were able to escape from it. Subsequent investigations—conducted among a total of 236 diverse communities, covering 25,866 households in India, Kenya, Uganda, Peru, and North Carolina, United States—also showed that escape and descent have occurred concurrently in all locations. While some households have escaped from poverty, other households in the same community simultaneously fell into poverty. New poverty was created even as some old poverty was overcome.

To conceptualize this simultaneous process, a bathtub serves as a useful metaphor to characterize the findings of this and other studies. The "bathtub of poverty" is emptied by a drain, but it is refilled simultaneously by a continuously running faucet. The water exiting down the drain represents the individuals and families that are effectively escaping from poverty, and water filling the tub from the faucet stands for those who are concurrently falling into poverty. The level in this bathtub has not been lowered fast enough because the inflow from the faucet has offset the outflow from the drain, meaning that although the individuals mired in poverty are not necessarily always the same, the total poverty count remains relatively constant. This metaphor will be referenced throughout the chapter.

The first section of this chapter briefly outlines the stages-of-progress methodology. This methodology relies upon communities' understandings of poverty that are expressed in terms of discrete bundles of assets and capabilities. These robust, asset-based understandings of poverty have enabled communities to identify poverty groups and differentiate between individuals and households that have escaped from poverty and those that have fallen into it, and to single out the reasons associated with escapes and descents, respectively. In each particular context, a specific sequence of assets is defined, corresponding to incremental improvements in material status. This progression of assets serves as a marker of material progress, which communities utilize to evaluate different people's situations. Poor individuals are commonly identified by their communities in this manner. Ecological, cultural, and economic situations vary, and context-related progressions of sequentially acquired valuable assets differ across the different regions that were studied using this method. While many rungs in these ladders are similarly defined across regions and countries, many rungs are also different within particular contexts.

The second section presents the results from seven separate studies carried out using the stages-of-progress methodology. Other studies—in other countries, using other methods—have arrived at a similar conclusion: poverty is being created everywhere even as people move out of poverty. Yet little is being done to halt or slow down the creation of poverty. With our minds firmly fixed on widening and hastening the drain, we have practically ignored the fast-flowing faucet.

Different policies will be required, respectively, to promote escapes and prevent descents. Escaping poverty and falling into poverty are not symmetric in terms of reasons, as will be shown. While one set of reasons is associated with households' escape from poverty, a different set of reasons is associated with descents into poverty. Both sets of reasons need to be targeted by appropriate policies. Instead of any one ideal policy, *two* sets of policies must be pursued in tandem, one set to accelerate escapes out of poverty (widening the drain) and another set that help stem descents into poverty (turning off the faucet).

Both sets of policies will need to be regionally contextualized. Considerable differences in rates and reasons exist not just across countries, as could be expected, but also within countries and regions. Thus promoting escapes and preventing descents will require somewhat different interventions in different regions. A more decentralized approach is required to identify important factors operating within each specific context. The stages-of-progress methodology is additionally useful on this account.

The third section reviews some advantages and shortcomings of this methodology. The concluding section presents some policy consequences, dwelling on the need to more effectively *prevent descents* into poverty. This will require, in particular, improving quality and cost in health care provision.

The Stages-of-Progress Methodology

This approach was developed after extensive field investigations were undertaken in five countries. Building on a rich history of participatory approaches (for example, Chambers 1997; Narayan and others 2000; Salmen 1987), this methodology is rigorous but relatively simple to apply. After initial training, community groups can even utilize these methods on their own to track and explain poverty and to uncover appropriate solutions. It relies upon working with community groups to develop a ladder of successive steps consisting of capabilities and assets that people acquire sequentially as they move upward out of poverty. The first study was undertaken in the summer of 2002 in Rajasthan, India (Krishna 2004).

Seven Steps

The methodology has seven steps that are recounted briefly below.[1]

STEP 1. ASSEMBLING A REPRESENTATIVE COMMUNITY GROUP. This group included males and females, higher-status and lower-status community members, and older as well as younger members. In some instances advance notice had to be given to the community and its leaders.

STEP 2. PRESENTING OBJECTIVES. My coworkers and I (hereafter referred to as "we") introduced ourselves as researchers, making it clear that we did not represent any government agency or nongovernmental organization, so there would be no benefits or losses from speaking freely and frankly to us. These facts were mentioned to remove any incentives people might have for misrepresenting the poverty status of any household in their village.

STEP 3. DESCRIBING "POVERTY" COLLECTIVELY. Community groups in each village were asked to delineate the locally applicable stages of progress that poor households typically follow on their pathways out of poverty. "What does a household in your community typically do," we asked the assembled community members, "when it climbs out gradually from a state of acute poverty?" "Which expenditures are the very first ones to be made?" "Food," was the answer invariably in every single village. Which expenditures follow immedi-

Table 4-1. *Stages of Progress and the Poverty Cutoff*[a]

Stage	Peru (Cajamarca and Puno)	Kenya (western)	Uganda (western and central)	India Andhra Pradesh	India Gujarat	India Rajasthan
1	Food	Food	Food	Food	Food	Food
2	Clothing	Clothing	Clothing	House repairs	Clothing	Primary education
3	House repairs	House repairs	Primary education	Debt payments	Primary education	Clothing
4	Purchase small animals	Primary education	House repairs	Clothing	Debt payments	Debt payments
5	Primary education	Small animals			House repair or roof	
6	Purchase small plot of land				Renting a small tract of land to farm as sharecropper	

Sources: For Peru, Krishna and others (2006c); for Kenya, Krishna and others (2004); for Uganda, Krishna and others (2006b); for Andhra Pradesh, Krishna (2006); for Gujarat, Krishna and others (2005); for Rajasthan, Krishna (2004).

a. Dashed line indicates the poverty cutoff, as defined by the community groups.

ately after? "Some clothes," we were told almost invariably. As more money flows in incrementally, what does this household do in the third stage, in the fourth stage, and so on? Lively discussions ensued among villagers in these community groups, but the answers that they provided, particularly about the first few stages of progress, were relatively invariant across all communities of each region studied. "After crossing which stage is a household no longer considered poor?" we asked the assembled community members, after drawing up the progression of stages.

The placement of this poverty cutoff and the nature of the initial stages (that is, those below the poverty cutoff) differed somewhat across communities belonging to the different regions studied. However, remarkably similar understandings existed across diverse communities within each particular region. Across regions as well, there were considerable similarities in terms of these understandings of poverty, as table 4-1 shows. It was community members and not researchers who defined these stages of progress; the similarity in stages is more remarkable for this reason.

After crossing this cutoff, households are no longer considered poor, either by themselves or by their neighbors. Notice the progression in stages shown in table

4-1 as households gradually make their way out of poverty. In villages of Rajasthan, India, for example, the first four stages are food (or rather, the *capacity* to acquire basic food), primary education for children, clothing, and debt repayment (the capacity to repay debts in regular installments). The poverty cutoff is drawn immediately after this fourth stage. In Andhra Pradesh villages, similarly, the poverty cutoff is drawn immediately after the fourth stage. Three of these first four stages are similar between Rajasthan and Andhra Pradesh villages.

Later stages of progress beyond the first few are not reported in table 4-1. These stages included, for example, digging an irrigation well on one's own land; purchasing larger animals, particularly cattle; starting a small retail business; constructing a new house; purchasing jewelry; acquiring radios, fans, and tape recorders; and purchasing a motorcycle, tractor, or a small car. These are, however, discretionary expenses, and depending upon the taste of a household's members, purchasing a radio or tape recorder can precede or come after acquiring ornaments. There was, consequently, more variation in the ordering of these later stages in different villages.

Notice how people's understandings of poverty and movements out of poverty are shaped in terms of acquiring sequentially a particular set of assets and capabilities. These locally constructed understandings of poverty constitute the criteria within these communities for identifying who is poor. They also constitute a threshold or an objective that defines the goals and the strategies of poor people.

STEP 4. INQUIRING ABOUT HOUSEHOLDS' POVERTY STATUS TODAY AND IN THE PAST. In this step a complete list of all households in each village was prepared. Referring to the shared understanding of poverty developed in the previous step, the assembled community groups identified each household's status at the present time, twenty-five years ago, and also during an intervening period, eight to ten years ago.[2] Households of today formed the unit of analysis for this exercise.[3]

STEP 5. ASSIGNING HOUSEHOLDS TO PARTICULAR CATEGORIES. After ascertaining each household's poverty status for the present time and for twenty-five years ago (or ten years ago), each one was assigned to one of four separate categories:

—Category A: Poor then and poor now (remained poor);[4]
—Category B: Poor then but not poor now (escaped poverty);
—Category C: Not poor then but poor now (became poor); and
—Category D: Not poor then and not poor now (remained not poor).[5]

STEP 6. INQUIRING ABOUT REASONS FOR ESCAPE AND DESCENT FROM A RANDOM SAMPLE OF HOUSEHOLDS. We took a random sample of about 30 percent of all households within each category and inquired in detail about causes and contributory factors associated with each household's trajectory over the past twenty-five years. For each selected household, these event histories were checked independently with the community groups convened in each village, and these accounts were cross-checked with individual households.

STEP 7. FOLLOWING UP BY INTERVIEWING HOUSEHOLD MEMBERS. Reasons given by the community groups for each selected household's trajectory were cross-checked separately through individual interviews with members of the household concerned. At least two members of each household were interviewed separately in their homes.

Multiple sources of information were thus consulted for ascertaining reasons associated with the trajectories of each selected household. It took a team of six to eight individuals three to four days on average to complete these inquiries in one rural community (which has on average about 150 households). These were not standard eight-hour days, but it was an enjoyable learning experience.

Correspondence with Assets

The stages-of-progress approach provides a useful methodological device, a benchmark or yardstick, for assessing how high up the ladder of material prosperity a particular household has climbed within a particular region. Some limitations and required improvements are discussed in the concluding section.

Quite remarkable, however, is the fact that communities' understandings of poverty are expressed clearly in asset-based terms (broadly defined). A close correspondence also exists between the stage at which any household is placed during community discussions (step 4 above) and the total number of *tangible* assets possessed, including animals, radios, household furniture, and so on. Box 4-1 shows these results for communities studied in two regions of Uganda.

The average number of tangible assets possessed increases monotonically as a household advances along the stages of progress, that is, there is a close relationship between a household's present stage and its average number of tangible assets. Other visible characteristics—housing type, cattle ownership, education levels—also align neatly with a household's position on the stages of progress. Thus, whether assets are defined more broadly—for example, as "a stock of financial, human, natural or social resources that can be acquired, developed, improved and transferred across generations"—or whether a narrower definition is adopted, communities' understandings of (material) poverty are expressed in terms that are fundamentally asset based.[6]

Box 4-1. *Stages of Progress and Asset Ownership for Thirty-Six Communities in Uganda*

HOUSEHOLD STAGE AT PRESENT	AVERAGE NUMBER OF HOUSEHOLD ASSETS (OUT OF 10)
1	2.46
2	3.08
3	3.58
4	4.08
5	4.94
6	5.24
7	5.55
8	5.71
9	6.42
10	6.72
11	7.31
12	8.01

Source: Krishna and others (2006b).

The Faucet and the Drain

Between 2002 and 2006, seven separate studies were conducted using the stages-of-progress methodology, considering a total of 236 communities and tracking the pathways followed by 25,866 households. In chronological order, these studies were undertaken in Rajasthan, India (Krishna 2004); western Kenya (Krishna and others 2004); Gujarat, India (Krishna and others 2005); Andhra Pradesh, India (Krishna 2006); central and western Uganda (Krishna and others 2006b); two regions of Peru (Krishna and others 2006c); and thirteen communities in rural North Carolina, United States (Krishna and others 2006a). What follows is a brief summary of some key findings from these studies.

In every region studied, escape and descent have occurred in parallel. Even as some households have risen out of poverty in each region, other households have concurrently fallen into poverty, raising the level in the "bathtub." This simultaneity of escape and descent was evident in every community that was studied; there was no community in which only escape or only descent was experienced.

Everywhere, people are simultaneously both moving out of poverty and falling into poverty. New poverty is being created even as some old poverty is being destroyed. Yet the need to prevent the creation of poverty is hardly recognized in most policy.

Table 4-2. *Escape and Descent over Twenty-Five Years*
Units as indicated

Regions	Number of communities	Number of households	Percent of total households	
			Escaped poverty	Became poor
India				
Rajasthan	35	6,376	11	8
Gujarat	36	5,817	9	6
Andhra Pradesh	36	5,536	14	12
Kenya (western)	20	1,706	18	19
Uganda (central and western)				
	36	2,631	24	15
Peru (Cajamarca and Puno)	40	3,817	17	8
North Carolina, United States[a]	13	312	23	12

Sources: For North Carolina, Krishna and others (2006a). For other locations, see footnote to table 4-1.
a. Ten-year period.

Table 4-2 presents the aggregate data from seven separate regions studied so far. The first row of this table shows, for example, that of all households resident in thirty-six communities of Rajasthan (India), 11 percent escaped from poverty over the twenty-five-year period from 1977 to 2002. They were poor earlier, but they are not poor any more. Concurrently, however, another 8 percent of households fell into poverty; they were *not* poor in the earlier period, but they have become poor since.

Data from our other six studies are similar. In the western Kenyan communities, a total of 18 percent of all households escaped from poverty during 1980 to 2004, but another 19 percent fell into poverty over the same period. Poverty increased overall by 1 percent—even as large numbers of households escaped from poverty.

Studies conducted by other scholars, using other methods and studying other countries, have also reached a similar conclusion: poverty is simultaneously created and destroyed. Everywhere a drain and faucet operate in parallel; the bathtub of poverty is continually replenished.

Over a period of thirteen years, from 1987 to 2000, 26 percent of a panel of 379 Bangladeshi households considered by Sen (2003) escaped from poverty. Simultaneously, however, another 18 percent of households fell into poverty. Carter and May's (2001) study of 1,171 households in KwaZulu-Natal, South Africa, shows that over a five-year period from 1993 to 1998, 10 percent of households moved upward out of poverty, but another 25 percent of households fell into poverty in the same period. Analyzing results from their nationally representative sample of 1,300 Ugandan households, Deininger and Okidi (2003) found that while 29 percent of households came out of poverty over the eight-year period from 1992 to 2000, another 10 percent of households fell into poverty. Even within the short period of three years, from 1997 to 1999, considered by Haddad and Ahmed (2003), six percent of a sample of households in Egypt escaped from poverty, and another 14 percent of households fell into poverty. No matter the country studied or the length of time period considered, escapes from poverty have occurred concurrently with descents into poverty.

It is not as if falling into poverty were some fringe phenomenon, one that is rare, affects a tiny proportion of households, or is easily reversed. An accumulating body of evidence shows that large numbers of households move into poverty each year—and it is not only borderline households that are affected by these flows.

Even formerly well-to-do households have fallen deeply into poverty. Households in Rajasthan, India, that fell into poverty have lost all or large parts of the productive assets that they previously owned. Many among these households have become entirely landless, and they see little hope of restoring their previous well-to-do status. Of the 344 Ugandan households that fell into poverty within the communities that we studied, as many as 24 percent can no longer afford food and clothes, and another 29 percent have pulled their children out of school. They have fallen so deeply into poverty that coming back out is at best a remote possibility.

Movements into poverty are not reversible in a very substantial number of cases. Some who fall into poverty are able to bounce back—in some cases the flow into poverty can be reversible—but many households that fell into poverty have remained persistently poor. Of households that fell into poverty in these Ugandan communities during the period from 1979 to 1994, only one-third had emerged out of poverty ten years later, in 2004. The remaining two-thirds of newly impoverished households continue to remain poor.

A poverty trap, corresponding to a low-level equilibrium, tends to ensnare many freshly impoverished people. Carter and Barrett (2006) show how such a poverty trap operates in practice. High health care costs or droughts force households to sell off their assets. Selling off a few cows and goats is not so bad, but as successively more assets are sold off by this household, there comes a point when a critical threshold is crossed. Households falling below this threshold of asset ownership find themselves occupying a poverty trap. Their capacity to earn has been impaired so much that it is well nigh impossible to make an escape out of poverty. Evidence that my colleagues and I gathered in Uganda

Table 4-3. *Principal Reasons for Descent into Poverty*
Percent of descending households

Reasons	India			Kenya (western)	Uganda (central and western)	Peru (Puno and Cajamarca)
	Rajasthan	Gujarat	Andhra Pradesh			
Poor health and health-related expenses	60	88	74	74	71	67
Marriage, dowry, or new household-related expenses	31	68	69		18	29
Funeral-related expenses	34	49	28	64	15	11
High interest private debt	72	52	60	. . .	. . .	. . .
Drought, irrigation failure, or crop disease	18	. . .	44	. . .	19	11
Unproductive land or land exhaustion	. . .	. . .	. . .	38	8	. . .
Number of households	364	189	335	172	202	252

Sources: See footnote to table 4-1.

and Peru shows that a majority of newly impoverished households have become entangled in such a poverty trap.

Introducing a separate focus on falling into poverty is an important contribution of the stages-of-progress method. Why is so much poverty still seen, even in areas where programs are in place, where the economy has been growing and many households have managed to escape poverty? It is because large numbers of households continue to fall into poverty. In Rajasthan and Peru, for example, *more than one-third* of currently poor households were not always poor; they have acquired poverty within their lifetimes (Krishna 2004; Krishna and others 2006c).

Asymmetric Reasons for Escape and Descent

Different policy sets will be required to deal separately with escape and descent. The second important set of results from the stages-of-progress studies shows that escaping poverty and falling into poverty are *not symmetric* in terms of reasons. Everywhere, one set of reasons is associated with escapes out of poverty, but another and different set of reasons is responsible for descents. Tables 4-3 and 4-4 briefly outline the asymmetric nature of these reasons. Consider first table 4-3, which provides aggregate data about reasons for descent.

Health and health-related expenses have been most prominently associated with descents into poverty, followed in order by social expenses on funerals and marriages, and high-interest private debt. In communities of Kenya, Uganda, India, and Peru, health care is overwhelmingly the most important reason for households' descents into poverty. Health and health-related expenses were associated with nearly 60 percent of all descents recorded in villages of Rajasthan, India, 74 percent of all descents examined in Andhra Pradesh, India, and as many as 88 percent of all descents studied in villages of Gujarat, India. In communities of Kenya, Uganda, and Peru that we studied, 74 percent, 71 percent, and 67 percent of all descents, respectively, were associated with ill health and health-related expenses. In rural North Carolina as well, the majority of descents into poverty featured health and health care costs as a prominent factor.

Health problems operate commonly across all regions to drive households into poverty. Evidence collected in other countries, including Cambodia, Ethiopia, Haiti, Sierra Leone, Senegal, and Vietnam, points unambiguously to the deleterious effects of health care costs upon households' welfare (Asfaw and Braun 2004; Barrett, Reardon, and Webb, 2001; Deolalikar 2002; Fabricant, Kamara, and Mills 1999; Farmer 1999; Strauss and Thomas 1998). Households in China facing one serious health situation suffer average long-term income drops of 13 percent. When two or more health incidents are experienced consecutively, a household's slide into poverty becomes steeper and more assured (Gan, Lixin, and Yao 2005). "Rises in out-of-pocket costs for public and private healthcare services are driving many families into poverty and increasing the poverty of those who are already poor. The magnitude of this situation—known as 'the medical poverty trap'—has been shown by national household surveys and participatory poverty alleviation studies"(Whitehead, Dahlgren, and Evans 2001, p. 833). Not only does ill health reduce the earning capacity of a household's members but in the absence of affordable and easy-to-access health care facilities, it also adds considerably to the household's burden of expenditure, thereby striking a double blow, which quite often results in tragedy. The resulting dependence of survivors, including orphans, upon other households contributed further to descent in many cases. More than half of all personal bankruptcies in the United States are attributable to medical costs.[7]

Escaping poverty is not merely the reverse of falling into poverty. As Table 4-4 shows, very different reasons have been associated with escape. Diversification of income sources and jobs are the principal reasons related to escapes out of poverty. Irrigation and other land improvements in agriculture have constituted the second set of pathways leading people out of poverty.

Table 4-4. *Principal Reasons for Escaping Poverty*
Percent of escaping households

	India			Kenya (western)	Uganda (central and western)	Peru (Puno and Cajamarca)
Reasons	Rajasthan	Gujarat	Andhra Pradesh			
Diversification of income	70	35	51	78	54	69
Private sector employment	7	32	7	61	9	19
Public sector employment	11	39	11	13	6	10
Assistance from government or nongovernmental organization	8	6	7	. . .	. . .	4
Irrigation	27	29	25	. . .	. . .	. . .
Number of households	499	285	348	172	398	324

Sources: See footnote to table 4-1.

Because different reasons are responsible for escapes and descents, different policies need to be in force simultaneously. One set of policies is required to accelerate escapes out of poverty (widening the drain), and another and parallel set of policies is required to slow down descents into poverty (turning off the faucet). Without having the second set of policies also in place, the number of households in poverty cannot be reduced to any tolerable level.

A third important result from these investigations shows that considerable variations in rates and reasons exist both across countries, as could be expected, but also *within* countries and regions. For example, in the Panchmahals district of Gujarat, India, the village of Balaiya saw great success in reducing poverty, with 23.7 percent of the population escaping poverty and only 4.2 percent descending into it. Meanwhile, a neighboring village fared much worse. In Chikhali 9.3 percent of the population drained out of the bathtub of poverty as 20.6 percent poured in. (See Krishna and others 2005.) The disparity in poverty flows noted in these two communities is the trend, not the exception, and similar results were found repeatedly in other regions as well. This phenomenon was observed over a twenty-five-year period, and intraregional poverty disparity is still widely prevalent today

In addition, reasons (for escape and descent) also differ considerably across communities within a region. For example, diversification of income sources has been the most important reason associated with escaping poverty in all regions studied in India (and elsewhere), but different *kinds* of diversification are more important in each particular state and subregion. As a result different types of support will need to be provided in different regions and communities. A more decentralized and participatory approach, such as the stages-of-progress methodology, will help elicit these context-specific reasons.

Limitations and Strengths

Some limitations will need to be addressed as this methodology is extended further. First, the methodology will need to deal better with intrahousehold differences, particularly those based on gender. Females within households and female-headed households are more likely to be poor. In our thirty-six Gujarat villages, for instance, we interviewed members of a random sample of 133 female-headed households (Krishna and others 2005). Of these households, ninety-nine (74 percent) have remained poor over twenty-five years, and another 15 percent have become poor during this time, making for a total of almost 90 percent who live in poverty at the present. It is important, however, to supplement these investigations with inquiries about differences between males and females within households.

Second, the methodology will need to be adapted for dealing better with newly formed communities, particularly those in large cities. Because it relies upon commonly shared community memories, this methodology works better among more long-standing and close-knit communities. Ascertaining stages and reasons in the community meeting for each household presumes that community members are knowledgeable *and* willing to speak publicly about each other. Such communities are easier to find in rural areas but less prevalent in metropolitan areas.

The North Carolina study presented an exception to this trend. Because "poverty" is more stigmatized and less easily discussed publicly in the United States compared to the other countries we studied, and because communities are less stable in this region compared to others, the stages-of-progress methodology needed to be modified for application in North Carolina. Relatively more reliance was placed upon household interviews, which compromised to some extent the triangulation and verification that we can derive when each selected household's reasons and stages are additionally discussed in community meetings. Further refinements are being made in the course of an ongoing country-wide study in rural and urban Kenya.

Another potential weakness, common to all longitudinal studies, arises on account of the changing compositions of communities and households. Households twenty or even ten years hence will not be the same as the households of today. Some new households will be set up by young adults and new immigrants, and some will not be in the same place when the later study is conducted. Because households do not remain the same over time, some simplifying assumptions need to be made in longitudinal studies. While panel data studies consider households in the starting year of the study, neglecting all households newly arisen since that time, the stages-of-progress method entails an equal though opposite neglect. By considering households at the end of this period, this method neglects all households that have faded away during this time. Each method is useful for answering a different set of questions. By studying households that exist at the present time, one can elicit, particularly in the case of younger households, the difference between some individuals' inherited and acquired status: Did a person who was born to poverty remain poor at the end of the period, or did the individual manage to escape from poverty in the past several years? Is another person who was part of a nonpoor household ten years ago still nonpoor, or has she or he, regrettably, fallen into poverty?

Compiling these trajectories—of stability and change—helps us to assess the overall disposition of poverty over time. More important, learning about the reasons for change in each individual case helps to identify chains of events associated with escaping poverty and falling into poverty, respectively. Suitable context-specific interventions can be identified, resulting in more efficient and better targeted use of public resources for poverty reduction.

It is important to recall, however, that what can be ascertained using the stages-of-progress method are proximate causes as they are experienced at the microlevel. More distant causes, operating at the national and international levels, are also important to identify and address. Thus different methodologies will need to be brought together for a more comprehensive understanding of poverty.

Policy Consequences: Emptying the Bathtub of Poverty

Instead of being seen in terms of a rising tide, with all boats lifted equally, poverty is better conceptualized by a different image. Recent microlevel studies show consistently that in all communities and countries, some households are lifted up by a rising tide while others are simultaneously plunged into abiding poverty. The bathtub image captures these opposite dynamics better: a drain takes people out of the bathtub of poverty, but a faucet simultaneously adds more people in. Policies intended to move people out of poverty will not suffice to rid the bathtub of poverty. Unless the inflow from the faucet is simultaneously controlled, more newly impoverished people will simply replace those who have moved out.

Provision of protection and creation of positive opportunities are simultaneously required. Preventing descents into poverty is not a natural consequence of promoting more escapes. Different policies must operate simultaneously: one set to widen the drain and another set to slow down the faucet.

Descents are not automatically reduced just because economic growth is faster. In Gujarat, for instance, a state in India that has regularly achieved 9 percent growth rates for many years, health care continues to remain a severe problem for many. In thirty-five of the thirty-six Gujarat communities that we studied, large numbers of people have fallen into poverty because of health-related reasons (Krishna and others 2005). Affordable and effective health care services provided by a local nongovernmental organization have staved off the poverty trap in one exceptional community. Overall, health care in fast-growing Gujarat is no better than in other (and poorer) states of India. In fact, Gujarat ranked fourth from bottom among twenty-five states in terms of proportion of state income spent on health care (Mahadevia 2000).

Improving health care—making it more affordable, accessible, and effective—will go a long way toward emptying the bathtub of poverty. Relying upon economic growth alone to fix this problem will not suffice.

Japan presents an important example of simultaneously pursuing the two sets of policies. At 2 percent Japan's poverty rate is among the lowest in the world. Sustained economic growth undoubtedly helped reduce poverty in this country, but quite early in its growth process, Japanese government officials also recognized the critical interrelationship between illness, health care services, and poverty creation. Not convinced that poverty creation would be reduced merely as a side benefit of economic growth, the Japanese government initiated innovations in universal health coverage in the 1950s that, with several modifications, are still in place at the present time (Milly 1999). Other countries that have single-digit poverty rates also provided affordable high-quality health care to all residents, thereby addressing the most prominent reason for descent into poverty.

Other reasons for descent are not similar across contexts, and reasons for escape also differ from place to place. Fashioning contextually appropriate policies will require studying trends and reasons in context. Community-based methods, including those grounded in asset-related understandings of poverty, are likely to helpful for this purpose.

The Stages of Progress is one such method. It cannot be categorized as either qualitative or quantitative; it is a mixture of both. It captures many of the advantages of quantitative approaches, for instance, the ability to aggregate numerical information. At the same time, by working with a community-based understanding of poverty, it helps illuminate processes and strategies operating at the household and community levels. The more collaborative and communicative nature of this approach leads to results that are also more immediately useful to the communities concerned.

Different methods of studying poverty are variously useful for examining different aspects. While the stages-of-progress approach is helpful for ascertaining microlevel reasons for escape and descent, other methods are better for understanding macrolevel operations. Combining methods suitably will help clarify different facets of poverty. Progress in poverty reduction will be better as a result.

Notes

1. For a more detailed description of these steps and a complete training manual, see Anirudh Krishna, "Stages of Poverty: Disaggregating Poverty for Better Policy Impact" (www.pubpol.duke.edu/krishna [November 2006]).

2. A period of twenty-five years was selected for most regions because it corresponds roughly to one generation in time, and households' strategies are made in terms of generational time horizons. In addition, we also inquired about an interim period of eight to ten years ago. In order to denote the earlier periods clearly, we made reference to some significant event that is commonly known. For instance, in India, we referred to the national emergency of 1975–77, which is clearly remembered, particularly by older villagers. In Kenya, similarly, we referred to the year of President Kenyatta's demise.

3. Households of today are not strictly comparable to households of twenty-five years ago. However, household composition has been relatively stable in all communities studied; relatively few households, less than 2 percent in all, have either migrated in or migrated out permanently. Local inquiries also revealed that the households that had disappeared belonged to both ends of the wealth distribution. A few households that no longer remained in these villages had done extremely well by migrating to cities. A few others that had done extremely poorly had also entirely vanished, leaving no trace behind.

4. This category corresponds to the persistent or chronically poor, as identified by the Chronic Poverty Research Centre (2004) and Hulme and Shepherd (2003).

5. A residual category, E, was also defined, and households that could not be classified otherwise because of lack of information were assigned to this category. Very few households, less than 0.5 percent in all, were placed within this category.

6. See Moser, chapter 1 in this volume.

7. See David Himmelstein and others, "Marketwatch: Illness and Injury as Contributors to Bankruptcy," *Health Affairs*, Web Exclusive, February 2, 2005 (content.healthaffairs.org/cgi/content/full/hlthaff.w5.63/DC1).

References

Asfaw, Abay, and Joachim von Braun. 2004. "Is Consumption Insured against Illness? Evidence on Vulnerability of Households to Health Shocks in Rural Ethiopia." *Economic Development and Cultural Change* 53, no. 1: 115–29.

Barrett, Christopher B., Thomas Reardon, and Patrick Webb. 2001. "Nonfarm Diversification and Household Livelihood Strategies in Rural Africa: Concepts, Dynamics, and Policy Implications." *Food Policy* 26, no. 4: 315–31.

Carter, Michael R., and Christopher B. Barrett. 2006. "The Economics of Poverty Traps and Persistent Poverty: An Asset-Based Approach." *Journal of Development Studies* 42, no. 2: 178–99.

Carter, Michael R., and Julian May. 2001. "One Kind of Freedom: Poverty Dynamics in Post-Apartheid South Africa." *World Development* 29, no. 12: 1987–2006.

Chambers, Robert. 1997. *Whose Reality Counts? Putting the First Last*. London: Intermediary Technology Publications.

Chronic Poverty Research Centre. 2004. *The Chronic Poverty Report 2004–05*. Manchester, U.K.

Deininger, Klaus, and John Okidi. 2003. "Growth and Poverty Reduction in Uganda, 1992–2000: Panel Data Evidence." *Development Policy Review* 21, no. 4: 481–509.

Deolalikar, Anil B. 2002. "Access to Health Services by the Poor and the Non-Poor: The Case of Vietnam." *Journal of Asian and African Studies* 37, no. 2: 244–61.

Fabricant, Stephen, Clifford Kamara, and Anne Mills. 1999. "Why the Poor Pay More: Household Curative Expenditures in Rural Sierra Leone." *International Journal of Health Planning and Management* 14, no. 3: 179–99.

Farmer, Paul. 1999. *Infections and Inequalities: The Modern Plagues*. University of California Press.

Gan, Li, Lixin Xu, and Yang Yao. 2005. "Health Shocks, Village Governance, and Farmers' Long-Term Income Capabilities: Evidence from Rural China." Working Paper FE20050066. Beijing: Forum for Economic Development.

Haddad, Lawrence, and Akhter Ahmed. 2003. "Chronic and Transitory Poverty: Evidence from Egypt, 1997–99." *World Development* 31, no. 1: 71–85.

Hulme, David, and Andrew Shepherd. 2003. "Conceptualizing Chronic Poverty." *World Development* 31, no. 3: 403–24.

Krishna, Anirudh. 2004. "Escaping Poverty and Becoming Poor: Who Gains, Who Loses, and Why?" *World Development* 32, no. 1: 121–36.

———. 2006. "Pathways Out of and into Poverty in 36 Villages of Andhra Pradesh, India." *World Development* 34, no. 2: 271–88.

Krishna, Anirudh, and others. 2004. "Escaping Poverty and Becoming Poor in 20 Kenyan Villages." *Journal of Human Development* 5, no. 2: 211–26.

———. 2005. "Why Growth Is Not Enough: Household Poverty Dynamics in Northeast Gujarat, India." *Journal of Development Studies* 41, no. 7: 1163–92.

———. 2006a. "Escaping Poverty and Becoming Poor in Thirteen Communities of Rural North Carolina." Working Paper. Sanford Institute of Public Policy, Duke University.

———. 2006b. "Escaping Poverty and Becoming Poor in 36 Villages of Central and Western Uganda." *Journal of Development Studies* 42, no. 2: 346–70.

————. 2006c. "Fixing the Hole in the Bucket: Household Poverty Dynamics in Forty Communities of the Peruvian Andes." *Development and Change* 37, no. 5: 997–1021.

Mahadevia, Darshini. 2000. "Health for All in Gujarat: Is it Achievable?" *Economic and Political Weekly* 35 (August 26): 3193–204.

Milly, Deborah J. 1999. *Poverty, Equality, and Growth: The Politics of Economic Need in Postwar Japan.* Harvard University Press.

Narayan, Deepa, and others. 2000. *Voices of the Poor: Can Anyone Hear Us?* Oxford University Press.

Salmen, Lawrence. 1987. *Listen to the People: Participant-Observer Evaluation of Development Projects.* Oxford University Press.

Sen, Binayak. 2003. "Drivers of Escape and Descent: Changing Household Fortunes in Rural Bangladesh." *World Development* 31, no. 3: 513–34.

Strauss, John, and Duncan Thomas. 1998. "Health, Nutrition and Economic Development." *Journal of Economic Literature* 36, no. 2: 766–817.

Whitehead, Margaret, Goran Dahlgren, and Timothy Evans. 2001. "Equity and Health Sector Reforms: Can Low-Income Countries Escape the Medical Poverty Trap?" *Lancet* 358 (September 8): 833–36.

II

Asset Policy—
Social Protection or
Asset Accumulation Policy?

5

Asset Accumulation Policy and Poverty Reduction

CAROLINE MOSER

This chapter provides an introduction to asset accumulation policy and its contribution to sustainable poverty reduction.[1] It distinguishes between an asset index conceptual framework for poverty diagnosis and asset accumulation policy as an associated operational approach. This distinction is further clarified as follows:

—An asset index conceptual framework is an analytical and diagnostic tool for understanding poverty dynamics and mobility.

—An asset accumulation policy is an operational approach for designing and implementing sustainable asset accumulation interventions.

In describing these two components, the chapter seeks to demonstrate the value added by asset-based approaches, for both better understanding poverty and developing appropriate long-term poverty reduction solutions.

Asset-based approaches to poverty reduction are discussed in terms of some basic but pertinent questions. What is an asset? What new insights can an understanding of asset accumulation give us about poverty reduction? What is an asset-based approach? How does an asset index conceptual framework contribute to

I would like to acknowledge Pablo Farias at the Ford Foundation for his commitment and support to this work, and Anis Dani, Andrew Norton, and Peter Sollis for their substantive contributions.

83

Box 5-1. *Definition of the Most Important Capital Assets*

Physical capital: the stock of plant, equipment, infrastructure, and other productive resources owned by individuals, the business sector, or the country itself.

Financial capital: the financial resources available to people (such as savings and supplies of credit).

Human capital: investments in education, health, and the nutrition of individuals. Labor is linked to investments in human capital, health status determines people's capacity to work, and skills and education determine the returns from their labor.

Social capital: an intangible asset, defined as the rules, norms, obligations, reciprocity, and trust embedded in social relations, social structures, and societies' institutional arrangements. It is embedded at the microinstitutional level (communities and households) as well as in the rules and regulations governing formalized institutions in the marketplace, political system, and civil society.

Natural capital: the stock of environmentally provided assets such as soil, atmosphere, forests, minerals, water, and wetlands. In rural communities land is a critical productive asset for the poor whereas in urban areas land for shelter is also a critical productive asset.

Sources: Bebbington (1999), Carney (1998), Moser (1998), Narayan (1997), and Portes (1998).

---

the diagnosis of poverty? What is an asset accumulation policy? The chapter ends by briefly highlighting contexts where an asset accumulation framework and associated policy can usefully inform researchers and policymakers.

What Is an Asset?

Generally, an asset is identified as a "stock of financial, human, natural or social resources that can be acquired, developed, improved and transferred across generations. It generates flows or consumption, as well as additional stock" (Ford Foundation 2004).[2] In the current poverty-related development debates, the concept of assets or capital endowments includes both tangible and intangible assets, with the capital assets of the poor commonly identified as natural, physical, social, financial, and human (see box 5-1).

In addition to these five assets, which are grounded in empirically measured research (see Grootaert and Bastelaer 2002), more "nuanced" asset categories are being identified. These include aspirational (Appadurai 2004), psychological (Alsop, Bertelsen, and Holland 2006), productive, and political assets, the last being associated increasingly with human rights.[3] These examples illustrate the growing importance of thinking "outside the box" and moving beyond well-established categories of capital assets.

Understanding Asset Accumulation: New Insights about Poverty Reduction

Longitudinal research in Indio Guayas, a slum community in Guayaquil, Ecuador, highlights some of the limitations of static "snapshots" of poverty and illustrates a relative success story of asset accumulation and long-term poverty dynamics.[4] Over twenty-six years the majority of households have moved out of poverty. More than four out of five families were below the income poverty line when they originally "invaded" watery mangrove swampland and marked out the plots for their future homes. Today less than one in three is poor; they live in a built-up settlement with land titles and physical and social infrastructure; and their adult children are on average twice as educated as their parents. How did they do it?

Looking at the assets of the poor is essential in understanding upward mobility and particularly transitions out of poverty. A number of asset accumulation stories from Indio Guayas stand out. In the early days, the trust and collaboration forming the basis of community social capital were essential to households, which were squatting in bamboo houses connected by perilous walkways without land, roads, running water, lighting, or sewerage, let alone education or health. From 1975 to 1985, a vibrant community organization fought political leaders successfully to acquire social and physical infrastructure. From 1985 to 1995, welfare benefits and child care based on voluntary community delivery systems (primarily by women) were provided through UNICEF and Plan International. Thus community social capital continued to be important. Over the past decade, services were acquired and community welfare support was withdrawn, resulting in the decline of community social capital.

Social capital helped households to accumulate the physical capital associated with building their houses, acquiring land titles, and filling in their plots with earth. Over time, as households incrementally upgraded their houses, replacing bamboo walls with cement blocks and earth or wooden floors with cement, the value of this asset was consolidated. From 1978 to 1992, housing, the first critical asset that households seek to accumulate, grew the fastest of all assets. However, the asset accumulation rates reversed order from 1992 to 2004. Once housing was established, parents made trade-offs between their own consumption and their children's human capital, either investing in their education as a longer-term strategy for poverty reduction or spending it on "luxury" consumer durables.

Today, their adult sons and daughters, better educated but with greater expectations and aspirations, face different challenges in a globalized context. Nearly half still live on the family plot and benefit from the assets accumulated by their parents. Household social capital has increased over time, particularly among poorer households. Low wages, the high expenditure on human capital (health and education) associated with privatization of social infrastructure, and increasing demand for conspicuous consumption leave households needing more income earners than before. Others of the next generation have left to acquire homes of their own, repeating their parents' experience but this time squatting on the hills that form the city's new periphery. A third group has migrated, primarily to Barcelona, Spain, where the employment opportunities, labor rights, and access to financial capital such as mortgages all contribute to far more rapid asset accumulation than that of their peers in Guayaquil. There, increasing alienation, associated with a lack of wage employment opportunities, has resulted in a dramatic rise in violent robbery, theft, and drug dealing. Insecurity and fear predominate in all households (Moser 2005).

For the current generation, getting out of poverty may not be enough. Inequality and exclusion are also important issues to address. Thus different assets are important at different times. In totality, the history of asset accumulation illustrates the pathways by which individuals, households, and communities make it out of poverty. But does this provide useful lessons?

What Is an Asset-Based Approach?

Asset-based approaches to development are rooted in the international poverty alleviation–reduction debate of the 1990s. This dialogue raised questions about conventional measurements of poverty; identified the multidimensionality of poverty and the relationship between inequality, economic growth, and poverty reduction in the south; redefined the meaning of poverty itself; and elaborated new poverty-reduction strategies. Heavily influenced by the work of Amartya Sen (1981) on famines and entitlements, assets, and capabilities, as well as by that of Robert Chambers (1992, 1994) and others on risk and vulnerability, an extensive debate distinguished between poverty as a static concept and vulnerability as a dynamic one. It focused on defining such concepts as assets, vulnerabilities, capabilities, and endowments, and on developing policies to address the impacts of shocks by focusing on the assets and entitlements of the poor. The issue of risk and insecurity lies at the core of this "new poverty" focus. Insecurity is defined as exposure to risk, with the outcome being vulnerability in terms of a decline in well-being.

As the name implies, asset-based approaches are concerned specifically with assets and associated asset accumulation strategies. This emphasis is closely linked to the concept of capabilities. Thus assets "are not simply resources that people use to build livelihoods: they give them the capability to be and act" (Bebbington 1999). As such, assets are identified as the basis of agents' power to reproduce, challenge, or change the rules that govern the control, use, and transformation of resources (Sen 1997). A review of current asset-based approaches shows there is no single analytical framework or operational approach but a range of both. It is also useful to distinguish between researchers, who have constructed an analytical framework around assets, and practitioners, who have applied this to operational approaches.

As summarized in table 5-1, asset-based frameworks and associated operational approaches can be loosely divided into four types:

—The asset vulnerability framework that emphasizes the relationship between assets, risks, and vulnerability. At the operational level, this relationship is at the core of social protection policy and programs.

—The asset-based research approach closely associated with the BASIS Collaborative Research Support Program. Operational work connected with this includes asset-based assessments that identify poverty traps and productive safety nets.[5]

—In the United States, the asset-building approach developed by Sherraden (1991) and Oliver and Shapiro (1990) and operationalized through the Ford Foundation's Asset Building and Community Development Program. A range of formal interventions (such as Individual Development Accounts and the U.K. Child Trust Fund) are connected with this, as well as a range of community-based asset-building programs and associated methodological tools.

—Internationally focused longitudinal asset accumulation research and associated asset accumulation policy, which this paper describes.

Using an Asset Index Conceptual Framework to Diagnose Poverty

Asset index conceptual approaches to poverty diagnosis and analysis are not new but have not, to date, been widely recognized. However, they represent an important shift in focus in the historical development of poverty research methodology and its associated policy. While traditional 1960s and 1970s research emphasized income poverty, the new wave of pro-poor policy created by the World Bank's 1990 and 2000 world development poverty reports (World Bank 1990, 2000) and the UN's Millennium Development Goals shifted the focus to consumption. Asset accumulation shifts the focus even further by connecting it to production and providing the link between individual and household enterprises, labor market participation, and poverty reduction (see appendix 5A).

Table 5-1. *Summary of Asset-Based Analytical Frameworks and Their Associated Operational Approaches*[a]

Analytical frameworks	Examples of authors or institutions	Operational approach	Authors or institutions	Examples of implementation: tools and techniques
Asset vulnerability framework	Moser (1998); Siegel (2005); Sabates-Wheeler and Haddad (2005); CPRC (2004)	Social protection	World Bank (1990, 2000)	Risk and vulnerability assessment
BASIS CRSP asset-based research approaches	Carter and May (2001); Hoddinott and others (2005); Adato, Carter, and May (2004)	Asset-based assessments	BASIS CRSP, for instance, Kerr and others (2005); Little (2002)	Tools to identify poverty traps
Asset building	Sherraden (1991); Ford Foundation (2004); Oliver and Shapiro (1990)	Asset building and community development	Ford Foundation (2004)	Asset building in financial holdings, natural resources, social bonds, and human capital
			Coady International Institute (Mathie and Cunningham 2003)	Asset-based community development "transformative" methodology
			Morad (2003); Fossgard-Moser (2005)	Community asset mapping
	Sherraden (1991)	Asset-based welfare policy	Corporation for Enterprise Development (U.S.); U.K. government	Individual development accounts; Child Trust Fund (U.K.)
Longitudinal asset accumulation research	Moser (1998); Moser and Felton (2006)	Asset accumulation policy	Moser (2007)	Nexus linking assets-opportunities-institutions; distinction between first- and second-generation policy

While standard poverty measures provide static backward-looking measures, asset-based approaches offer a forward-looking dynamic framework that identifies asset-building thresholds and measures movements in and out of poverty. This systematic, integrated approach identifies the links between different assets and their transformative potential through effective risk management. As such, it seeks to identify how to strengthen opportunities and dilute constraints. In focusing on how the poor construct their asset portfolios, this approach recognizes the importance of individual and collective agency and the links between asset accumulation and inequality, security, and political stability.

The evidence for asset-based approaches comes from a range of research. Of particular methodological importance have been different initiatives to construct asset indexes, by such researchers as Sahn and Stifel (2000), Filmer and Pritchett (1999), and Carter and May (2001). The longitudinal research project on intergenerational asset accumulation and poverty reduction in Guayaquil, Ecuador (1978–2004), described in chapter 2, used a fourfold asset index as a diagnostic tool to understand poverty dynamics and mobility, and to examine the long-term investment choices made by households. The range of assets held by households were categorized, as were the processes by which each asset was accumulated or eroded over time and the relative importance of different assets for intergenerational poverty reduction. According to the data, the asset accumulation potential of households depends on the interrelationship between their original investment asset portfolio and the broader opportunity structure in terms of the internal life cycle, the external politicoeconomic context, and the wider institutional environment (Moser and Felton 2006)

Asset index analysis adds value to understanding upward mobility and transitions. It shows how different assets can be accumulated at different points in time and clarifies the interrelationship between different assets. The Guayaquil study, for instance, showed that households started by heavily investing in housing capital. This was the first priority for those invading swampland and living under very basic conditions. As basic housing needs were met, however, households accumulated other types of capital, both for production and consumption purposes. As a result housing capital accumulation leveled off and was replaced by the accumulation of consumption capital. Education and financial capital increased fairly steadily across the entire time period. Finally, while community social capital actually fell between 1992 and 2004, household social capital rose.

What Is an Asset Accumulation Policy?

Asset accumulation policy is the associated asset-based operational approach that focuses directly on creating opportunities for the poor to accumulate and consolidate their assets in a sustainable way. It identifies asset accumulation as a precondition for empowerment, particularly economic empowerment.

Asset Accumulation and Social Protection: Differences and Complementarities

How does asset accumulation policy relate to other poverty reduction policies? At the overall level, the dominant paradigm has relied on at least three critical components: growth-led poverty reduction, targeted cash transfers, and social safety nets.[6]

Over the past decade, alongside the range of poverty-focused frameworks using similar concepts—such as capabilities, assets, livelihoods, vulnerabilities, institutions, agency, and opportunities—there has been the parallel design of a number of new antipoverty programs. Foremost among these in the late 1990s was sustainable livelihoods, given priority by bilateral institutions such as the U.K. Department for International Development and international nongovernmental organizations such as CARE and Oxfam. Today, influenced by the World Bank's 2000 world development report on poverty, donors, governments, and nongovernmental organizations have widely adopted a social protection policy approach. (See box 5-2). Social protection policy has an extensive breadth of coverage, ranging from ex-ante protective measures to ex-post safety nets. Such safety nets go beyond food aid to "productive" safety nets that ensure that those experiencing asset-based shocks remain above the poverty threshold and do not fall into a poverty "trap," with the associated longitudinal chronic poverty.[7]

For example, the Ford Foundation–funded social protection program in Asia seeks to be welfare enhancing while also contributing to growth and efficiency objectives, and while not explicitly adopting an asset-based approach, the initial analysis and framework had a strong focus on various forms of asset building as the underpinning of sustainable development and social protection. The program maintains that assets reduce dependence on social protection, but social protection will remain the dominant, essential element of social policies for poor countries. The program states that it needs to look at social protection as developmental and not just as relief assistance. Responses to crisis should be demand led and community driven (see Cook, Kabeer, and Suwannarat 2003).

What can an asset framework offer that social protection cannot? The apparent overlap between these different approaches makes it important to clarify

---

Box 5-2. *Definitions of Sustainable Livelihoods and Social Protection*

Livelihoods: A livelihood comprises the capabilities, assets, and activities required for a means of living. A livelihood is identified as sustainable when it can cope with and recover from stresses and shocks and maintain or enhance capabilities and assets, both now and in the future, while not undermining the natural resource base (Carney 1998, p. 1; Department for International Development 2000).

Social protection: This has been defined as "longer-term policies that aim to protect and promote economic and social security or well-being of the poor. Social protection policies are designed to . . . provide a buffer against short-term shocks, and also enhance the capacity of households to accumulate assets and improve their well-being so that they are better protected in times of hardship" (Cook, Kabeer, and Suwannarat 2003). The World Bank's Social Risk Management framework identifies social protection as consisting of "public interventions to assist individuals, households and communities in better managing income risks" (Holtzmann and Jorgensen 1999, p. 1008) by "preventing, mitigating and coping with risks and shocks" (World Bank 2000).

---

more specifically how asset accumulation policy differs from, or complements, social protection policy. Table 5-2 provides a brief summary and shows the differences in emphasis in operational approaches. With such closely aligned objectives, interventions associated with one framework can contribute to those of another. However, there are distinct entry points that result in prioritizing different objectives in operational practice.

One difference relates to the way each regards and deals with the issue of risk. As the name implies, asset-based frameworks are concerned more specifically with assets and their associated long-term accumulation strategies. Assets are more closely linked to growth and risk management. From the asset accumulation perspective, risk is an opportunity. Managing such risk is about proactively identifying and investing in opportunities, so the biggest risk is not taking a risk.

Table 5-2. *Recent Policy Approaches to Poverty Reduction and Associated Objectives*

Analytical framework	Primary objectives of operational approach
Sustainable livelihood approach	Sustaining activities required for a means of living
Social protection	Providing protection for the poor and vulnerable against negative risks and shocks that erode their assets
Asset-based social policy	Creation of positive opportunities for sustainable asset accumulation

From the social protection perspective, risk is a danger, so risk management strategies are designed to defensively reduce or overcome the associated shocks, stresses, and vulnerabilities. Thus social protection focuses more on protecting the poor from erosion of assets or on helping the poor recover them. When people reach a "poverty threshold," below which it becomes extremely difficult for them to accumulate assets on their own, productive safety nets provide a policy solution (Barrett and Carter 2005). Research indicates that health shocks, such as sickness and disease, are the most powerful force for pushing people below this threshold.[8] Livelihood strategies also overlap with assets and social protection approaches. They are an evolving set of strategies to improve well-being through investing in assets, and through providing protection where necessary to deal with vulnerabilities. As the name implies, these strategies are primarily concerned with well-being per se.

Asset accumulation policy can be useful in its own right only if policy interventions, along with different objectives, are clearly distinguished from those of livelihood strategies and social protection. Table 5-3 illustrates this distinction in the case of international migration and transnational asset accumulation (see Hall 2007). It shows how these three policy approaches complement one another, and highlights the distinctions between interventions designed to strengthen livelihood (well-being), protect those most vulnerable, and enable the accumulation of long-term sustainable assets.

Components of Asset Accumulation Policy

Asset accumulation policy focuses on creating opportunities for long-term asset accumulation. Figure 5-1 provides a visual representation of the framework, which incorporates an iterative asset-institutions-opportunities nexus. There are four basic principles.

First, the process by which the assets held by individuals and households are transformed into accumulated capital assets does not occur in a vacuum. Outside factors such as government policy, political institutions, and nongovernmental organizations all play important roles in determining how easily households can accumulate assets. Entry points to strengthen strategies for asset accumulation depend on context but may be institutional or opportunity-related in focus. The accumulation of one asset often results in the accumulation of others, while insecurity in one asset can also affect the others.

Mahajan, for instance, argues succinctly that in a globalized world, financial capital is becoming central to the other forms of capital assets, as each in turn becomes "financialized."[9] Natural capital, connected with land in many rural areas, is no longer communally owned but tradable, with forests privatized and

Table 5-3. *Ecuadorian International Migration: Operational Approaches and Associated Interventions in Ecuador and Spain*

Operational approach	Primary objectives	Interventions	Formal and informal institutions
Short-term strengthening of livelihoods for family in Ecuador	To provide immediate coping strategies	Remittances —provide income toward basic family needs for food, clothing, health care —act as cushion against lack of domestic employment opportunities	Migrant families
Provision of welfare support and social protection both for family in Ecuador and for migrant in Spain	To help mitigate the heavy costs of migration	Measures to assist with —psychological outcomes of changing family structure, particularly children left with extended family relatives —initiatives to equip migrants to cope better in destination country —legal protection of migrants in Spain	Church and nongovernmental organizations (funded by church in Ecuador; by European Union in Spain) Spanish government
Longer-term enhancing, diversifying, and consolidating the asset base of migrant families in Ecuador	To accumulate sustainable assets	Promotion of remittance-supported productive activities through —human capital (education training) —physical capital (water, electricity, land, housing) —financial capital (saving, loans) —communications to increase social status and retain homeland links to strengthen social capital	Civil society organizations such as Ecuador—Plan for Migration in high out-migration provinces (funded by AECI)[a] Small migrant self-help organizations Solidarity Bank (*Banco Solidario*)

Source: Constructed from Hall (2007).

a. Agencia Española de Cooperación Internacional (Spanish Agency for International Cooperation).

sold. Even air becomes financialized with carbon credits, while pollution, too, will be financialized in the future. In the case of social capital, this financialization includes the purchase of access to clubs and networks, and membership in circles that once required kinship. Human capital costs relate to the privatiza-

Figure 5-1. *Asset Accumulation Policy*

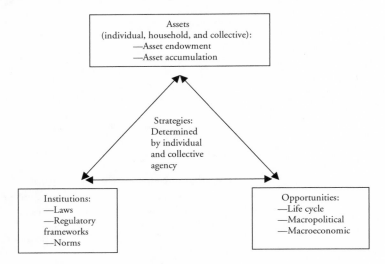

tion of both health and education. Private physical capital has always been financialized, but access to public goods is now being controlled and priced.

Second, institutions—in the form of laws, norms, and regulatory and legal frameworks—either block, allow, or positively facilitate asset accumulation in a variety of ways. These include the composition of the labor markets and unemployment, the linkages between education and employment, and government and donor social protection policies.

Third, with regard to opportunities, the formal and informal context within which actors operate can facilitate asset accumulation. This relates to the dynamics of microlevel household life-cycle opportunities and constraints and issues of individual agency. It also relates to meso-, macro-, and sector level economic growth, associated market opportunities, and constraints relating to the broader political and economic context.

Finally, the actual "strategy"—whether it is termed livelihood, coping, or survival—can best be identified as the means by which social actors transform endowed into accumulated assets. This process is determined by individual as well as collective agency. In some contexts the lack of returns on individual assets and capabilities has resulted in initiatives that focus on group-based, collective agency. Asset accumulation strategies are tailored to the different types of assets. Issues relating to trade-offs, sequencing, and prioritization are all critical and context specific.

Distinction between First- and Second-Generation Asset Accumulation Policy

Asset accumulation policy is not static but changes over time. Thus it is useful to distinguish between first- and second-generation policies.

First-generation asset accumulation policy provides the social and economic infrastructure essential for acquiring such assets as human capital, physical capital (for example, housing), and financial capital (durable goods). It is commonly assumed that acquisition of such capital is the precondition for individuals and households to further accumulate assets on their own and move out of poverty. Current pro-poor policies still focus almost exclusively on such first-generation strategies, as exemplified by the Millennium Development Goals. These include the provision of water, roads and electricity, housing plots, better health and education, and microfinance. Once these are provided, it is assumed that well-being improves and "development" occurs.

However, important though these are, they do not guarantee further asset accumulation. For instance, when such strategies do not bring the expected development returns, and increased human capital (higher education levels and health) does not result in the expected job opportunities, rising aspirations and growing despair can lead to increasing violence, exclusion, and alienation.

Second-generation asset accumulation policy is designed to strengthen accumulated assets, ensure their further consolidation, and prevent erosion. Given the traditional microlevel focus on assets, this is particularly important in a globalizing institutional context. New development opportunities, associated with increased trade and international migration, are accompanied by risks. These come from global warming and natural disasters, corruption, failing states and postconflict contexts, accelerated urbanization, increasing inequality, and growing violence. Without good governance, accountability, and security, returns on assets may not be achieved and sustainability may not be maintained.

Second-generation asset accumulation policy forges coherent links between a rapidly changing macrocontext (economic or political) and achieving structural transformations, rather than addressing stochastic changes (Barrett and Carter 2005). Such strategies go beyond issues of welfare and poverty reduction to tackle a range of concerns relating to citizen rights and security, governance, and the accountability of institutions.

Ultimately, the design of second-generation asset accumulation interventions must be context specific. In Guayaquil, Ecuador, for instance, this included

—strengthening social justice through the judicial system, including a broader range of preventative and punitive interventions;

—empowering local communities to access information about legal, economic, and social rights;

—identifying appropriate institutional structures for strengthening financial capital in households that have moved out of poverty but are still highly vulnerable; and

—developing city-level employment strategies to ensure that the gains in human capital are not eroded.

However, the range of experience that has focused, directly or indirectly, on asset accumulation also yields some more general policy principles.

Conclusion

The asset accumulation approach, comprising both an asset index conceptual framework and an asset accumulation policy, is still in exploratory stages of development. Subsequent chapters in this book contribute to this process by showing how application of asset accumulation strategies in a number of sector and cross-sector contexts can be informed by the framework outlined in this chapter. These discussions cover communal assets in rural and urban contexts, the erosion of assets in postdisaster and fragile state contexts, financial assets associated with making markets work, and transnational asset accumulation associated with international migration. One of the most challenging topics discussed is the issue of assets, rights, and citizenship. Practices in these contexts are linked not only by the identification of opportunities for the accumulation of assets but also by the range of institutions involved.

The examples presented in this volume identify a continuum of assets accumulated by households moving out of poverty. Such observations can pinpoint which assets are more important for reducing vulnerability versus those more likely to facilitate sustainable asset accumulation. Generally, physical capital assets related to land and housing and human capital assets associated with health can be considered "protective" or "preventative," buffering against shocks that precipitate households into falling into poverty. By contrast, financial capital, educational human capital, and even political capital can be identified as "promotional assets" that actively provide opportunities to move out of poverty in a sustainable way. Finally, social capital acts as the "glue" that holds it all together. While considerably more research and associated policy application remain to be done, experience thus far suggests that the framework is useful for researchers and policymakers alike as they seek to better understand poverty and provide more robust and sustainable solutions for poverty reduction.

Appendix 5A: Asset-Based Analytical Frameworks and Their Associated Operational Approaches

This section draws on Moser (1998). See also Davies (1993), Devereux (1993), and Maxwell and Smith (1992).

Vulnerability, Risk, and Assets

The asset vulnerability framework highlights the relationship between vulnerability, risks, and asset ownership, identifying not only risks (or threats) but also resilience in resisting or recovering from the negative effects of a changing environment. Vulnerability is closely linked to asset ownership.[10] The poor are managers of complex asset portfolios; different household capital assets contribute to well-being outcomes, with the associated capacity to manage assets cushioning households and limiting the impact of shocks (Moser 1998, p. 3). Siegel's asset framework (2005) shows that a household's capital assets determine its opportunities, while the broader "policy and institutional environment" influences a household's livelihood strategies. Researchers working on the "chronically" poor (those considered most vulnerable and multidimensionally deprived) also use a vulnerability framework (Chronic Poverty Research Centre 2004; Sabates-Wheeler and Haddad 2005).

In terms of operational practice, risk, vulnerability, and asset accumulation are at the core of the social protection framework developed by the World Bank (World Bank 2000; Holzmann and Jorgensen 2000). This framework uses a twofold typology of risk to distinguish between microlevel idiosyncratic risks that affect individuals or households, mesolevel covariant risks affecting groups of households and communities, and macrolevel risks affecting regions or nations. The related risk-management framework makes an important distinction between reducing and mitigating risk versus coping with shocks.

Asset-Based Approaches

Asset-based approaches have been developed to address the causes and dynamics of longer-term persistent structural poverty (primarily in rural Africa and Asia). The BASIS Collaborative Research Support Program, a policy-focused research group of U.S.-based economists with partners in the south, has drawn on longitudinal data to identify "dynamic asset poverty" and to distinguish between "deep-rooted persistent structural poverty and chronic and other forms of poverty that the passage of time will alleviate"(Adato, Carter, and May 2005).

This asset-based approach differentiates between stochastic poverty or "churning" (movement into or out of poverty due to short-term shocks) and structural mobility associated with gains or losses of productive assets. It identifies poverty traps, defined as a critical minimum asset threshold below which households cannot take advantage of positive changes or recover from negative ones (Barrett and Carter 2005).

In terms of operational practice, BASIS recommends programs that reduce long-term poverty effectively "through some combination of helping households to accumulate assets, providing access to institutions that increase the returns on those assets and minimizing the impact that shocks can have on a family's asset holding" (Hoddinott and others 2005). In addition, asset-based evaluations have assisted policymakers working on building assets for sustainable recovery and food security in Ethiopia (Little 2002) and improving property rights and environmental services in Indonesia (Kerr and others 2005).[11]

Asset Building

One of the best known approaches is the U.S. asset-building (or asset-based) policy. First developed by Michael Sherraden (1991), it is based on two premises: first, that the poor can save and accumulate assets, and second, that assets have positive social, psychological, and civic effects independent of the effects on income (Boshara and Sherraden 2004). Sherraden distinguished between assets (identified as the stock of wealth in a household) and income (the flows of resources associated with consumption of goods and services and maintaining a standard of living). He argued that welfare policy had been constructed mainly in terms of income and proposed that it should be based instead on savings, investment, and asset accumulation.

Sherraden's U.S. research showed that saving and accumulation are shaped by institutions, not merely by individual preference. The poor are not only asset poor but have few institutional structures within which to accumulate assets. For impoverished welfare recipients, asset accumulation is not encouraged, if even permitted: the "asset test" associated with means-tested income transfer programs prevents accumulation of more than minimal financial assets. And yet an extensive range of asset-based policies does exist, operating mainly through the tax system, such as homeownership tax benefits and 401(k)s. Thus an asset-based welfare policy can be designed to promote and institutionalize asset accumulation for the poor through approaches that are progressive (with greater subsidies for the poor), inclusive (asset inequality in the United States is largely racially based), lifelong, and flexible (Sherraden 1991, pp. 7–9).

In terms of operational practice, this asset-building framework has been effectively implemented since 1991 through a range of pilot programs aimed to broaden asset ownership both in the United States and, more recently, the

United Kingdom. Best known is the "American Dream" Individual Development Account (IDA) Demonstration, with 300 IDA programs throughout the United States supporting 15,000 account holders. IDAs are savings accounts provided to low-income families in which the deposits they make are matched with resources from a "blend of public and private funding" (Boshara 2005). Recent evaluations show that participants can save successfully in structured accounts, and such results have been instrumental in promoting federal IDA legislation. At the same time, there is no evidence that IDAs raise the net worth (assets minus debts) of savers (Lerman 2005). Supporters of this approach argue that even if accumulations are not large, they start early and enjoy the benefits of compounding: "what matters is not the amount, but the existence of accumulation" (Boshara 2005).

Alternative Bottom-Up Community Asset-Building Programs

A number of programs in both the north and south have extended the asset-building concept beyond individuals and households to incorporate community assets. They have also shifted from a more northern "top-down" concern with the "apathy" of an alienated welfare-dependent population to a "bottom-up," demand-driven approach. Foremost among these is the Ford Foundation's Asset Building and Community Development Program, designed to "reduce poverty and injustice." Building on the work of Sherraden (1991), Sen (1981), Putnam (1993), and others, the program's asset framework proposes that when low-income people gain control over assets, they gain the independence necessary to resist oppression, pursue productive livelihoods, and confront injustice (Ford Foundation 2004). The program proposes that an asset offers a way out of poverty because it is not simply consumed but rather constitutes a "stock" that endures and can be used to generate economic, psychological, social, and political benefits that foster resilience and social mobility. The program highlights inequalities in asset distribution across race, ethnicity, and gender, and supports grantees in building assets that communities can acquire, develop, or transfer across generations. This includes financial holdings, natural resources, social bonds and community relations, and human assets such as marketable skills.

Along with asset-building programs, participatory methodologies have been developed to operationalize a community, asset-based approach. Coady International Institute in Nova Scotia, Canada, has designed asset-based community development, a "transformative" methodology used to motivate community leaders to identify assets, link their mobilization for community activities, and strengthen their communities' capacities to sustain economic and social development over the longer term (Mathie and Cunningham 2003). Morrad Associates has designed an asset-mapping technique as a tool to map community assets and begin the process of building assets (Morrad 2003). This has been used in participatory community assessments conducted by private sector companies such as Shell in their operations in South Africa, Oman, and the United States (Fossgard-Moser 2005).

Notes

1. This chapter draws heavily on a background paper on assets, livelihoods, and social policy commissioned by the World Bank for their conference on New Frontiers of Social Policy: Development in a Globalizing World, Arusha, Tanzania, December 2006 (see Moser 2007).

2. This term has evolved over time, adapted for different purposes. Thus, according to the *Shorter Oxford English Dictionary* (Oxford: Clarendon Press, 1973), assets were originally defined as "sufficient estate or effects" (1531) and extended to "all the property a person has that may be liable for his or their debt" (1675).

3. Appadurai actually discusses "the capacity to aspire," but the concept is reworded here to better "fit" with the other types of assets mentioned. For a discussion of productive and political assets, see, respectively, Moser and Felton, chapter 2 in this volume, and Ferguson, Moser, and Norton, chapter 17.

4. By way of illustration, this section very briefly summarizes some of the findings presented in detail in chapter 2.

5. See Carter, chapter 3 in this volume

6. See Solimano, chapter 7 in this volume.

7. See Carter, chapter 3 in this volume.

8. See Krishna, chapter 4 in this volume.

9. See Mahajan, chapter 12 in this volume.

10. Vulnerability is defined as exposure to hazard or risk and the ability to manage risks stemming from such exposure (Moser 1998; Sabates-Wheeler and Haddad 2005).

11. Asset-based evaluations have also assisted policymakers in addressing poverty traps and environmental disasters in Ethiopia and Honduras. Michael Carter, personal communication.

References

Adato, Michelle, Michael Carter, and Julian May. 2004. "Sense in Sociability? Social Exclusion and Persistent Poverty in South Africa." Paper written for BASIS Collaborative Research Support Program. University of Wisconsin–Madison.

Alsop, Ruth, Mette Bertelsen, and Jeremy Holland. 2006. *Empowerment in Practice: From Analysis to Implementation.* Washington: World Bank.

Appadurai, Arjun. 2004. "The Capacity to Aspire: Culture and the Terms of Recognition." In *Culture and Public Action*, edited by Vijayendra Rao and Michael Walton, pp. 59–85. Stanford University Press.

Barrett, Christopher, and Michael Carter. 2005. "Risk and Asset Management in the Presence of Poverty Traps: Implications for Growth and Social Protection." Background note prepared for World Bank–Department for International Development Project "Linking Social

Protection and Growth: Assessing Empirical Evidence, Developing the Future Agenda." Workshop, Leuven, Belgium, June 23–24.

Bebbington, Anthony. 1999. "Capitals and Capabilities: A Framework for Analyzing Peasant Viability, Rural Livelihoods and Poverty." *World Development* 27(12): 2021–44.

Boshara, Ray. 2005. "Individual Development Accounts: Policies to Build Savings and Assets for the Poor." Policy Brief Welfare Reform and Beyond 32. Brookings.

Boshara, Ray, and Michael Sherraden. 2004. "Status of Asset Building Worldwide." Report. Washington: New America Foundation.

Carney, Diana. 1998. "Implementing the Sustainable Livelihoods Approach." In *Sustainable Rural Livelihoods. What Contribution Can We Make?* edited by D. Carney, pp. 3-23. London: Department for International Development.

Carter, Michael, and Julian May. 2001. "One Kind of Freedom: Poverty Dynamics in Post-Apartheid South Africa." *World Development* 29, no. 12: 1987–2006.

Chambers, Robert 1992. "Poverty and Livelihoods: Whose Reality Counts?" Discussion Paper 347. Brighton: Institute of Development Studies.

———. 1994. "The Origins and Practice of Participatory Rural Appraisal." *World Development* 22: 953–69.

Chronic Poverty Research Centre. 2004. *The Chronic Poverty Report 2004–5.* University of Manchester, Institute for Development Policy and Management.

Cook, Sarah, Naila Kabeer, and Gary Suwannarat. 2003. *Social Protection in Asia.* New Delhi: Har Anand.

Davies, Susanna. 1993. "Are Coping Strategies a Cop Out?" *Institute of Development Studies Bulletin* 24, no. 4: 60–72.

Department for International Development. 2000. *Sustainable Livelihoods—Current Thinking and Practice.* London.

Devereux, Stephen 1993. "Goats before Ploughs: Dilemmas of Household Response Sequencing during Food Shortage." *Institute of Development Studies Bulletin* 24, no.4: 52–59.

Filmer, Deon, and Lant Pritchett. 1999. "The Effect of Household Wealth on Educational Attainment: Evidence from 35 Countries." *Population and Development Review* 25, no. 1: 85–120.

Ford Foundation. 2004. *Building Assets to Reduce Poverty and Injustice.* New York.

Fossgard-Moser, Titus. 2005. "Social Performance: Key Lesson from Recent Experiences within Shell." *Journal of Corporate Governance* 5, no. 3: 105–18

Grootaert, Christiaan, and Thierry van Bastelaer, eds. 2002. *Understanding and Measuring Social Capital: A Multidisciplinary Tool for Practitioners.* Washington: World Bank.

Hall, Anthony. 2007 (forthcoming). "International Migration and the Challenges for Social Policy: The Case of Ecuador." In *Assets, Livelihoods and Social Policy*, edited by Caroline Moser and Anis Dani. World Bank

Hoddinott, John, and others. 2005. "Pathways from Poverty: Evaluating Long-Term Strategies to Reduce Poverty." Collaborative Research Support Program Brief 30. Madison: BASIS, University of Wisconsin.

Holzmann, Robert, and Steen Jorgensen. 1999. "Social Protection as Social Risk Management: Conceptual Underpinnings for the Social Protection Sector Strategy Paper." *Journal of International Development* 11, no. 7: 1005–27.

————. 2000. "Social Risk Management: A New Conceptual Framework for Social Protection and Beyond." Social Protection Discussion Paper 0006. Washington: World Bank.

Kerr, John, and others. 2005. "Property Rights, Environmental Service and Poverty in Indonesia." Brief 29. Madison: BASIS, University of Wisconsin (May).

Lerman, Robert. 2005. "Are Low-Income Households Accumulating Assets and Avoiding Unhealthy Debt?" Opportunities and Ownership Project Brief 1. Washington: Urban Institute.

Little, Peter. 2002. "Building Assets for Sustainable Recovery and Food Security." Brief 5. Madison: BASIS, University of Wisconsin (January).

Mathie, Alison, and Gord Cunningham. 2003. "Who Is Driving Development? Reflections on the Transformative Potential of Asset-Based Community Development." Occasional Paper Series 5. Antigonish, Nova Scotia: Coady International Institute, Francis Xavier University.

Maxwell, Simon, and Marisol Smith. 1992. "Household Food Security: A Conceptual Review." In *Household Food Security: Concepts, Indicators, and Measurements: A Technical Review*, edited by Simon Maxwell and T. Frankenberger, pp. 1–72. Rome and New York: International Fund for Agricultural Development and UNICEF.

Moser, Caroline. 1998. "The Asset Vulnerability Framework: Reassessing Urban Poverty Reduction Strategies." *World Development* 26, no. 1: 1–19.

————. 2005. "The Development Implications of Daily Violence in Indio Guayas, Guayaquil." International Workshop on Youth Violence in Latin America. London School of Economics, May.

————. 2007 (forthcoming). "Assets and Livelihoods: A Framework for Asset-Based Social Policy." In *Assets, Livelihoods and Social Policy*, edited by Caroline Moser and Anis Dani. Washington: World Bank.

Morrad, Moustafa. 2003. "Mobilizing Community Assets." Washington: One Global Economy.

Moser, Caroline, and Andrew Felton. 2006. "The Construction of an Asset Index: Measuring Asset Accumulation in Ecuador." Paper presented at workshop on Concepts and Methods for Analyzing Poverty Dynamics and Chronic Poverty. University of Manchester, October.

Narayan, Deepa. 1997. "Voices of the Poor: Poverty and Social Capital in Tanzania." Environmentally and Socially Sustainable Development Studies and Monograph Series 20. Washington: World Bank.

Oliver, Melvin, and Thomas Shapiro. 1990. "Wealth of a Nation: A Reassessment of Asset Inequality in America Shows at Least One Third of Households Are Asset-Poor." *American Journal of Economics and Sociology* 49, no. 2: 129–51

Portes, Alejandro. 1998. "Social Capital: Its Origins and Applications in Modern Sociology." *American Review of Sociology* 24, no. 1: 1–24.

Putnam, Robert. 1993. *Making Democracy Work: Civic Traditions in Modern Italy*. Princeton University Press.

Sabates-Wheeler, Rachel, and Lawrence Haddad. 2005. "Reconciling Different Concepts of Risk and Vulnerability: A Review of Donor Documents." Sussex: Institute of Development Studies.

Sahn, David E., and David Stifel. 2000. "Assets as a Measurement of Household Welfare in Developing Countries." Working Paper 00-11. St. Louis: Center for Social Development, Washington University.

Sen, Amartya. 1981. *Poverty and Famines: An Essay on Entitlement and Deprivation.* Oxford: Clarendon Press.

————. 1997. "Editorial: Human Capital and Human Capability." *World Development* 25, no. 12: 1959–61.

Sherraden, Michael. 1991. *Assets and the Poor: A New American Welfare Policy.* Armonk, New York: M.E. Sharpe.

Siegel, Paul. 2005. "Using an Asset-Based Approach to Identify Drivers of Sustainable Rural Growth and Poverty Reduction in Central America: A Conceptual Framework." Policy Research Working Paper 3475. Washington: Environmentally and Socially Sustainable Development Departments, World Bank.

World Bank. 1990. *World Development Report 1990: Poverty.* New York: Oxford University Press.

————. 2000. *World Development Report 2000/2001: Attacking Poverty.* Washington.

6

Addressing Vulnerability through Asset Building and Social Protection

SARAH COOK

The Asian financial crisis of the late 1990s dramatically exposed the vulnerability of populations across the region. From Thailand and Indonesia to South Korea, incomes had been steadily rising. But in the absence of formal social protection, and as structural change and mobility undermined traditional family and community "safety net" arrangements (which are rarely able to cope with covariant shocks), the crisis thrust large numbers of people back into poverty. In the wake of the crisis, the Ford Foundation's Asia offices initiated a program of research on Social Protection in Asia.[1] This chapter presents an overview of the program, highlighting key findings from selected projects and drawing on these to reflect on the relationship between assets, social protection (SP), and poverty reduction. The program did not explicitly adopt an assets framework, and individual projects were wide-ranging in content, methodology, and scope. Nonetheless, convergence is seen around the role of SP in addressing vulnerability and the types of assets that are important in securing livelihoods.

The analysis points to some tentative conclusions. SP is increasingly seen as social policy for poor countries or people. As such, it needs to be linked to wider developmental goals, including enhancing productivity and empowering recipients as citizens, rather than viewed merely as residual relief and social assistance. Equally, however, SP cannot be subsumed entirely within a poverty reduction agenda. Instead, policies and interventions should be complementary to, rather than a substitute for or subordinate component of, economic interventions. Within this context various types of assets play an important role in reducing vulnerability, acting as a buffer, and promoting further development. Assets, however, are themselves vulnerable to erosion or loss, directly or indirectly, as a result of shocks. While assets may contribute to poverty reduction, households will continue to require social welfare provision (for example, for catastrophic health events), or they may face severe or covariant shocks where accumulated assets can provide only limited protection. Institutional mechanisms of *social* (or publicly provided) protection and provision will therefore remain essential, but dependence on these can be reduced through asset accumulation and other poverty-reducing interventions.

Vulnerability to Crisis, Safety Nets, Social Protection, and Assets

To better understand the relationship between vulnerability and SP, Ford Foundation analysts conducted a research project to explore the nature and experience of vulnerability across Asia (Cook, Kabeer, and Suwannarat 2003). A critical distinction emerged between problems of chronic disadvantage and exclusion experienced by the long-term poor (predominant in South Asia), and "new" forms of vulnerability associated with globalization, transition from plan to market (China and Vietnam), and—most immediately—financial crisis across much of Southeast Asia. Sources and socioeconomic markers of vulnerability—economic, natural shocks, or marginalization based on education, location, and identity (such as ethnicity, caste, and gender)—were mapped across the region, with the most vulnerable and marginalized identified as those experiencing multiple forms of disadvantage (for example, illiterate, low-caste, elderly women). Seasonal food deficits, physical insecurity, exposure to violence, corruption, violation of rights, and discrimination are all forms of vulnerability experienced disproportionately by those with other forms of socioeconomic insecurity and with least access to means to protect their rights. Sources of vulnerability are thus not only economic or a dimension of poverty but "may lie in the specific nature of the social and economic environment in which households and individuals live" (Rahman 1995, p. 113).

With the focus initially on response to crisis, a tension emerged between these "old" and "new" forms of poverty, which required different responses. A distinction was drawn between narrow and wider views of SP: a narrow goal would be to keep income flows steady and smooth consumption through a crisis; a broader conceptualization would attempt to engage with the underlying causes, including the the resistant structures of oppression that underpin severe poverty and exclusion.[2]

While the dominant SP discourse at that time was around *ex post safety nets and social funds*, a key message of the initial report was the need for more *institutionalized ex ante mechanisms of social protection*. These were defined as longer-term policies to protect and promote the welfare of the poor or vulnerable, which would also help reduce exposure or increase resilience to shocks. A second message was the need to see SP as "investment," thus returning in part to a developmental or "productivist" approach. In contrast to a crisis-triggered safety net perspective, this reflects the view that "social protection is not only a welfare or safety nets issue, but also a social and economic development issue. By extension, mechanisms of SP for the extreme poor and vulnerable should enable them to *build up their assets* [emphasis added] so as to escape the threat of poverty in a sustainable way and to withstand the shocks of crisis and change" (Cook, Kabeer, and Suwannarat 2003, pp. 7–8).

These messages can be encapsulated within the threefold approach to social security or protection proposed by Guhan (1994):

—protective: coping with crisis and guaranteeing relief from deprivation;

—preventive: directly seeking to avert deprivation or mitigate risk; and

—promotional: aiming to improve real incomes and capabilities, reduce risks, and enable the accumulation of assets.

Two further sets of challenges for SP were identified in the initial phase. One set concerned the governance dimension, encompassing both technical concerns over the implementation of programs that deliver services to the intended beneficiaries, as well as more fundamental issues recently described as the transformative agenda of SP (Devereux and Sabates-Wheeler 2004). This agenda focuses on the realization of rights and entitlements and on the potential of SP as a mechanism of empowerment by building citizenship and the collective capabilities of the poor.

A second set of challenges concerned how to create a demand-led process that responded to real and articulated needs. This had been the focus of social fund programs prominent in Latin America and adopted in Thailand and other countries in response to crisis. However, given the criticisms of some community-based or social fund programs, the "supply" side challenge—production and delivery of pro-poor accessible social services—was also recognized as essential for meeting demand.

During a workshop sponsored by the Ford Foundation and held in Bangkok, June 2002, scholars, officials, and activists from across Asia framed the issues to be addressed within the projects. Core issues under discussion included what type of SP interventions could be protective, productivity enhancing, and transformative. In more conventional terms, can SP interventions be both welfare enhancing while also contributing to growth and efficiency objectives? Given the wide range of SP mechanisms available (including residual social assistance and safety nets, community social funds, social insurance, and social security programs), the resulting research program aimed to explore the kinds of needs to which SP interventions should respond and the most appropriate mechanisms for doing so.

While not explicitly adopting an assets-based approach, the analysis underlying the program had a strong focus on various forms of asset building as an underpinning of sustainable and developmental SP. It was recognized that "a broader perspective on SP could involve interventions such as investment in building up assets among the poor to provide resilience to resist sudden shocks or losses" (Cook, Kabeer, and Suwannarat 2003, p. 18). There was also an emerging critique of the then-dominant view that investments in education and health and in other social assistance measures constituted direct consumption, were unproductive, fiscally unaffordable and unsustainable, and crowded out private expenditures.[3] Donors in the region were starting to debate the need for a shift in focus from relief and social assistance to examination of the developmental potential of safety net interventions. Empirical evidence was emerging of the value of current investments that reduce social costs in the future.[4] Thus stronger arguments were available to support strategies that increased *human capital investments* and maintained and strengthened the *productive assets* of households, which "together with social provision of basic public goods and services, better protect households from falling into the safety net and requiring social assistance" (Cook, Kabeer, and Suwannarat 2003, p. 22). The perspective from Asia was starting to emphasize the important role social or public expenditures could play in both protective and developmental terms.

The Program: Addressing Vulnerability in Different Contexts

Through a call for proposals after the 2002 workshop, the Ford Foundation selected ten projects involving researchers or research sites across the region. These are summarized in the appendix (table 6A). This section presents key findings and themes highlighted in final reports and at a workshop held in May 2006.[5] This is followed by a discussion of findings specifically related to assets and some reflections on the relationship between assets and SP.

Social Protection: A Policy Framework to Address Vulnerability

A consensus emerged of SP as a policy framework to address vulnerability (as distinct from, but substantially overlapping with, poverty). Projects tended to identify vulnerability and forms of risk or, more frequently, vulnerable groups. Through research on specific groups (such as homeworkers, migrants, and poor farmers), projects assessed both the forms of structural disadvantage and the kinds of contingencies that can lead to poverty, as well as interventions for addressing these vulnerabilities.

The Fuzzy Boundaries of the Economic and the Social

The realities of people's lives and livelihoods are not compartmentalized: what may be useful distinctions for analysts or policymakers may not be meaningful at the level of the household. However, there is value in understanding *sources* of insecurity (for example, social, economic, physical, or political). Policy responses require an understanding of the linkages between these categories. Interventions considered social are often developmental—investments in health and education enhance labor as a factor of production—while even residual social assistance interventions can have productivity-enhancing impacts. Thus dialogues on SP need to be integrated with economic and, perhaps more broadly, political, environmental, and other policy discussions.

Clearer Articulation of Macro-, Meso-, and Micro-Linkages

The forces fueling migration, informalization of employment, loss of land or agrarian livelihoods, and other insecurities generally lie far beyond the boundaries of local geography, specific sectors, or particular vulnerable groups; increasingly such forces are a product of integration into the global economy. Without explicit attention to these wider processes, SP (and many poverty reduction interventions) may become principally reactive.[6] By extension, this reality may imply the need for a regional or wider framework for SP.

Policies or Institutional Arrangements
Can Exacerbate Insecurity for the Poor

Studies of home-based workers showed how national infrastructure and economic and industrial policies are often skewed in favor of larger formal units and enterprises. Subsidies provided to power loom units in India, for example, hurt the competitiveness of hand loom weavers. Administrative requirements are often more burdensome for poor workers. On the social side, public expenditures—for health and education, for instance—are frequently regressive.

Box 6-1. *Key Social Protection Messages from the Equitap (Equity in Asia-Pacific Health Systems) Project*

National systems and policies matter, not projects and programs.
Reaching the poor requires universalism, not targeting.
Health protection is feasible even in low-income economies.
Social insurance is no panacea or substitute for taxation; pro-poor social insurance requires taxation.
Pessimism about tax-funded integrated health delivery systems must be countered.
High tax and social protection are not inconsistent with public opinion or globalization.
Regional comparative perspective and knowledge are necessary.

From Rannan-Eliya (2006).

Universalism, Targeting, Conditionality, and "Projectization"

The arguments for universal approaches to SP are emerging more strongly in Asia than elsewhere. Conclusions drawn from the multicountry Equitap health equity study are worth reproducing here because they provide an important evidence-based challenge to the dominant paradigm (see box 6-1).

Specifically in the case of health, the study shows the effectiveness of tax-funded universal provision. Public subsidies for health care do not benefit the poor in many countries: in Bangladesh, Indonesia, and Vietnam, subsidies are pro-rich, biased toward inpatient hospital care. Overall, universalistic tax-funded systems and national health insurance systems perform better than non-universalistic tax-funded systems with user fees, means testing, and projects for reaching the poor. The best targeted systems in Asia are tax funded with integrated provision, a universalistic approach, and minimal access barriers to the poor. Social insurance systems only reach the poor if they are universal in nature, but these are generally unattainable in the poorest countries. Equity requires substantial tax financing to pay premiums, for example, for unemployed or informal sector workers. Equity schemes (for example, to target specific groups such as migrants) do not work if they are not integrated into mainstream programs.[7] Many of these findings extend to other social insurance schemes: organizations representing homeworkers, for instance, advocate the inclusion of workers into national programs. Assessment of the Thai 30-baht health care scheme found that although the plan was generally well received, some users felt discriminated against as beneficiaries and resentful of what they perceived to be lower-quality services and treatment by providers (Doane and others 2006).

Governance and Politics Matter

State capacity, (relatively) good governance, political will, and accountability mechanisms were all recognized as prerequisites for effective program implementation. The importance of politics was illustrated by the Indonesian political debate over shifting from a fuel subsidy to a cash transfer program.[8] In several contexts government coordination and the need for a policy framework for SP was raised: the introduction of multiple schemes creates fragmented systems. In China funding for rural areas is channeled through seventeen agencies, increasing the opportunity for leakage, rent seeking, and corruption.

Anticipating the Future:
From Piecemeal Thinking to a System of Social Protection?

The implication of many of the above points is the need for a more systematic approach. What would an ideal system look like? What steps can be taken to get there? This requires looking ahead and assessing the impacts of changing demographic and epidemiologic pressures, for example. Given greater mobility and the rise of cross-border insecurities (such as trafficking), this may also require some regional SP policies or at a minimum some coordination of approaches.

Finally, there was recognition that some issues were inadequately addressed. Chief among these was the financing of various SP policies or programs. Other issues included reaching the poorest and concerns about rights, citizenship, and empowerment.

What about Assets?

As noted earlier, most studies did not explicitly adopt an asset-based approach. Nonetheless, the following types of assets were highlighted through the studies.

Land, Housing, and Shelter

The importance of housing as an asset base for protection and promotion—for home-based workers (particularly women), the rural and urban poor, and migrants—emerged from a number of the studies. One of the most powerful sets of findings directly associated with property comes from the International Center for Research on Women (2006), in a project that explicitly sought to explore the hypothesis that property ownership was critical to women's protection from domestic violence. It thus diverged from the narrow, income-based

Box 6-2. *Women's Property and Protection from Violence*

Women worldwide experience gender-based disadvantage in access to and control of productive resources, which severely limits their ability to manage economic shocks and social risks. A particularly significant but unrecognized manifestation of the social and economic risks women face on account of their gender is domestic violence. Very often, the lack of a place to stay or viable economic options forces women to remain within violent relationships.

Argument: Women's ownership of immovable property has the potential to extend their capabilities, expand their negotiating power, and enhance their ability to address vulnerability, therefore serving as a critical factor of social protection against the experience of domestic violence.

Key findings: A multisite survey (West Bengal, Kerala, Sri Lanka) with nearly 10,000 respondents revealed the following:

—On average over 50 percent reported some form of domestic violence (36 percent in Sri Lanka, 64 percent in West Bengal, and 65 percent in Kerala), and over 40 percent reported physical violence from husbands (12.4, 55, and 35.7 percent, respectively).

—Violence compromises personal and household security, employment, income, and productivity. In West Bengal 30 percent missed work due to violence for an average of 2.7 days.

—In Kerala and West Bengal, approximately 34 percent of women owned property; on Sri Lanka, 30 percent. More women owned a house than land.

—In West Bengal 57 percent of women without property experienced violence compared to 35 percent of those who owned property. In Kerala the difference was larger: 49.1 percent without property experienced physical violence versus 6.8 percent with property. In Sri Lanka there was little difference.

—In both Kerala and West Bengal, housing was more protective than land.

See Bhatla, Chakraborty, and Duvvury (2006).

conception of social protection to focus on domestic violence as a key source of vulnerability and insecurity for women—both economically, in terms of their ability to work and generate an income, and physically—and thus as a "social protection" issue. (See box 6-2.) Findings about the importance of housing relative to land have wider implications for asset-building strategies because they indicate that, in this context, housing as a site of *protection* and *production* is not necessarily mediated by male labor to the same extent as land is.

Studies of Southeast Asian homeworkers concluded that asset reforms involving land and housing were particularly important in communities where low-income workers (including the growing numbers of female informal workers

Box 6-3. *A Promising Intervention?*

PATAMABA (Pambansang Tagapag-ugnay ng mga Manggagawa sa Bahay) is a nonprofit membership organization in the Philippines with a mission to organize and expand the network of informal self-employed and subcontracted workers; to provide social, economic, and personal support, and to campaign for social protection for its members. It supports a number of social protection schemes.

In Angono PATAMABA has partnered with the Community Mortgage Program of the national government to create a housing association. Members are allocated a lot on which they can build a house, amortized over twenty-five years at a cost of approximately $4.40 to $5.50 a month. With local government support, a new community is being created. The sustainability of the project (currently in an early stage) will depend on livelihood and social protection interventions that strengthen the community and each household's capacity to cope with unstable employment or income, illness, death, disability, and old age. It may also depend critically on the continued support of local politicians.

See Doane and others (2006).

engaged in outsourced and subcontracted work for global supply chains) and migrants are under constant threat of eviction or rent increases. In turn, inadequate or insecure housing and limited access to land and property (particularly for women) limits the ability of the poor to borrow and imposes other social constraints on mobility and participation. An example from the Philippines illustrates a constructive asset-building response, drawing attention to the need for *complementary* livelihood and social protection schemes (see box 6-3).

The Vietnam study identified lack of land as a critical challenge for the poorest farmers. This was partly due to lack of cultivable land (most acute among ethnic minorities) but also due to land loss through production failures, natural disasters, illness, accidents, gambling, or other losses—again suggesting the need for complementary asset-building strategies (Duong and others 2005, p.173). In the transitional context of Vietnam and China, the shift toward market allocation of urban housing has also created difficulties of access and affordability for the new urban poor and for migrants. Household registration systems in both countries create specific problems of access to secure residential shelter for migrants. Here, however, the issue is not one of housing *ownership*, which cannot be the solution for mobile populations, but rather one of secure rights of access and freedom from discrimination.

Shelter, however, can also be vulnerable. A community of pearl collectors in Bangladesh is exposed to bad weather that regularly damages or destroys their boats—their home and only asset—putting the lives of family members (particularly children) at risk. None of the respondents reported owning other assets such as land or tools. Although development organizations operate in the area, the lack of standard housing poses an obstacle for these workers to gain benefits. Even microfinance institutions do not recognize the boats as a fixed residence and thus will not provide loans.

Shelter and the lack thereof have an important impact on other assets such as opportunities and capabilities. Residence grants legality and may be required for employment and for access to education, health care, services, and credit. The type of shelter and its location affect health, sanitation, time use, and ultimately well-being. Shelter may be used for productive activity as well as residence and thus emerges as a fundamental prerequisite for both protection and development.

Nontangible Assets: Human Capital and Labor

A second type of asset building involves contributions to human capital—health, education and related skills, and capabilities. From a human development or rights perspective, these are essential components of human well-being. From an economic efficiency perspective, they are inputs that enhance labor productivity. In parts of Asia (particularly transitional economies), a feature of recent decades has been the rapid commercialization and privatization of even basic education and health care. In these contexts ill health and high medical expenditures have become a major cause of poverty. Evidence from the Equitap study shows how unpredictable *health* expenditures push people into poverty. In Bangladesh, Vietnam, and China, 6 to 10 percent of households have medical expenditures amounting to over 15 percent of household consumption. An additional 2 to 4 percent of households in Bangladesh, India, and China fall below the $1-a-day poverty line after expenditures on medical care (Rannan-Eliya, 2006).

While there was less direct focus on *education* within the projects, there was significant evidence of its importance, with strong correlations between low education and other types of vulnerability or exclusion. Education is both a cause and effect of poverty; adequate education requires money, and low education limits employment opportunities and incomes. It is also affected by other vulnerabilities. For example, among poor farmers in Vietnam, ill health in the household was the second major reason for withdrawing children from school (Duong and others 2005).

Financial Assets: Access to Credit or Financial Instruments

Microcredit, savings associations, and other forms of financial asset building were noted in the studies, particularly those dealing with homeworkers across South and Southeast Asia. While indicating the importance of such mechanisms, these studies also showed the exclusion of the most vulnerable from access to financial institutions. Getting the poorest or most excluded, who have no initial capital, onto the first rung of the ladder of asset accumulation remains a challenge even for institutions such as the Bangladesh Rural Advancement Committee (BRAC). Strategies for assisting this group to accumulate assets require complex institutional arrangements and interventions that may be difficult to scale up.[9]

Other Productive Assets

A range of other assets or opportunities, both tangible and nontangible but particularly directly productive, were also mentioned as critical for enhancing livelihood security. These included employment, productive techniques, and market information. Some are not assets in themselves but rather reflect the institutional environment and arrangements (information flows, market access, rights protections, and the like) that are needed to translate labor or other assets into commodities, functionings, and, ultimately, capabilities.

A constant theme for the region, regardless of the specific type of asset or intervention under discussion, concerns appropriate developmental strategies for mobile populations where portability is critical. For internal and regional migrants, vulnerability arises from institutional discrimination (job entry barriers and housing), lack of rights protection (for example, wages paid in arrears) or access to social security, and high costs of housing, education, and medical treatment. Social protection mechanisms are required to address the insecurities such workers face, but any programs (such as unemployment compensation, medical insurance, or pensions) or accumulated assets need to be portable.

Summary

Across the projects the types of assets discussed vary widely, but in general the importance of housing and property, human capital, and other productive assets is highlighted. Clear messages emerge about *complementarities* among different types of assets and about the *vulnerability* of assets themselves to loss or damage and the consequent need for mechanisms to protect or replace them. How assets are converted into income flows or other resources that increase capabilities is influenced by wider institutional and market arrangements, for example, the impacts of global or macroforces on the price of inputs, labor, and products. While some households recover quickly from shocks, others are pushed into a downward spiral of asset depletion and increasing vulnerability. The factors that combine to determine resilience include the private and collective assets to which people have access, the nature of the shock, and the broader institutional context, including systems of SP and access to basic services (Chronic Poverty Research Centre 2004).

The studies generally have less to say about asset accumulation leading to sustained poverty reduction, largely because this was not the question they set out to address. They did not involve longitudinal research. Many studies focused on groups that were still poor or exposed to high levels of vulnerability. In many cases the responses are aspirational—the assets people would like to have or which they identify as needs. Alternatively, strategies of accumulation are inferred from the disaccumulation or drawing down of certain assets observed in times of difficulty. A more general point, however, is the need to understand better the dynamics of the relationship between different strategies of asset accumulation and disaccumulation, and between (chronic) poverty and vulnerability. The very poor may undertake proactive strategies to avoid opportunities involving risk, but that may be costly in developmental terms. Some level of asset accumulation may assist households to engage in more risk taking. Similarly, basic social protection mechanisms or a "fall-back" guarantee (for example, in the form of a cash transfer or a guarantee of work) may enable the poorest or low-asset households to take opportunities or risks to which they are currently averse—thus potentially contributing to asset accumulation and development. These issues warrant further research.

Looking Ahead: Assets, Poverty Reduction, and Social Policies

While building assets may enable households to move out of poverty and better protect themselves against future shocks, a number of questions remain as to the potential "autonomy" of an asset-based approach, the extent to which it addresses vulnerability as well as poverty, and the security of accumulated assets themselves. Questions of concern include:

—What kinds of protections are needed in the process of moving toward some (to be defined) level of asset "security"?

—How are assets themselves to be protected against shocks, whether direct (disasters that damage land, housing, productive assets) or indirect (through depletion in response to other shocks)? This question suggests a need for other institutional arrangements, such as insurance or credit markets.

—What kinds of assets work best for the poor or vulnerable? This question, in turn, leads to others: Which ones most effectively translate into commodities and capabilities in different contexts? What wider institutional arrangements are needed? What happens when threats to livelihoods cannot be protected by accumulated assets or lead to the rapid depletion of assets?

While asset accumulation may be complementary to other social protection or policy interventions, it is unclear to what extent it can address a number of SP issues raised above. Examples from the health sector have already illustrated the point: catastrophic health care needs can impose major costs on the poor, leading to withdrawal of children from school, increasing borrowing and selling of assets, and pushing people back into poverty. Without some form of SP system, those who are asset or income poor (in relative terms) will remain vulnerable. One positive extension of an asset-based approach may be to consider health or human capital accumulation as an integral part of a poverty reduction or SP strategy. This still raises the issues of who pays and how, as well as how access to quality health care is guaranteed to all. In general, then, an asset-based poverty reduction strategy will need to be complemented by other forms of SP.

It should also be noted that many existing social assistance and cash transfer programs already contribute to asset building or are directly productive. School feeding programs (for example, Food for Education in Bangladesh and Programa de Educación, Salud y Alimentación [PROGRESA] in Mexico) provide nutrition and education, reducing the likelihood of children being poor in the future (Chronic Poverty Research Centre 2004, p. 57). Pensions have created unexpected assets by providing funds for education. Namibia is an example where pensioners have become a valuable resource for the family after the introduction of a social pension system (Devereux 2001). Similarly, public works programs may provide the capital for small-scale business start-ups (Chronic Poverty Research Centre 2004, p. 57).

A potential limitation of the asset-based approach is its essentially individual (private property or ownership) focus on the mechanisms for addressing risk. Although collective and natural assets can be included within asset-based approaches, in practice much of the focus of discussion and application tends to be on individual or household risk and response. The nature of collective or community assets as a mechanism for poverty reduction and a buffer against risk deserves more attention. Undervaluing such assets may contribute to the marginalization of groups most dependent on them—generally the poorest. Public goods and services could also be seen as collective assets. From a SP perspective, ensuring entitlements to (rather than ownership of) such goods is critical. Other essentially private assets, such as housing, may not require ownership. In certain circumstances, but not all, it may be sufficient or more appropriate to have an entitlement (provided, for example, through rental housing allowances). Finally, ensuring that the poorest and most excluded are reached by and benefit from an asset-based approach elicits many of the same challenges and complexities of design, implementation, and institutional arrangements that confront other kinds of interventions.

Social protection policies will remain important in preventing and mitigating shocks and insecurities and in giving the poor a more secure position from which to seize opportunities and demand their rights. This, however, cannot be done without real transfers of resources and sustained and predictable funding. While a developmental SP approach should contribute to asset building and could be more explicitly asset based, there will continue to be a need for a variety of SP approaches and interventions as complements to asset building and poverty reduction. SP policies are necessary to serve as a buffer when assets fail and to protect those individuals who are unable to accumulate assets due to a lack of labor, ill health, or other deficits in functioning.

Appendix Table 6A. *Ford Foundation Asia Regional Social Protection Program: Summary of Projects*[a]

Area of study	Project title	Implementing organization	Objectives and methods
Regionwide	Asia social protection dialogue	WIEGO with Homenet Thailand	Create a regional forum for discussion of SP for informal workers.
	The role of health systems in social protection, and the views of the poor in Asia	Institute of Policy Studies of Sri Lanka	Partial contribution to large regional network and program of research on health equity (Equitap).
Bangladesh, India, Nepal, Pakistan, Sri Lanka	Social protection for home-based workers in South Asia	Homenet South Asia and Institute of Social Studies Trust, India	Examine existing approaches to social protection for informal and home-based workers, identify best practices, perform studies of particular groups of home-based and informal workers and their priorities and needs for social protection.
China	Alternative approaches to rural health care	China Academy of Health Policy, School of Public Health, Peking University	Research on alternative approaches to rural health care financing and provision. Focus is on access to health care for rural poor, given that ill health is a major source of vulnerability and cause of poverty in rural China.
	Social protection for the urban poor in China	Chinese Academy of Social Sciences, Institute of Population and Labor Economics	Focus on "shock-induced" poverty arising from state sector reform and unemployment; household surveys in 5 cities. Explore urban poverty and employment links, informal employment, and access to social protection.
	The role of the family in social protection	Institute of Social Development and Public Policy, Beijing Normal University, China	Household survey on how family type, structure, and life cycle affect vulnerability and need for social protection. How the state engages with families—

			through forms of assistance, targeting, and so forth—to meet the challenges of social protection.
India and China	The challenge of social protection in rural India and China	Centre for Development Studies, India, and Chinese Academy of Social Sciences, Rural Development Institute	Examine the case for basic social security as an entitlement or right for the poor, and explore potential for universal coverage in China and India. Identify rural vulnerable and constraints, and examine alternative mechanisms for delivering social protection.
India (West Bengal, Kerala), Sri Lanka	Property ownership and inheritance rights of women for social protection: the South Asian experience	International Center for Research on Women, India	Multisite research: household survey, narratives, and focus groups. Women's ownership of immovable property has the potential to extend their capabilities, expand their negotiating power, and enhance their ability to address vulnerability, therefore serving as a critical factor of social protection for them against the experience of domestic violence.
Indonesia	Developing a poverty map for Indonesia: a tool for better targeting in poverty reduction and social protection programs	SMERU Research Institute, Indonesia	Expansion of pilot methodology for poverty mapping to all of Indonesia, disaggregated at provincial, district, subdistrict, and village levels; field verification study to assess validity of poverty-mapping estimates.
Vietnam	Social protection for the needy in Vietnam	Institute of Social Development Studies, Hanoi, Vietnam	Research in eight provinces, three largest cities; three "vulnerable" populations—rural poor, rural-to-urban migrants, people with disabilities and HIV/AIDS. Identify vulnerability, coping strategies, unmet needs, and access to social protection among these groups.

a. Abbreviations: Equitap, Equity in Asia-Pacific Health Systems; SMERU, Source Monitoring and Early Response Unit; WIEGO, Women in Informal Employment: Globalizing and Organizing

Notes

1. The author was involved in this program as a consultant to the Ford Foundation on the initial scoping study and later as program officer in the Foundation's Beijing office.

2. The findings pointed to a broader approach to social protection than the World Bank's social risk management framework (World Bank 2000), with its focus on reducing and managing specific forms of risk, rather than (additionally) the underlying sources of vulnerability.

3. For examples of these debates, see Stephen Devereux (2002).

4. See, for example, Bezuneh and Deaton (1997, p. 676).

5. This discussion draws on contributions made by participants at the final program workshop, "Social Protection in Asia," sponsored by the Ford Foundation, May 15–16, 2006, in Bangkok, Thailand. However, I am solely responsible for how the ideas are presented here.

6. See for example Mkandawire (2006).

7. From a presentation and report by Rannan-Eliya (2006).

8. In October 2005 the Indonesian government more than doubled fuel prices by slashing the level of subsidies. This move ramped up inflation and slowed consumer spending, which, many argued, unfairly hurt the poor. Amid great controversy over how to deal with the crisis, the government announced an unconditional cash transfer program to provide subsistence support of roughly $10 a month for one year to about 15.5 million poor households, at a cost of about $480 million in 2005. The fiscal resources conserved by the cut in subsidies enabled the government to prepare a $1.4 billion spending program to upgrade education and health facilities and village infrastructure in 2005–06. See Asian Development Bank, "Outlook 2006: II. Economic Trends and Prospects in Developing Asia: Southeast Asia" (www.adb.org/Documents/books/ADO/2006/ino.asp [October 16, 2006]).

9. Imran Matin (2006) of the BRAC discussed the challenges of reaching the ultrapoor at the Bangkok workshop. See also Chronic Poverty Research Centre (2004).

References

Bezuneh, Mesfin, and Brady Deaton. 1997. "Food Aid Impacts on Safety Nets: Theory and Evidence: A Conceptual Perspective on Safety Nets." *American Journal of Agricultural Economics* 79, no. 2: 672–77.

Bhati, Nandita, Swati Chakraborty, and Nata Duvvury. 2006. "Property Ownership and Inheritance Rights of Women as Protection from Domestic Violence: Cross-Site Analysis." In *Property Ownership and Inheritance Rights of Women for Social Protection—The South Asia Experience*, pp. 71–101. Washington: International Center for Research on Women.

Chronic Poverty Research Centre. 2004. *The Chronic Poverty Report 2004–05*. Manchester, U.K.

Cook, Sarah, Naila Kabeer, and Gary Suwannarat. 2003. *Social Protection in Asia*. New Delhi: Har Anand.

Devereux, Stephen. 2001. "Social Pensions in Namibia and South Africa." Discussion Paper 379. Brighton, U.K: Institute of Development Studies.

———. 2002. "Social Protection for the Poor: Lessons from Recent International Experience." Working Paper 142. Brighton, U.K: Institute of Development Studies.

Devereux, Stephen, and Rachel Sabates-Wheeler. 2004. "Transformative Social Protection." Working Paper 232. Brighton, U.K: Institute of Development Studies.

Doane, Donna L., and others. 2006. *Social Protection for Homebased Workers in Thailand and the Philippines*. Quezon City, Philippines: Homenet Southeast Asia.

Duong, Le Bach, and others. 2005. *Social Protection for the Most Needy in Vietnam: The Cases of Poor Farmers, Rural-to-Urban Labor Migrants, People Living with Disabilities and with HIV/AIDS*. Hanoi: Gioi Publishers.

Guhan, S. 1994. "Social Security Options for Developing Countries." *International Labour Review* 133, no. 1: 35–53.

International Center for Research on Women. 2006. *Property Ownership and Inheritance Rights of Women for Social Protection—The South Asia Experience*. Washington.

Matin, Imran. 2006. "Social Protection for the Poorest: Reflections from BRAC Experiences." Presentation at the Ford Foundation workshop on Social Protection in Asia. Bangkok, May 15–16.

Mkandawire, Thandika. 2006. "Targeting and Universalism in Poverty Reduction." Social Policy and Development Paper 23. Geneva: UN Research Institute for Social Development.

Rahman, Hossain Zillur. 1995. "Rethinking the Land Reform Question." Paper presented at the conference on Bangladesh Agriculture in the 21st Century. World Bank, Dhaka, November 6 and 8.

Rannan-Eliya, Ravi. 2006. "The Role of Health Systems in Social Protection and the View of the Poor in Asia: Findings from the Equitap Project." Presentation at the Ford Foundation workshop on Social Protection in Asia. Bangkok, May 15–16.

World Bank. 2000. *World Development Report 2000/2001: Attacking Poverty*. Washington.

7

Social Protection and Asset Accumulation by the Middle Class and the Poor in Latin America

ANDRÉS SOLIMANO

Globalization, new technologies, and the market economy offer new opportunities but at the same time introduce new risks and vulnerabilities to the poor and the middle class in Latin America, who have few ways to protect themselves against economic crises, health crises, and natural disasters. This fact has led to an increased demand for social protection, a term carrying a slightly paternalistic flavor, as it implies that the state or special agencies will protect vulnerable citizens. Of course, a deeper question is, Should the focus instead be on how to design and reform the economic systems that generate such risks and volatility?

The antipoverty and social protection policies of Latin America during the (neo)liberal era largely failed to reduce poverty levels: in 2005 close to 40 percent of the population (more than 200 million people) was considered to be poor. The reasons that current policies have failed to reduce poverty go beyond specific social programs and are linked to the macroeconomic and developmental performance of the economies. For instance, growth in gross domestic product has not exceeded 3 percent a year (with lower GDP per capita gains). Growth crises have been frequent, often leading to cuts in employment and real wages (Solimano 2006). Finally, persistent inequality has reduced the impact on poverty even where economic growth occurs.

Social policies have tried to mitigate these macroeconomic and structural developments. However, the practice of targeting in the delivery of social goods and services has faced some unanticipated problems, as its information requirements were often underestimated. In addition, some of these policies excluded those individuals not considered "very poor." Moreover, targeted social policies affect the middle class adversely; they do not fully receive the social benefits that their taxes pay for. The role of assets in social policy has been a largely neglected topic in Latin America, although a few scholars emphasize the importance of assets for antipoverty programs and to reduce the vulnerability of low-income groups, and other scholars show that the adverse effects for saving and capital mobilization stem from the fact that a vast amount of wealth held by the poor in developing countries is untitled (De Soto 2000).[1]

This chapter highlights the role that asset accumulation by the middle class and the poor can play in fostering economic autonomy, reducing vulnerability, and improving wealth distribution in economies subject to volatility. Differences as well as complementarities between social protection policies and asset-building mechanisms are identified as well as some priority areas for new policies that protect growth, strengthen the middle class, and promote asset building.

Social Protection Policies

A main concern of social policies in Latin America has been to protect citizens from the adverse effects of unemployment, economic crises, health problems, and aging (Economic Commission for Latin America and the Caribbean 2006). The specific modalities of social policies have evolved according to the broader development strategies adopted by the region and the demands from different social groups for redistribution and social protection.

Under the development strategy of import substitution, in place from the 1930s to the 1980s, the main objectives of social policy were social modernization and the formation of human resources needed by the industrialization process. These policies included the expansion of education, including higher education, housing policies to cope with the housing needs of a growing urban population, and national public health systems and pay-as-you-go social security. Labor policies resulted in legislation on minimum wages, severance pay, and restrictions on firing and hiring. Land reform was also implemented to correct a highly concentrated pattern of land tenure. The social constituency behind these policies included labor unions, various organizations in the public and private sectors, and rural workers.

This development strategy-cum-social policy delivered respectable growth (by today's standards) until the late 1970s and a degree of social modernization. However, the economic model of import substitution also involved microinefficiencies associated with high import tariffs and expansion of the public sector. The debt crisis of the early 1980s and its legacy of inflation, fiscal deficits, exchange rate instability, and debt-servicing problems led to a crisis of that development model.

The criticism of the old economic model was also extended to its social protection model. Many argued, for example, that social spending was not necessarily reaching the most needy in urban and rural areas and that the subsidy of certain basic goods and services was fiscally expensive. Furthermore, public universities, often tuition free, implicitly subsidized the children of rich households and the upper middle class. Finally, critics contended that the social security system based on pay-as-you-go delivered low pensions and failed to contribute to the development of domestic capital markets.

The economic reforms of the 1990s included macroeconomic stabilization, external opening, financial liberalization, privatization, and market deregulation. (Chile implemented similar policies earlier in the mid-1970s under the Pinochet regime.) These policies were oriented to expand the possibilities of wealth creation through private sector activity and the use of markets and international trade in goods and financial assets. However, the application of these policies had social costs, and the new policy regime of open markets brought new forms of economic instability and risks that needed mitigation.

The main objective of social protection policies in the 1990s was poverty reduction. Policymakers believed that poverty reduction would be led by faster economic growth following the adoption of market-based reforms. The main variable to be protected was income, defined as the level above or below a certain poverty line. Clearly, the definition focuses on flows rather than stocks (assets). In fact, the reduction of wealth and income inequality was not an explicit priority of these policies (Solimano 1998). This is in contrast to several experiments, of various degrees of success or failure, with income and wealth redistribution in the 1960s, 1970s, and 1980s.[2]

These social protection policies focused on assisting the most vulnerable segments of the population (the poor, the elderly, children, and the handicapped). The principle of targeting is to reach the neediest part of the population, appealing both to the viewpoint of simple common sense and the more instrumental logic of minimizing fiscal costs and encouraging macroeconomic stabilization. Nevertheless, targeting is not free of problems, as its informational and operational requirements are not minor.

Figure 7-1. *Latin America and Caribbean GDP per Capita as a Percentage of U.S. GDP per Capita, 1975–2004*

Percent

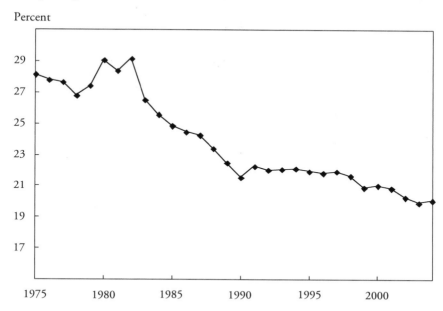

Source: Author's calculations based on World Development Indicators online database. See World Bank, WDI Online (publications.worldbank.org/WDI/Indicators (WDI) [November 2006]).

Targeting was complemented by social emergency funds oriented toward providing support income and public works programs for low-income groups in the wake of severe macroeconomic crises or natural disasters. The private sector was encouraged to participate in the delivery of education, health, and pensions as a natural corollary of private sector–led development. Labor market policies were in turn oriented to ensure more labor "flexibility" by relaxing firing rules and reducing severance payments. Minimum wages were deemphasized as an income support policy.

A full evaluation of the results of these economic and social policies is beyond the scope of this chapter. However, the results of these social and development policies are not encouraging in terms of rapid and sustained growth, poverty reduction, and lower inequality. As a consequence of such modest growth, Latin America's GDP per capita as a share of the GDP per capita of the United States has been stagnant or declining in the last ten or fifteen years (see figure 7-1). In addition, modest average growth has been accompanied by volatility and growth

Table 7-1. *Growth Crises in Latin America versus a Reference Group, 1960–2003*
Units as indicated

| Countries | Number of years with negative GDP per capita growth rates | | | Percent of time in crisis in total period |
	1960–80	1981–2003	1960–2003	
Latin America				
Argentina	6	11	17	38.6
Bolivia	4	9	13	29.5
Brazil	2	11	13	29.5
Chile	4	3	7	15.9
Colombia	2	5	7	15.9
Costa Rica	3	8	11	25.0
Dominican Republic	4	6	10	22.7
Ecuador	3	8	11	25.0
Mexico	0	8	8	18.2
Peru	4	10	14	31.8
Uruguay	5	9	14	31.8
Venezuela	10	13	23	52.3
Average	3.9	8.4	12.3	28.0
Reference group				
Korea	2	1	3	6.8
Philippines	0	7	7	15.9
Thailand	0	2	2	4.5
Ireland	2	2	4	9.1
Spain	2	2	4	9.1
Turkey	5	6	11	25.0
Average	1.8	3.3	5.2	11.7

Source: Solimano (2006).

crises (see table 7-1). Needless to say, those with fewer assets and lower incomes tend to suffer more in downturns and crises that destroy jobs and increase poverty.

The reality is that in several countries the private systems of delivery of social services offer quality education and health services (although probably below the standards of advanced countries) to the upper middle class, but the poor and the lower middle class cannot afford private provision unless they receive a subsidy. Most of these people have access to only insufficiently funded public education and public health systems. Education is often better in urban areas than in rural areas, in affluent neighborhoods than in poor ones, and in private schools than in public schools. In the health sector, public hospitals are often underfunded, and queuing for patients is routine. In Chile in recent years, thousands of families have left the private health insurance system, ISAPRES (Instituciones de Salud Previsional), and switched to the state-run FONASA system (Fondo Nacional de Salud) because of the escalation of costs in the private system and the limited coverage of the services offered (Solimano and Pollack 2006).

The asset accumulation approach to social protection identifies assets that affect the well-being of individuals and communities, including material assets (land, capital, and housing), financial assets, social capital (the network of contacts, norms, and culture among individuals in a certain community), and natural capital.[3] The approach goes beyond the purely economic to the issue of asset formation and focuses also on the role of social interaction and social support in helping people to cope with adverse circumstances. From an economic perspective, assets (under certain conditions) can provide protection against unexpected shocks, helping to reduce vulnerabilities. If a person suffers a temporary loss of income, an asset can provide collateral to borrow money for daily needs. In the event that the loss of income is of a more permanent nature, a person (or household) can sell the asset, although this will reduce the individual's net worth. Assets must have an economic value, be traded in certain markets, and be potentially liquid to be accepted as collateral for borrowing or to be sold. In addition, property rights to the asset must be clear. Not all assets comply with these conditions. Noneconomic assets, such as social capital, have a different value from a liquid economic asset. Still, social capital can help cushion negative shocks through nonmarket mechanisms, such as social interaction and the support of community groups.

Social protection policies can operate through the asset side or through the flow side. If a pension system is based on the individual accumulation of assets, as in a privatized system, then individual assets are a cushion against the decline in income associated with aging. If social protection is based on the provision of temporary income or jobs to the unemployed, it will operate more on the flow side and will rely on the decision of government to provide that protection. In a way, individual assets are like self-insurance, whereas social protection is a form of social insurance. Social capital is based on civil society organizations rather than on the direct intervention of the state.

The empirical relevance of the asset approach will depend on the pattern of ownership of assets: what type of assets the middle class and the poor hold, their liquidity, and the structure of property rights. These issues are taken up in the following sections.

Asset Distribution

Income distribution is (and has historically been) quite unequal in Latin America: cross-country average Gini coefficients, a measure of income concentration, are around 0.5—well above the levels for countries of East Asia and the Organization for Economic Cooperation and Development.[4] Furthermore, a recent study of patterns of asset ownership in Latin America reveals that housing is the most widespread asset held by households (69 percent own their homes); for the vast majority of the population, this is their only asset (Torche and Spilerman 2006). The proportion of home ownership in Latin America is similar to that of the United States and is relatively uniform across socioeconomic levels. The pattern of homeownership is associated with housing policy for the poor and the middle class and also with the (illegal) settlement of public land in cities by *pobladores* (squatters).

The study also finds that education has expanded at all levels (primary, secondary, and tertiary). Education is widespread, but high-quality education is within the reach of only the upper middle class and the wealthy. Land ownership is highly concentrated, although agrarian reform in some countries has led to a decline in concentration. The growing urbanization of the region has diminished the importance of land inequality. Ownership of capital assets is also concentrated among the few.

Distribution is thus clearly not uniform across types of assets. In addition, in some countries a formal titling procedure for the resources and property owned by lower-income classes is absent. The lack of titles impedes the use of such assets as collateral for bank loans (De Soto 1989, 2000).

Segmentation in access to credit and high-quality education by socioeconomic status prevents a more egalitarian distribution of assets. In addition, family background (income, wealth, education level of the parents, occupational status, and social connections) tends to reproduce inequality in wealth, access to political power, and influence in society across generations.

Growth, the Middle Class, and Asset Accumulation

The main macroeconomic accomplishments of the 1990s and early to mid-2000s in Latin America have been the reduction and stabilization of inflation, the improvement of the fiscal budget, and a stronger external sector position.[5] This is important for the poor, as inflation affects them more severely than other groups. In addition, macroeconomic stability creates conditions for more sustained growth if the growth impulse is there. Unfortunately, except in the early

1990s, with the resumption of capital flows and the launching of reforms, and during 2004–06, with commodity price booms, sustained and high growth has been elusive in most of Latin America when considered in a medium-term perspective. It is hard to think of lasting solutions for social problems without some basic economic stability and steady growth. In recent years the main gains in poverty reduction in Latin America (Chile) and elsewhere (China) have occurred in countries that experienced rapid GDP growth. Of course, growth is not the whole story, and policies to strengthen the middle class, reduce inequality, and widen access to productive assets and social capital are also important.

Latin America is a continent of large inequalities, as income is concentrated at the top. As a consequence, mean income is often greater than median income, a feature typical of concentrated income distributions. The size of the middle class, measured both as a share of total income and of total population, is often smaller in Latin America than in countries of the Organization for Economic Cooperation and Development and in former socialist countries of Eastern Europe (see figure 7-2).[6] The small size of the middle class is related to the fact that income is concentrated.

Stable, higher-income democracies often have a strong middle class and relatively low levels of inequality. In contrast, countries with low-to-medium income per capita that are politically more unstable and divided often have a weak middle class and concentrated patterns of income distribution. The political correlate of this system is often volatile and populist politics (Solimano 2005). A stronger and more stable middle class is often considered a stabilizing factor in politics and economics, since private investment is sensitive to instability and political polarization. More universal social policies can strengthen social cohesion and stabilize politics, thereby favoring social peace and economic growth. A higher share of income for the middle class, as well as reduced ethnic polarization, is empirically associated with higher income, higher growth, more education, and other favorable development outcomes (Easterly 2000).

Building a stronger middle class requires providing people better access to housing and education, the two main assets that the population as a whole accumulates. In addition, the middle class is the owner of small and midsized enterprises, which are often in need of finance capital investment and working capital. Moreover, as the savings capacity of the poor and middle class grows over time, they need access to financial assets. Such access can mobilize the hidden productive potential of these groups, with positive effects on economic efficiency, growth, and social welfare. A strong asset position helps protect against negative shocks.

Three main impediments to a more even distribution of assets exist in Latin America. One is the limited savings capacity of low-income groups (even

Figure 7-2. *Size of the Middle Class, by Share of Total Income, 1990s*[a]

Percent

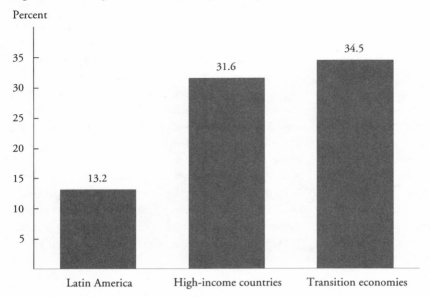

Latin America   High-income countries   Transition economies

Source: Birdsall, Graham, and Pettinato (2000).

a. The *middle class* refers to those households with per capita income between 75 and 125 percent of the median income. *Latin America* includes Brazil, Chile, Costa Rica, Mexico, Panama, and Peru. *High-income countries* include Australia, Austria, Belgium, Canada, Denmark, Finland, France, Germany, Ireland, Israel, Italy, Luxembourg, Netherlands, Spain, Sweden, Switzerland, Taiwan, the United Kingdom, and the United States. *Transition economies* include the Czech Republic, Hungary, Poland, the Russian Federation, and the Slovak Republic.

though their savings capacity is not zero). Usually, however, low-income families can save to finance the down payment for a house or other type of property. In addition, they have a certain economic capacity to acquire durable goods. During economic development the relationship between savings rates and per capita income is nonlinear, and relatively large increases in savings can take place after per capita income rises.

Second, for assets to be able to mobilize capital, property rights must be well defined and enforceable. In Latin America low-income groups have acquired their main asset (housing) often through nonmarket mechanisms: occupation of urban dwellings or subsidized housing. Some owners have titles to their property; others do not. The legal system, unfortunately, is expensive and often unfriendly to the poor. In fact, the design and enforcement of contracts is costly, and it requires some legal education and access to lawyers. The poor often cannot afford all that.

Third, capital markets are segmented, serving the elites better than the poor and the middle class. The traditional routes to accumulating material assets and also to acquiring higher education—borrowing and access to capital markets—are largely restricted to the nonpoor. (The elite hold assets that can be used as collateral or have the right connections to access credit and get their children into good quality schools.) The reform of judiciary systems—to make access to justice more expeditious for the poor and middle classes—is essential if asset accumulation is to be more egalitarian.

Conclusion

This chapter has reviewed the conceptual underpinnings of social protection policies in Latin America as implemented under various policy regimes, including import substitution policies, market-oriented reforms of the Washington Consensus, and hybrid regimes. The results of this analysis highlight the need to define social policies that go beyond growth-based poverty reduction and targeted subsidy policies (the centerpieces of social policy in the 1990s in Latin America), and that also consider addressing the needs of the middle class as well as income and wealth inequality as valid objectives. In addition, a new approach should emphasize the potential of asset building and asset ownership by the poor and middle class as a mechanism to promote economic autonomy, boost savings and investment, promote upward social mobility, and also help the poor cope more effectively with adverse shocks.

The literature on asset building identifies a range of assets, including material assets—such as housing and land—financial assets, and social and communal assets. Economists stress the role of assets in coping with negative shocks. However, for assets to be economically valuable for that purpose, two conditions must be met: first, property rights must be reasonably well defined, and second, the assets must have liquidity. Other social scientists emphasize family and community relationships as mechanisms of social protection. In fact, individual assets and social capital complement each other in providing social protection. The economic and social views of assets, ultimately, have useful complementarities for defining renewed social policies.

In the last two decades or so, modest and unstable growth, persistent inequality, and narrowly defined social policies have hampered more rapid social progress in Latin America. The chapter stresses the importance of economic stability and steady growth as the underpinning for poverty reduction and broad social improvement; the chapter also underlines the need to broaden the objectives of social policies to include a concern for strengthening the middle class and widening access to assets by the poor and the middle class. A more widespread and equal ownership of assets can unleash creativity, entrepreneurship, and innovation latent in groups that traditionally have had little access to formal capital markets and the legal system. Egalitarian asset accumulation could also be expected to help democratize traditionally elitist Latin American societies.

Notes

1. See also Caroline Moser, chapter 5 in this volume.
2. The cases of Cuba in the early 1960s, Chile under Allende in the early 1970s, and Nicaragua in the 1980s under the Sandinistas were the most radicalized experiments with redistribution. More gradual policies with a redistributive bent were implemented in Costa Rica and Uruguay, among others.
3. See Moser, chapter 5 in this volume.
4. Historically, Latin America has had a quite unequal pattern of wealth distribution linked to concentrated land tenure and a social structure of relatively limited social mobility.
5. See also Economic Commission for Latin America and the Caribbean (2006) for specific proposals in the areas of pensions, health systems, and other policies of social protection.
6. Birdsall, Graham, and Pettinato (2000) define the middle class as the group whose income is in the range of 75–125 percent of the median income in a given country.

References

Birdsall, Nancy, Carol Graham, and Stefano Pettinato. 2000. "Stuck in the Tunnel: Is Globalization Muddling the Middle Class?" Center for Social and Economic Dynamics Working Paper 14. Brookings (August).

De Soto, Hernando. 1989. *The Other Path: The Invisible Revolution in the Third World.* New York: Harper and Row.

———. 2000. *The Mystery of Capital. Why Capitalism Triumphs in the West and Fails Everywhere Else.* New York: Basic Books.

Easterly, William. 2000. "The Middle Class Consensus and Economic Development." Policy Research Working Paper 2346. Washington: World Bank.

Economic Commission for Latin America and the Caribbean (ECLAC). 2006. "La protección social de cara al futuro: Acceso, financiamiento y solidaridad." Report prepared for the Thirty-First Session of ECLAC. Montevideo, Uruguay, March 20–24.

Solimano, Andrés, ed. 1998. *Social Inequality.* University of Michigan Press.

———. 2005. "Towards New Social Policies in Latin America: Growth, the Middle Class and Social Rights." *ECLAC Review* no. 87: 45–60.

———, ed. 2006. *Vanishing Growth in Latin America. The Late Twentieth Century Experience.* Cheltenham, U.K.: Edward Elgar.

Solimano, Andrés, and Molly Pollack. 2006. "The Search for Stability and Growth under Persistent Inequality: The Case of Chile." In *Pro-Poor Macroeconomics: Potential and Limitations*, edited by Giovanni Andrea Cornia, pp. 217–47. Basingstoke, U.K.: Palgrave Macmillan.

Torche, Florencia, and Seymour Spilerman. 2006. "Household Wealth in Latin America." Paper prepared for the project meeting on Personal Assets from a Global Perspective. World Institute for Development Economics Research. Helsinki, May 4–6.

PART III

Asset Accumulation and Consolidation in Practice

8

Building Natural Resource–Based Assets in Southern Africa: Workable Scenarios

PAULA NIMPUNO-PARENTE

Most of southern Africa's people live in environments that are rich in natural resources. However, people have not been able to use these resources to generate sustainable livelihoods because in many instances conservation has been prioritized at the expense of the people neighboring or living in these protected areas. The focus on conservation has ignored the fact that a peaceful and profitable coexistence between people and protected areas is possible. The purpose of this chapter is to examine strategies that will enable low-income groups in environments that are rich in natural resources to build a sustainable economy by wise and measured use of these resources.

Historically, many of the people who inhabited these areas were dispossessed of their land. Today they are still not able to fully maximize access to these resources for investment or even for sustainable livelihoods because of their lack of knowledge and capital—even though three-fourths of the population of southern Africa lives in rural areas, and their natural resources are all they depend on. Land-based livelihoods are often more important than many policymakers acknowledge. Their hidden economic value derives in part from contributions that are not monetized but provide a variety of benefits that research is only now beginning to reveal. Nontimber forest products alone account for 19.4 percent of all livelihoods; 38.2 percent comes from agropastoralism (excluding trade values). Every year each household derives an estimated $311 worth of benefit from fuel wood collected, $193 worth of benefit from edible wild fruits and herbs, and $41 worth of benefit from medicinal plants. These examples are indicators of the extent and importance of natural resource use. Omitting such values in national accounting and macroeconomic policy could undermine sustainable development and further expose biodiversity to overexploitation (Dovie, Shackleton, and Witkowski 2001).

In southern Africa most poor people still live on the land and depend on natural resources for their livelihoods and well-being. Some policy analysts argue that land-based livelihoods can make a significant contribution to poverty reduction among these people if policies are pursued that both widen access to productive resources and enhance the productivity and output of such activities. For several years the Ford Foundation has supported work in community-based natural resource management in southern Africa. This work has mainly focused on resource rights of access. Although right of access is critical, it is not the sole factor that will enable communities to secure ownership and control, use these resources for their livelihood, and build assets. Serious attention must also be paid to access to finance, gender equity, new forms of leadership and the good governance of community organizations, and social justice outcomes when poor people gain access to natural resources.

The Assets Program of the southern Africa office of the Ford Foundation has adopted an integrated approach to strengthen the economic base of families and communities to address their vulnerability. The program does this by supporting organizations that build natural and financial assets as well as design policy reforms that increase the social and economic safety nets of families and communities. In addition, the program also aims to help build systems of good governance and contribute to policy analysis and changes for maximum impact. This strategy makes sense when one considers the high levels of poverty and inequality that are still prevalent in southern Africa. Although there has been some economic growth, several decades of democracy, and government policies designed to address legacies of the past, poverty and unemployment persist and remain the core challenges of governments and the development sector in general. Some policies, such as those for housing, water, and land, have been relatively successful in addressing some of the legacy issues, but the reality is that the gap between rich and poor appears to be widening, and there is an increasing realization that economic growth alone does not in itself reduce poverty and inequality.

A contributing factor to the skewed regional growth is the differential allocation of resources, which affects the extent to which poverty and unemployment are reduced. Given the large number of people still living in rural areas across the region, some analysts are now urging a reconsideration of the potential contribution of agriculture, land, and natural resources to growth and development, alongside other asset redistribution measures and policies to help poor people. A potential solution to this challenge would be to include partners such as nongovernmental organizations and private sector organizations to enhance the capacity of governments to assist the poor to enter and participate in the market economy. However, this partnership will not be effective if the impact of global economics is not factored into its plan for regional growth, since globalization has, in many instances, had a negative impact on structural change. For example, most of the markets for tourism are in the Northern Hemisphere. To make a shift so that the Southern Hemisphere receives more of the market share, the south must prove that it can weather currency fluctuations as well as satisfy the north's need for ensured safety. Structural change is therefore essential, through localized development programs, to foster greater community and private sector partnerships, to create sustainable growth in the local economy, and to make enterprises more resilient in the marketplace.

But what disadvantages vulnerable groups is their limited access to financial services, such as funding from formal financial institutions, which means that it is very difficult for low-income households and communities to gain credit, savings, and insurance. Poor people are particularly vulnerable to unpredictable events such as illness, death, poor harvest, or price fluctuation for their produce. Moreover, HIV/AIDS is on the increase in the region and has become a principal cause of financial vulnerability.

Because of a highly skewed income distribution and economic structure in southern Africa, a large number of households are considered unbankable. Commercial banks regard them as risky investments because they have been traditionally dependent on a combination of postal banking, rotating savings, and credit schemes such as *stokvels* (informal rotating and savings credit schemes among friends and families) as well as unscrupulous microlenders.[1] It becomes critical, therefore, to provide to these poor people such financial resources as savings accounts, insurance, credit, and regular remittances or pensions. Access to finance and information about markets and prices will increase their capacity to prepare for periods of vulnerability and adversity.

Policy and Legislation

Most southern African governments have developed legislation and policies that aim to create land and resource rights for those who were denied them under colonialism. Policies were created to give communities rights to both access to and management of their natural resources so as to address land distribution imbalances, poverty, and conservation. The governments of South Africa, Namibia, and Mozambique developed policies, constitutions, and legal frameworks and embarked on various experiments to transfer user rights and control over resources.[2] With this reality, policies were designed to facilitate and provide community-based natural resource management programs to create a conducive environment for national economic growth and local economic development in rural and marginalized areas. These programs have in some cases led to promising results, with previously dispossessed rural communities acquiring significant equity in agriculture and tourism enterprises.

Yet in too many cases the support systems that enable growth are lacking or limited. The extent to which communities have been able to add value to natural resources and to assert meaningful ownership and control over these resources depends on whether these policies are translated into action and whether mechanisms are in place to enforce the policy. Such mechanisms should address the challenges of empowering communities to use their access and user rights provided by existing policy and legal frameworks; developing strategies for the poor to access capital and other services so they can use the land and other natural resources in economically viable, sustainable, and job-producing ways; promoting access and rights for women, who are largely excluded from access and decisionmaking due to the widespread acceptability of patriarchy in customary tenure; and addressing the high HIV/AIDS infection rate and resultant vulnerability of poor women and poor households.[3]

This chapter presents case studies for creating the necessary foundation upon which low-income groups and communities can be empowered to build assets in three economic sectors: tourism, agriculture, and the informal economy.

Tourism

There are two distinct international trends in the tourism industry. The first is conventional tourism, largely based in the global north and owned and controlled by large corporations. The second is the ecotourism industry, which is decentralized and based in the global south. Ecotourism offers visitors the opportunity to make a contribution to the sustainable use of natural resources and also to the socioeconomic growth of the largely poor host communities. The Ford Foundation's strategy in southern Africa adheres to the principles of ecotourism and tourism in aid of the poor. This strategy enhances the linkages between tourism and poor people so that tourism's contribution to poverty reduction is increased and poor people are able to participate in product development. Ecotourism is widely regarded as a significant generator of jobs and wealth and as economically empowering rural communities. And it is increasingly promoted as a robust strategy to grow the economies of these countries.[4] To date several organizations are working to ensure that local communities do benefit from tourism growth (estimated at 15 percent growth in sub-Saharan Africa in the first quarter of 2005). Recent research indicates, however, that tourism does not necessarily translate into poverty reduction because a lack of local economic capacity and skills and the skewed patterns of land ownership lead to external commercial interests capturing most of the benefits. The concentration of benefits in the hands of international operators and local urban elites undermines local social and economic development in the rural and remote areas where ecotourism destinations are located. Local employees remain indefinitely in low-paying, low-skilled jobs. Moreover, investors often choose to import the required materials and staff rather than source them locally. Developing tourism to benefit the poor in the local economy therefore requires significant effort by the government and the private sector to ensure that the benefits accrue to local communities.

There is also a gender dimension in tourism, according to the Overseas Development Institute (Ashley 2005). Compared to other industries, a higher percentage of tourism's benefits in terms of employment and the development of small businesses go to women. This is confirmed by tourism investments in the region, in which women represent 35–40 percent of beneficiaries. Furthermore, ecotourism provides economic opportunities for isolated rural communities.

Against a background of people-centered reforms in conservation, the Africa Safari Lodge Foundation is consciously promoting beneficial linkages with the rural poor.[5] The foundation is effectively building the capacity of communities in South Africa, Mozambique, and Namibia to take full ownership of tourism lodges through innovative private and community partnerships. As an organic and home-grown model, it builds on devolving tenure and tourism rights to communities in the region. Despite the different types of tenure rights in the region (communal land, protected areas, and private property), the foundation's program enables low-income communities to contribute significantly to sustainable rural development in remote areas, where tourism investment is often the major source of economic growth, job creation, and poverty alleviation. The foundation's approach demonstrates the positive economic impacts that game lodges or clusters of game lodges can have on the livelihoods of rural people.

However, technical assistance is critical to generating successful outcomes for both community groups and the private sector. Technical assistance must be able to support initiatives for the poor and simultaneously intersect with markets, a logic often lacking among nongovernmental organizatons and conservation groups. Commercial viability and profitability are preconditions for the lodges and tourism market if they are to contribute to local livelihoods in a sustainable manner and on a significant scale. Therefore it is vital that support programs target only commercially viable ventures and avoid initiating or supporting enterprises that are vulnerable in a market framework.

A case in point is the Balete-ba-Lekgopung lodge, called the Buffalo Ridge Community Wildlife Lodge. It is owned by the people of Balete-ba-Lekgopung and is located in the Madikwe Game Reserve in the Northwest Province of South Africa. The Northwest Parks and Tourism Board is the lead agency in the Madikwe Initiative, an agreement to grant long-term concessions to local rural communities living in the vicinity of the game reserve. The Buffalo Ridge Lodge is a pilot in an experiment in wildlife tourism and community-owned enterprise designed to provide jobs and to generate lease fees and other benefits to rural people without jeopardizing wilderness conservation. The community of Balete-ba-Lekgopung holds all of the shares through a community development trust. Two local development finance institutions and the Ford Foundation provided a mix of grants and soft loans that leverage a bundle of public and commercial finance to deliver the lodge-owning company to the community. The mixture of loan and capital is to ensure an early flow of revenue to the community.

The trust has a forty-five-year lease agreement with the Northwest Parks and Tourism Board and has appointed a private sector partner to maintain and operate the lodge. The lodge generated more than a hundred jobs during the construction phase and employs more than thirty permanent people, at an average annual wage of approximately U.S.$5,000 (the average annual income was previously U.S.$1,200). Community members fill 90 percent of the permanent jobs. Comprehensive skills-training programs supported by the Madikwe Initiative and the Tourism Board are under way to ensure that trained local staff at all levels are available. Skills related to owning and operating small enterprises have been taught to enable the community to benefit from secondary-enterprise opportunities. Community enterprises so far include a laundry, cleaning services, and waste management.[6] The lodge is a valuable asset for a community in which unemployment is estimated at 58 percent (broadly in line with the national level).

The key values that underpin the Balete-ba-Lekgopung Trust are cultivation of social capital, leadership, and gender equity. Although the community has been relatively successful in maintaining traditional norms and values, it is clear that generational and gender tensions are a factor (Matose and others 2006).[7]

Traditional leaders have been given the status of founder trustees, but a younger and better educated generation is gradually acquiring the leadership positions. The trust also plays a critical role in retaining young people in the rural areas, especially in communities that have been accustomed to migrant labor and its concomitant remittances. The strongly patriarchal culture of the groups and the fact that only three of the twenty-one trustees are women will likely test the performance of the trust with regard to gender equity.

One challenge is to integrate the lodge into the regional economy to ensure that economic growth and jobs are maximized and that community members benefit from more than lodge revenues. It will be important to link into and strengthen the economic development programs of other localities where community lodges exist. In particular, the lodge industry has an interest in, and in some cases acts as a catalyst for, effective HIV interventions in deep rural areas where public health facilities are scarce. Tools and processes to track changes in the asset and livelihoods status of the different interest groups within the community are needed to enable decisionmaking over time.

Balete-ba-Lekgopung is proving to be a successful model across the region. Its demonstration approach holds many lessons with respect to technical assistance and learning opportunities for those engaged in increasing community equity share in high-value areas of the economy. A Fair Trade in Tourism certification is being explored to encourage equity and fair business practices.[8] It is anticipated that this will increase the Africa Safari Lodge Foundation's market share in regional and international markets.

Thakadu is another lodge built within the Madikwe Game Reserve that is owned by the Batlokwa Boo Kgosi Matlapeng community. Several others are planned in southern Africa. While the models of devolution of resource rights may vary from country to country and over time, the overall approach has increased the number of models based on equity shares and local ownership in the conservation and tourism industry. The challenge for community owners is to mobilize the right mixture of equity finance through grants and commercial loans.

Agriculture

Southern Africa has not had many successful land reform or emerging farmers' (newly emerging black farmers) projects. The South African government is gradually shifting its policy away from a willing buyer–willing seller policy in an attempt to deal with accelerated land reform as well as growth and development in the agricultural sector for previously disadvantaged people. These goals pressure governments to achieve a peaceful and planned transfer of land as well as to assist emerging farmers to farm successfully (and avoid a Zimbabwean type of situation).

The Elgin Learning Foundation (ELF) has developed a model to transform emerging farmers into successful small business entrepreneurs by four means: gradually transferring land to poor individuals and communities; addressing the reality that most land transfers still do not result in anything above subsistence level farming; promoting sustainable land use among beneficiary groups; and furthering the understanding of agricultural markets. The ELF considers land and its retention as critical to building the capacity of emerging farmers and offers financing and mentoring to ensure that these new entrants into the farming sector maximize production and income.

Over the past several years, the value of the agriculturally based economy in the Western Cape's Overberg region has dropped, partly due to the collapse of the fruit market and partly to the inability of local farmers to implement reform projects. The out-of-season unemployment rate for the area's 55,000 residents is about 70 percent. Unemployment of this proportion has resulted in vast squatter camps, which are fraught with social and health problems, including drug abuse, crime, and HIV/AIDS.

With Ford Foundation support, the ELF Trust developed an innovative model farm for demonstrating agrarian reform and entrepreneurship, a program targeted at farm workers and unemployed people who previously worked for large commercial farms. The government acquired twenty hectares of land from large commercial farmers through the land restitution program, and the ELF secured a thirty-year lease agreement at less than U.S.$20 a year. The aim is to transform this land into a profitable business with demonstrated value by securing the necessary infrastructure, equipment, and materials, and also to train and mentor emergent farmers. Commercial farmers will provide technical assistance and mentoring.

With Ford Foundation support, the ELF embarked on a subsector market study, which identified wine, organic vegetables, and essential oils as marketable products for the newly leased land. The ELF also undertook a socioeconomic baseline study to gain a better understanding of the new farmers—their communities, their levels of education, their vulnerabilities, and so on. This was a critical first step toward helping underserved communities access services and resources not generally available, and providing brokers to build links between the ELF, government officials, and commercial farmers. Finally, the ELF also developed an integrated training package for accredited farming programs.

Products from the farm will be sold in local, national, and international markets; import-substitution possibilities will also be explored. Successive classes of emerging farmers will rotate through the program, working systematically through all phases of agricultural production while attending training courses to prepare them for independent land ownership and stewardship. The demonstration farm will be sustained through profits from the sale of its products, which will also cover the costs of the training facility and provide seed capital to graduating emerging farmers to establish their own farming ventures.

The ELF model will have an impact on the livelihood of more than a thousand farm families through improved livelihoods, lower unemployment, and farm ownership for blacks in a region dominated by white commercial farmers. The model addresses the disappointing results of the many government-led initiatives aimed at increasing access to land for its poor, previously disadvantaged population, and it can be replicated throughout the region.

The Informal Economy

Most countries with a communal and informal economy do not have publicly supported or market-based social security schemes. Where they do exist, they tend to benefit only formal sector workers. Yet income insecurity and vulnerability are high in a communal and informal economy. The poor rural communities of southern Africa are being severely damaged by the HIV/AIDS pandemic through the direct loss of human capital and the diversion of resources and income to health and caring activities. Various activities on which rural families depend for securing food and income are no longer possible for those who are sick and those who are caring for the sick. Financial and human assets are gradually depleted while traditional support mechanisms break down, increasing the vulnerability of these communities to other shocks.

The rural situation is exacerbated by the fact that many urban migrants stricken with HIV/AIDS return to their rural homes to be supported by relatives. Women often bear the brunt of this home-based care while also being responsible for securing household food and income. The poor are caught in a further financial bind by their inability to borrow money, even though a loan might allow them to open a small business.

The general inadequacy of insurance markets also exposes the poor to substantial risks and insecurity. Microfinance clients rely on a number of formal and informal mechanisms to cope with the financial shock associated with a death in the family. Burial societies, for example, are effective for meeting the immediate burial needs. But these short-term mechanisms do not deal with such adverse effects of poverty as children not attending school due to the inability to pay fees. Microfinance institutions thus have a critical role to play in mediating between the conventional finance markets and the informal economy.

Organizations such as the Small Enterprise Foundation (one of the largest microfinance institutions in South Africa) and donor programs have traditionally worked to strengthen markets, widen access to financial services to rural informal traders, and build organizational capacity. In addition, microfinance and the empowerment of women can even reduce violence against women—which, in turn, makes it possible for women to access loans and insurance so they can better participate in the economy.

The Ford Foundation is supporting the Small Enterprise Foundation to partner with a commercial insurance provider to leverage its distribution network and provide clients with relevant insurance products. The model will be able to demonstrate how nongovernmental organizations and commercial entities can achieve synergies that neither group could achieve on its own to assist people in going beyond the mere protection of assets to accumulating them.

A high percentage of the HIV/AIDS global infections are concentrated in southern Africa and remain closely linked to conditions of poverty, underdevelopment, and gender-based inequalities that are endemic to much of the region. While nearly 60 percent of new HIV infections are among women and girls, the reality is also that more than 40 percent of African women are at risk of violence. Furthermore, violence against women has been identified as an independent risk factor for HIV infection.

To address these overlapping vulnerabilities, the Intervention with Microfinance for AIDS and Gender Equity (IMAGE) was established as a partnership between the Rural AIDS and Development Action Research Programme (at the School of Public Health at the University of the Witwatersrand) and the Small Enterprise Foundation. The pilot program, located in some of the most disadvantaged communities in rural South Africa, concentrates on three interrelated United Nations Millennium Development Goals: poverty reduction, the promotion of gender equality, and HIV/AIDS prevention. It combines a microfinance-based poverty alleviation program with a gender and HIV training curriculum (Pronyk and others 2006).

A rigorous evaluation of the intervention demonstrates clear changes in the economic well-being, social capital, and empowerment of the project participants. Among the 430 women participants in the loan program, the rate of gender-based violence was reduced by more than half. It is one of the first interventions of its kind in a developing country to demonstrate such effects. The impact of the project on the vulnerability of young people was also measured, showing significant changes in knowledge, communication, openness, and access to voluntary counseling and testing services. During the first three years of the program's operations, about 1,750 loans were disbursed, valued at more than U.S.\$290,000. There was a notably higher repayment rate (99.7 percent) to the microfinance provider, better attendance and fewer dropouts among microfinance clients, and a general increase in the welfare of the community. Women involved in the program reported increases in disposable income and in their leadership positions in the community (Pronyk and others 2006).

The Way Forward

The three projects outlined in this chapter for empowering poor communities are works in progress. They require further research, review, and evaluation. The evaluation should determine whether the commercialization of natural resources leads to sustainable use, whether the carrying capacity of the market for community lodges exists, and whether the projects show good governance and gender equity as livelihoods improve.

There is also a need for a multifaceted approach that addresses tenure rights, access to finance, enterprise support, and markets as critical components for escaping poverty and accumulating assets. The approach should recognize that all members of a poor community, women in particular, have vulnerabilities that need attention. The building of safety nets through conventional and informal mechanisms may prove critical for these vulnerable groups to move out of poverty and into sustainable livelihoods.

Notes

1. There is no commonly accepted definition of *low income* in southern Africa. The current household income poverty threshold is around U.S.\$200 for South Africa and U.S.\$40 for Mozambique. Current figures are unavailable for Zimbabwe.

2. Although the Ford Foundation's southern Africa office does work in four countries—Mozambique, Namibia, South Africa, and Zimbabwe—this program concentrates its grant making in Mozambique and South Africa. Namibia and Zimbabwe are included in different ways: Namibia provides relevant learning opportunities from the Foundation's past work in the environment and development field and is integrated into regional networks. Zimbabwe is home to natural resource trade organizations that have a regional scope and outreach.

3. In South Africa the Communal Lands Rights Act was passed in 2004, but it has not been put into practice because it has been contested by civil society organizations. The debate is centered on decisionmaking, and control of the land is now proposed to be in the hands of the traditional leadership. This contradicts the tenets of the previously operating Community Property Association, which despite its uneven implementation, gave the final decision to communities on how assets are controlled and used. A critical issue is gender: the act questions women owning land as communal property with men. The Legal Resource Centre has

lodged a complaint with the Constitutional Court on behalf of communities and women's organizations regarding the act. Most programs are operating in a vacuum while waiting for the courts to establish clear guidelines.

4. For example, in South Africa, tourism and agrarian reform are prioritized in the South African government's Accelerated and Shared Growth Initiative. The ten-year target is black-owned resources of at least 25 percent. Black economic empowerment, however, has come under criticism because it is seen as a vehicle not to address broad inequalities but to create a black elite closely related to the government and to one political party.

5. The Africa Safari Lodge Foundation is a nongovernmental organization that works toward maximizing pro-poor impacts of nature tourism enterprises in southern Africa. It has created a steering committee responsible for oversight and program direction. The committee has developed a scorecard for black economic empowerment that emphasizes outsourcing to entrepreneurs located in the vicinity of tourism markets. This scorecard forms the basis for advocating for broad-based empowerment in the economy, as opposed to empowering a small urban black elite.

6. Personal communications from Peter-John Massyn from Mafisa Planning and Research and Nick Swan, an independent consultant, 2004.

7. In the context of people-centered natural resource management, the term *community* refers to landholder and village community. It is understood that *community* is a group of members linked through a high level of social aggregation that has been given tenure security over resources. However, there is no simple definition, mainly because membership is established through negotiations and consensus and is therefore viewed as dynamic, with a complex set of variables that change over time.

8. Fair Trade in Tourism South Africa is a trademark that gives recognition to businesses that agree to local employment, local buying, skills development, health and HIV/AIDS awareness, environmental education, and community support. The group is working with South Africa and exploring regional links through the Africa Safari Lodge Foundation.

References

Ashley, Caroline. 2005. "Facilitating Pro-Poor Tourism with the Private Sector: Lessons Learned from 'Pro-Poor Tourism Pilots in Southern Africa.'" Working Paper 257. London: Overseas Development Institute.

Dovie, Delali B. K., Charlie M. Shackleton, and Ed T. F. Witkowski. 2001. "Valuing Non-Timber Forests: Indicator for Interplay between Poverty, Livelihoods and the Environment." Paper prepared for the open meeting of the Global Environmental Change Research Community. Rio de Janeiro, October 6–8.

Matose, Frank, and others. 2006. "Debating Land Reform, Natural Resources and Poverty: The Membership Problem in People-Centred Approaches to Natural Resource Management in Southern Africa." Policy Brief 20. Belleville, South Africa: Programme for Land and Agrarian Studies (February).

Pronyk, Paul, and others. 2006. "Effect of a Structural Intervention for the Prevention of Intimate-Partner Violence and HIV in Rural South Africa: A Cluster Randomised Trial." *Lancet* 368 (December 2): 1973–83.

9

Protecting Land Rights in Post-Tsunami and Postconflict Aceh, Indonesia

LILIANNE FAN

This chapter has two objectives. The first is to delineate some of the critical land rights issues that have emerged over the last two years in the Indonesian province of Aceh, the place worst affected by the earthquake and tsunami of December 2004, and one already deeply scarred by thirty years of armed conflict.[1] The second objective is to consider these developments within the conceptual framework provided by asset-based approaches to poverty reduction and development.

The tsunami caused a dramatic loss of life as well as huge damage to land and property in Aceh. One hundred sixty-seven thousand people were killed or declared missing, and 500,000 people were made homeless within a few hours; 252,323 houses and 300,000 parcels of land were totally or partially damaged, and whatever land records did exist were either destroyed or rendered illegible (Fitzpatrick 2005). The destruction of ownership records, erosion of boundaries, redistribution of inheritance on a massive scale, and loss of physical land itself meant that securing access to land and determining who owned which parcels of land became the first priority in the process of rebuilding houses for displaced tsunami survivors. In areas where land was still accessible, it became important to first clarify land and property rights to minimize potential disputes and provide sufficient legal and social certainty for rebuilding houses and recovering livelihoods. At the same time, clear policies and procedures were needed to assist some 50,000 families whose land was submerged or rendered unsafe as a result of the tsunami or who did not own land or housing before the disaster and therefore required relocation to new land before the rebuilding process could begin.[2]

The shock of natural disaster and need for cooperation among all elements of society in the massive recovery effort instigated a renewal of peace negotiations between the Indonesian government and the Free Aceh Movement.[3] These talks led to the signing of a memorandum of understanding in Helsinki on August 15, 2005, bringing an official end to three decades of armed conflict during which 15,000 people had lost their lives.[4] Rights over land and other natural resources lay at the heart of the conflict between Aceh and the central government, which coincided with the emergence of a political economy that effectively marginalized Acehnese at local, provincial, and national levels. The sustainability of the newly forged peace in Aceh depends largely on how the deep-rooted patterns that perpetuated grievance and distrust at multiple social and political levels are transformed, and the ways in which new forms of social, economic, and political institutions and relationships are developed. Issues related to the distribution of control over and access to land and natural resources will play a key role in these processes.

Concepts rooted in asset-based approaches to poverty reduction and development provide useful tools for analyzing the multiple implications of land rights for tsunami- and conflict-affected people in the province of Aceh. "In disaster contexts," writes Moser, "assets are often dramatically destroyed and need to be rapidly rebuilt. Prioritization among different assets is critical, with the relationship between accumulation of one often dependent on another" (Moser 2006). The earthquake and tsunami caused sudden and massive damage to natural, physical, financial, social, and human capital, primarily along Aceh's coast but also in the interior, where disruption of family and trade networks had severe social and economic consequences. While the physical reconstruction might be completed in ten years, full recovery could well take generations. The severity of the natural disaster was amplified because it occurred in a land where thirty years of conflict had eroded personal and livelihoods security, social coherence, and public services and infrastructure.

In a postdisaster and postconflict context, secure access to land directly influences the capacity of individuals, households, and differently positioned members of communities to begin the process of rebuilding their lives and accumulating assets needed to alleviate vulnerabilities, risks, and poverty.[5] Land is both a foundation for reconstructing houses and recovering livelihoods destroyed by disaster or war and a potential source of income and accumulation of financial assets through sale, rent, or use as collateral for credit. The accumulation of natural, physical, and financial assets often forms the basis for increasing investment in human capital (for example, through education and skills training). "But [land] is far more than just an asset," writes Robin Palmer, Oxfam's global land adviser. "For many in today's structurally adjusted and economically liberalized world, land often provides the ultimate form of social security. Access to land is particularly important to women and can contribute to the protection of widowed, abandoned or single women and to their economic security."[6] Thus secure rights to land also play an important role in protecting vulnerable groups, such as widows and orphans, and in promoting women's economic empowerment by allowing them greater control over household and communal assets as well as enhancing their capacity to invest in the development of future generations.

The following discussion describes the pretsunami context and the impact of the tsunami. It then considers specific land rights issues that emerged as a result of the tsunami, including the need to clarify ownership rights, the situation of landless tsunami victims, and the increase in evictions and development-related displacement. Land and resource issues that have emerged since the signing of the peace agreement are assessed next, highlighting potential areas of contestation that long-term peacebuilding and development strategies will need to address. Finally, the conclusion proposes some ways forward.

Aceh before the Tsunami

Before the disaster the security of the lives, possessions, and infrastructure in Aceh had already been threatened by three decades of armed conflict between the Indonesian military and an Acehnese insurgency, known as the Free Aceh Movement (*Gerakan Aceh Merdeka*, or GAM). Over the past twenty-five years, poverty had increased dramatically in Aceh even as the GDP of the province rose steadily as a result of natural resource exploitation. Since the discovery of natural gas and oil in 1971, Aceh became increasingly important to the national economy. With the development of natural gas exploration, Aceh's GDP increased at a faster rate than in most provinces. However, this pattern of growth was accompanied by increasing poverty, especially in the rural areas. Between 1980 and 2002, poverty in the province increased by 239 percent, even though poverty rates elsewhere in Indonesia fell by as much as 47 percent in the same period (Brown 2005). Between 1999 and 2002 alone, the poverty rate in Aceh doubled from 14.7 to 28.9 percent. According to the Indonesian government's own statistics, in 2002 nearly 48.5 percent of the population in Aceh had no access to clean water, 36.2 percent of children under the age of five were mal-nourished, and 38 percent had no access to health facilities (United Nations Development Program 2004).

The decades under the presidency of General Suharto (1967–98) saw the loss of thousands of lives, systematic human rights abuses against civilians, erosion of livelihoods and local economic development, and widespread disruption of public services such as water and sanitation, education, and health. Ethnic tensions emerged as natural resources in Aceh were exploited by a largely non-Acehnese business elite. This was further exacerbated by government-supported transmigration of ethnic Javanese into poor rural areas and by the appropriation of villagers' land and property by the state apparatus, including the increasingly prominent military. During this period Aceh's natural assets were systematically stripped, with 75 percent of Aceh's total land area carved up into huge logging and plantation concessions. In some districts (South and West Aceh), more than 60 percent of the forest resources have been exploited. In 2000 there were at least twenty-eight logging companies (seven in the district of South Aceh alone) and five timber estates in the province, and some 140,000 hectares had been set aside for oil palm plantations. Concessions for timber and agricultural planta-tions were, and still are, largely owned by state-sponsored conglomerates based in Medan and Jakarta, with very little participation by local entrepreneurs (Down to Earth 2000).

The unsustainable exploitation of Aceh's natural resources led to multiple ecological and social problems, including flash floods, landslides, devastation of agricultural land, food shortages, and water pollution. These conditions led to confrontations between local communities and big companies (such as in the districts of South and Central Aceh). In Lhokseumawe the natural gas facility run by PT Arun was guarded by the military, who were accused of committing human rights violations using company equipment (Down to Earth 1998). At the same time, violence and displacement caused by the armed conflict under-mined agricultural production and trade in many areas, with crops often destroyed. Extortion of payments from farmers, traders, and businesspeople became common, as was the military's control of illegal logging, marijuana, and mining businesses. GAM also frequently taxed villagers, occasionally coupled with intimidation (although this was by no means comparable to the Indone-sian military in scale or brutality).

Horizontal tensions were also fueled by the government's transmigration pro-gram, which gave large areas of land in Aceh to Javanese transmigrants to set up food-crop sites and wood-processing industries. This program generated signifi-cant inequality in land holdings between the Javanese, who were often given up to two hectares, and Acehnese landowners, the majority of whom held plots smaller than two hectares (Brown 2005).

These conditions led to the rise of an armed movement for independence and many years of brutal anti-insurgency operations by the military, which in turn led to more exploitation and abuse and further deepened Acehnese hostility toward Jakarta. Ultimately, these conditions gave rise to various forms of resistance to the central government. The most prominent form was the armed insurgency by GAM. But after the fall of Suharto in 1998, resistance visibly diversified, with the emergence of a nonviolent student-led civic movement leading calls for an end to military impunity, a peaceful resolution of the conflict, and greater control over resources by Acehnese. By 2000, however, the military increasingly targeted civic leaders for arbitrary arrests, intimidation, and even kidnapping and extrajudicial killings.

Impact of the Tsunami

On December 26, 2004, an earthquake measuring 9.0 on the Richter scale struck off the Indonesian island of Sumatra, triggering a massive tsunami that hit the coasts of Indonesia, Sri Lanka, India, Thailand, Malaysia, the Maldives, Burma, the Seychelles, and Somalia.

Within the space of a few hours, the giant waves devastated thousands of kilometers of coastline and the communities that lived there. While the final death toll will never be known, official estimates indicate that at least 223,492 people perished across twelve countries, and an additional 43,320 are presumed dead. A further 1.8 million people were displaced, seeking refuge in temporary camps and with host communities. The United Nations estimates that the disaster created some $10 billion in damages in twenty-four hours (United Nations Office of the Special Envoy for Tsunami Recovery 2005).

The Indonesian province of Aceh was the area hardest hit. According to the Rehabilitation and Reconstruction Agency for Aceh and Nias (*Badan Rehabilitasi dan Rekonstruksi untuk Aceh dan Nias*, or BRR NAD-Nias), the total losses in infrastructure, housing, and productive capacity have been estimated at more than $4.6 billion. In addition to the devastation caused by the tsunami, a second powerful earthquake struck on March 29, 2005, off the island of Nias, Sumatra, leaving another 1,000 people dead and some 70,000 people displaced. A large proportion of victims of both disasters were women and children (United Nations Office of the Special Envoy for Tsunami Recovery 2005).[7]

When the waves subsided, the survivors found their lives in ruins. Some 1,000 villages and towns, 127,000 homes, 14,800 schools, and 10,000 kilometers of roads were destroyed. In some areas what had been heavily populated land was, after the tsunami, flat and featureless, every landmark and structure swept away. The damage to the civil infrastructure, in terms of both personnel and property, was such that local government was unable to operate satisfactorily until mid-2005. With 600,000 people rendered homeless, the provision of shelter quickly emerged as the chief priority in the relief and reconstruction process. At the end of 2005, some 78,000 people still remained in tents in Aceh and Nias, with hundreds of thousands more living in temporary barracks or with host communities (BRR NAD-Nias 2005). At the time of writing, the recovery communities in Aceh and Nias are working on a joint plan of action to address the urgent situation of some 70,000 households still living in barracks, many of which are due to be decommissioned at the end of 2006.[8]

The loss of livelihoods was also devastating. The International Labour Organization estimated that 1.8 million jobs might have been lost to the tsunami across the region (International Labour Organization 2005). The Asian Development Bank calculated that the disaster threatened to plunge a further 2 million people into poverty in the region as a whole and that many of those already below the poverty line would slide even deeper into poverty as they lost what little earnings they had before (Asian Development Bank 2005). In Aceh alone some 600,000 people—about 25 percent of the population—lost their sole source of livelihood. The unemployment rate in Aceh rose from approximately 6.8 percent before the tsunami to at least 30 percent (International Labour Organization 2005).

Across the region fishing communities, small-scale agriculturalists, laborers, and those running small businesses were the worst affected by the disaster. Many fishing families who survived lost their boats, nets, and engines, and hence their ability to earn a living. In Aceh about 70 percent of the small-scale fishing fleet was destroyed. This also meant that laborers who worked on boats owned by others or in processing and associated activities also lost their means of earning a living. Others whose sole or main asset was land found their crops destroyed and their land ruined because of the salt water and mud that covered them. According to the Food and Agriculture Organization up to 40 percent of the 40,000 hectares of agricultural land destroyed in Aceh may be permanently lost.[9]

Defining Land Rights Problems in Post-Tsunami Aceh

Within ten days of the disaster, Oxfam was asked by a United Nations official to explore the issue of land and property rights in the affected regions. As one of the first international nongovernmental organizations (NGOs) to provide emergency relief on the ground, Oxfam recognized that the already fragile land and property rights of poor communities in the region were further threatened by the huge loss of land, livelihoods, and critical personal documents, such as identification cards and land records. Oxfam commissioned a rapid scoping survey of the key issues to inform its future program and advocacy work (Williams 2005). The report highlighted the complexities of emerging land and property problems in Aceh, Sri Lanka, and India and recommended sustained monitoring of and advocacy for the protection of land and property rights of the affected populations.

In March 2005 Oxfam and the United Nations Development Program jointly commissioned a more in-depth study on restoring and confirming land rights in Aceh (Fitzpatrick 2005). The report addressed two urgent issues: the need for sufficient tenure security to support the reconstruction and recovery efforts, particularly in the housing sector, and the need to avert land and property conflicts, such as land-grabbing and inheritance disputes. The report also looked at several cross-cutting issues, including international standards for sustainable return and restitution of land rights, relocation proposals and obligations of due process and compensation, the role of land consolidation, spatial planning, and protection of the land rights of vulnerable groups. The report described the extent of land-related damage in Aceh:

—Approximately 300,000 parcels of land (170,000 urban and 130,000 rural) out of an estimated 1,498,200 were affected by tsunami-related damage. Of these, only around 60,000 parcels were titled, mostly in urban areas.

—The provincial office of the National Land Agency (*Badan Pertanahan Nasional,* or BPN) in Banda Aceh was badly damaged.

—BPN's provincial office in Banda Aceh lost 30 percent of its staff.

—There was substantial loss of or damage to land records held at BPN and subdistrict offices, including all cadastral index maps.

—There was widespread loss of personal identity documents in tsunami-affected communities.

—A large amount of land had been submerged or rendered unsafe for return as a result of the tsunami.

The report distinguished the land rights situation in post-tsunami Aceh from other postdisaster and postconflict contexts where judicial institutions played an important role in property restitution. Unlike the former Yugoslavia, there were no secondary occupations in Aceh and therefore no need for legally sanctioned evictions before displaced communities could return. Unlike Rwanda, East Timor, and Afghanistan, Aceh had no layered history of dispossession or intercommunal tension, even though it had undergone years of armed conflict. The land rights situation in Aceh could be defined primarily as one of massive displacement and the need for sustainable return, the main challenge being sheer scale rather than underlying complexity. The priority, the report recommended, was to support government and community-based mechanisms for establishing land tenure security to allow for quick return of displaced populations.

The report identified, however, several challenges in need of particular attention:

—tensions between local communities and the local and central government as a result of the long-standing conflict between Acehnese secessionists and Indonesian security forces;

—significant mistrust between civil society organizations and government agencies (the government, and the security forces in particular, have long been suspicious of civil society groups in Aceh, and many were labeled as being pro-separatist);

—the need to integrate bottom-up community mapping and village-level planning processes with top-down land titling, spatial planning, and land consolidation programs;

—resettlement assistance for those whose land is now submerged or otherwise unfit for return, as well as related obligations to provide due process and adequate compensation; and

—the need for special attention and protective mechanisms for vulnerable landholding groups, including women (especially widows), orphans, leaseholders, and communities with insecure forms of tenure.

Confirming Land and Property Rights through Land Administration

The Indonesian government recognized the need for land rights protection in its official master plan for rehabilitation and reconstruction of Aceh and Nias, which was published in March 2005 (National Development Planning Board 2005). The document proposed two measures: an audit of the physical condition of tsunami-affected land, and replacement of lost land documents and issuance of new records for those who never held them. The government's Rehabilitation and Reconstruction Agency for Aceh and Nias (BRR) has also committed itself to the protection of land and property rights of affected communities, regarding this as a precondition for the reconstruction of housing and infrastructure as well as the recovery of livelihoods. Many civil society groups, including the Aceh Legal Aid Foundation and a network of the five largest NGOs in the province, have identified land rights as a priority issue in the post-tsunami context.[10] They also acknowledged a lack of experience working on land and property rights issues due to the fact that before the tsunami the majority of Acehnese civil society focused on human rights advocacy and community empowerment activities.

Responding to a proposal from the BPN, the Multi-Donor Fund for Aceh and Nias, managed by the World Bank, approved a U.S.$28.5 million grant for a project called RALAS (Reconstruction of Aceh's Land Administration System). The project has two main tasks: reconstruction of property rights through "community-driven adjudication" and the issuance of land titles, and reconstruction of the BPN in Aceh province. Through the RALAS project, the BPN aims to title up to 300,000 land parcels in tsunami-affected areas within eighteen months, as well as an additional 300,000 parcels in areas adjacent to tsunami-affected areas. The Ministry of Finance agreed to waive fees and taxes to guarantee that the land titling is done free of charge. According to a June 2006 progress report, 52,915 parcels have been surveyed, and 50,500 land titles were ready to be issued but were waiting on a governmental regulation on banking and land to go into effect (Multi-Donor Fund for Aceh and Nias 2006).

With so many people dead or missing as a result of the disaster, inheritance became a major issue in the process of establishing rights over land. Managing this process has also been challenging because inheritance is a family matter and thus can only be handled through supporting family-level decisionmaking processes in a highly decentralized manner. Families may seek advice from village-based religious leaders but rarely take inheritance cases up to the *shari'a* (Islamic law) court unless there is a serious dispute. *Adat* (customary law) principles on inheritance are not a static set of rules that are applied uniformly across all situations; in practice they always depend on the decisions of the particular people involved—and the final decision lies with the head of the household. This means that while particular principles may be generally acknowledged— for example, parents giving houses to daughters—this bears no relationship to how widely they are actually being applied at any given time. At the time of writing, the United Nations Development Program has just started collaborating with the RALAS project to support "mobile teams" from the shari'a courts to accompany the BPN adjudication teams to tsunami-affected communities. The aim is to provide education about Islamic principles of guardianship and inheritance as well as to encourage women's land ownership. Because shari'a recognizes women's land ownership, it is more likely to protect the property rights of women and children (including widows and orphans) than are local adat practices.

Protecting Land Rights of Landless Tsunami Survivors

Other land problems, however, were not addressed by the RALAS project, perhaps the most urgent being the need for resettlement assistance for those who had been rendered landless by the tsunami. The Indonesian government now estimates that 80,000 hectares have been submerged and that 35,000 households who lost their land will have to be resettled to new locations.[11] In addition, an estimated 15,000 households did not own land or houses before the tsunami (renters and squatters). Both groups require resettlement to new land before they can be provided with houses.

The resettlement process has been fraught with many problems: ongoing policy ambiguity and debates over who should be eligible to receive resettlement assistance, a lack of mechanisms supporting community-based reintegration as a resettlement option, lengthy and expensive processes of land acquisition by the government, and a lack of appropriate private and state land in many districts.

At the heart of the debate over who should receive resettlement assistance is the differential treatment that BRR housing policy offers to pretsunami land- and homeowners versus pretsunami renters and squatters. At the time of writing, BRR policy stipulates that the government will acquire land and provide free housing to pretsunami land- and homeowners who require resettlement but deny renters and squatters access to free BRR housing in favor of a cash-only option.[12] As laid out in the regulations, pretsunami owners will receive basic thirty-six-square-meter houses on new land with appropriate infrastructure, while pretsunami renters will receive approximately U.S.$2,800, and pretsunami squatters will receive approximately U.S.$1,150. Renters and squatters must use this cash as a deposit for a loan to obtain ownership of BRR land and housing.[13] A growing number of actors in the recovery community have voiced their criticism of these BRR policies, which are viewed as inadequate for addressing the housing needs of the large number of landless tsunami victims, who are among the most vulnerable and asset-poor households affected by the disaster.

The lack of clear policies and mechanisms for providing resettlement and housing assistance to landless tsunami victims has led to ongoing delays and uncertainty for this population, and as a result a large number of these landless survivors still remain homeless and without housing commitments almost two years after the disaster. Many are scattered across the 300 or so government-commissioned barracks in Aceh.[14] September 2006 saw two major demonstrations at the office of the BRR by some 2,000 people residing in temporary living centers (TLCs), also known as barracks. The demonstrators demanded that the

BRR pay more attention to the conditions of people living in TLCs, particularly to those who had not received commitments for housing assistance. While some of the demands issued and methods employed by the protesters were deemed by the BRR as disproportionate and inappropriate, the demonstrations succeeded in reminding all those involved in the recovery effort that there is a very real and complex crisis in the TLCs and that those who remain in these locations include the most vulnerable: renters and squatters, those who lost land to the tsunami, single-female-headed households, and unaccompanied children. In response to the crisis in the TLCs, the Office of the United Nations Recovery Coordinator for Aceh and Nias and UNICEF are working with the BRR to develop a Barrack Plan of Action, aiming to stabilize conditions in the TLCs with a push to provide equitable assistance to the most vulnerable. What has become very clear, however, is that many internally displaced persons (IDPs) remain in the barracks because they are unable to return to their original locations and that adequate policy solutions to this problem are urgently needed.

Evictions and Development-Related Displacement

Another problem that began to emerge toward the end of 2005 was the increase in eviction threats by landowners who had been allowing displaced communities to stay on their land temporarily. Delays in finding permanent housing solutions for displaced people put pressure on some landowners to claim back or seek returns for the use of their land. In one case that occurred in Aceh Besar district in mid-October 2005, over 1,200 people were evicted from a private sawmill where many had been for almost ten months. The population, nearly all from the western district of Aceh Jaya, had swelled over this period, and eventually the sawmill owner issued an ultimatum: move or start paying rent. Oxfam field staff, who had been delivering water and sanitation services to the camp since early 2005, were promptly informed about this threat but were unable to convince the landowner to reconsider his stance. When the community finally decided to move to an empty plot of government land across the road, Oxfam, UNICEF, and Concern helped them set up their tents in the new site and provided emergency water supply and other relief services. However, while the government granted permission for the IDPs to remain at the new site until they could be moved into permanent housing, the site was too small for proper drainage work to be done, and tents were tightly cramped together, making the camp both uncomfortable and unsanitary. Oxfam coordinated with the Australian Red Cross, which committed to build temporary shelter units for the entire camp if the government could give them a larger piece of land on which they could stay for up to two years. The government agreed, and the temporary shelter units are currently under construction. In the meantime, the community continues to wait, and agencies continue to provide short-term services.

Such cases are not uncommon in postdisaster Aceh nor on Nias Island, where eviction threats were also reported at several IDP camps in late 2005 and early 2006. In addition, major infrastructure projects also threaten to cause a new wave of displacement for tsunami victims, even as they promise to bring long-term benefits to affected populations and economic development to the province as a whole. Some communities have already staged protests in relation to the planned West Coast Highway, funded by the U.S. Agency for International Development, demanding compensation for land acquired for the road construction, including grave sites, and for the loss of newly constructed houses.[15] It is likely that the trend toward evictions and displacement will increase as time passes and the pressures mount on landowners to revive land-based income-generating activities or sell their land to developers.

The Place of Land Rights in Postconflict Aceh

The tragedy of the tsunami brought about a renewed commitment for peace, and on August 15, 2005, a historic memorandum of understanding (MOU) between the leaders of the Free Aceh Movement (GAM) and the Indonesian government was signed in Helsinki, Finland.[16] The European Union and the Association of Southeast Asian Nations (ASEAN) have supported the peace process by establishing the Aceh Monitoring Mission to track the implementation of the MOU, including the decommissioning of weapons, demobilization of GAM combatants, release of prisoners, and reintegration of GAM members into their communities.

The months immediately after the signing of the MOU saw the establishment of the Aceh Monitoring Mission (made up of European Union and ASEAN civilian monitors), phased withdrawal of nonorganic Indonesian National Army (*Tentara Nasional Indonesia*, or TNI) troops and Indonesian National Police, and decommissioning of GAM weapons. This process was completed in December 2005, with 25,890 TNI troops and 5,850 police relocated and a total of 840 GAM weapons surrendered. During 2006 MOU implementation has resulted in significant institutional changes in Aceh. On February 11, 2006, the governor of Aceh issued a decree establishing the Aceh Reintegration Agency (*Badan Reintegrasi Aceh*, or BRA) as the main entity responsible for coordinating government bodies, donors, and supporting agencies working on post-conflict assistance and peace-building programs.

In March 2006 the World Bank published the GAM Reintegration Needs Assessment, which reported that 70 percent of GAM ex-combatants were unemployed (World Bank 2006b). Respondents interviewed for the assessment also identified livelihoods recovery as the number one priority. Accordingly, post-decommissioning reintegration activities have focused on the dispersal of reintegration livelihoods funds. However, it has been widely admitted that the process remains lethargic, particularly around unequal funds committed to different categories of conflict-affected social groups.[17] At the same time, senior officials in the BRA and the World Bank have expressed concerns about the lack of strategy for long-term economic development, particularly employment generation, in the post-reintegration phase. They have expressed the need for a more comprehensive and coordinated recovery plan from government, donors, and supporting agencies, particularly in the area of livelihoods recovery but also in rehabilitating water, sanitation, and health services in conflict-affected areas.

In Articles 3.2.4 and 3.2.5 of the MOU, the Indonesian government promised to rehabilitate public and private property destroyed as a result of the conflict and to grant farming land or, in the case of incapacity to work, social security to three groups: GAM combatants, pardoned prisoners, and all civilians "who have suffered a demonstrable loss due to the conflict."[18] It is still unclear how this is to be implemented, and some scholars have warned that it is unlikely that sufficient land will be found to fulfill this pledge to all those who fit the criteria, which could lead to problems such as land disputes as demobilized combatants return to local communities and find unlawful occupation of land promised under the agreement (Foley 2005; International Crisis Group 2005). This ambiguity is not specific just to the articles regarding land but rather epitomizes a continued confusion around what particular articles of the MOU mean, as well as a lack of plans for how they will be implemented.

Natural Resources and the Law on Governing Aceh

On July 11, 2006, the Jakarta parliament passed the Law on Governing Aceh (LOGA), which effectively grants a legal basis to the implementation of the peace agreement. The following are the main features of the law, by category (Decentralization Support Facility 2006b):

—*General:* The Aceh government will regulate all public sectors except those that are under the authority of the central government, including foreign affairs, defense, security, justice, national fiscal affairs, and certain functions in the field of religion.

—*Economic:* Aceh will receive 70 percent of oil and gas revenues; 80 percent of forestry, fishery, mining, and geothermal energy revenues; and an additional 2 percent of General Allocation Funds for fifteen years and 1 percent of funds for the next five years.

—*Political:* Local political parties can be established.

—*Legal:* A human rights court will be established in Aceh as well as a truth and reconciliation commission based on existing regulations. Aceh will have the right to implement shari'a law.

—*Security:* The TNI will protect state unity and sovereignty.

—*Sociocultural:* The *Wali Nanggroe* (traditional "guardian" head of state) will be established as a nonpolitical, nongovernmental institution.

—*Subsequent required regulations:* These entail at least four national regulations, three presidential decrees, fifty-eight provincial *qanun* (shari'a-based regulations), and thirty-five district qanun.

While the large concession of natural resources revenues to Aceh was deemed acceptable to most Acehnese, there remained widespread dissatisfaction with the LOGA, most prominently (but not exclusively) from GAM, who claimed that it contravened the spirit as well as provisions of the MOU. GAM was particularly disappointed with the central government's continuing authority to make laws affecting Aceh, the continued role of the TNI in defense, and that the human rights courts established in Aceh would be nonretroactive. The mobilization of civil society groups to lobby on the LOGA process led to formation of the Aceh Democracy Network, a coalition of Acehnese and national activists. This included a women's policy network, which succeeded in getting many points of its advocacy agenda adopted into the final LOGA.[19] However, points on women's participation in religious decisionmaking bodies were not adopted.

Emerging Conflict-Related Land and Resource Issues

At the time of writing, it is still too early to predict the extent to which land issues might be a source of future conflict; however, it is possible to trace several potential areas of contestation through assessing some post-MOU developments. These include return of conflict-affected IDPs, repatriation of transmigrants, and contestation over land between local communities and the military.

The first major humanitarian crisis among conflict-affected IDPs after the MOU occurred in December 2005, when 4,500 refugees from Bireuen and Pidie decided to return on foot to their homes in Bener Meriah and Aceh Tengah, which they had fled in May and June 2001. A week later some sixty people, mostly women and children, collapsed of exhaustion and starvation (Decentral-

ization Support Facility 2006a). At the same time, institutions that have historically been involved in perpetuating and exacerbating conflict continue to create
tensions at the local community level. These include antiseparatist groups, who
continue to generate ongoing tensions with GAM and local communities—
particularly in Aceh Tengah, Bener Meriah, and Aceh Timur—and among
transmigrants.

The local government has started to implement plans to return tens of thousands of transmigrants (estimated 40,000) who fled during the conflict and
assist them with jobs on palm oil and paper plantations. There have been a
number of cases reported in the media of conflict-affected transmigrants being
repatriated to Aceh Barat district, and local governments have confirmed ver-
bally that transmigrant repatriation will continue over the next few years, along
with the development of plantations. This program of transmigrant return is
certain to revive old tensions as well as create new ones, including in tsunami-
affected areas where land for reconstruction is already scarce (such as in Desa
Patek, Aceh Jaya). While the right of return of transmigrant communities must
also be recognized, any repatriation program must be especially careful not to
replicate the patterns of control over land-based productive assets that led to
some of the very ethnic and class inequalities that fueled the conflict for so
many years.

Even while the peace process is under way, the military's continuing ability to
intimidate locals and claim control over resources is demonstrated by a number
of cases where communities have been faced with military land claims, such as
in Aceh Barat (Kelurahan Suak Indrapuri) and Aceh Besar (Kecamatan Seuli-
mum, Desa Meunasah Kulam, and Kecamatan Mesjid Raya). In the case of the
tsunami-affected village Desa Meunasah Kulam, some twenty-four households
are seeking new land since their own plots are being claimed by the military,
which has an office, residences, and a clinic in the same area. The Canadian Red
Cross has committed to building houses for all those who have land that is not
disputed. A few households that are affected by the military's claims have managed to buy new land nearby, but many others are unable to do so due to a lack
of funds and thus remain without housing commitments. The affected beneficiaries include a number of widows.[20]

Conclusion

The land rights problems in present day Aceh, the site of both a devastating
tsunami and decades of armed insurgency, are vast in both scale and variety. Two
years on from the disaster and over a year since the signing of the Helsinki

MOU, it is still too early to declare success in either the tsunami recovery or the implementation of the peace process. What is clear is that the protection of rights to land, property, and resources is a precondition for a sustainable recovery in post-tsunami and postconflict Aceh and that equitable access to land and resources lies at the heart of the province's physical, economic, social, and political development. With the reconstruction effort in Aceh and Nias currently representing the largest in the developing world, there is an unprecedented opportunity and commitment to "build back better" (World Bank 2006a). The realization and sustainability of this vision, however, depends on economic and social measures that recognize and address historical inequalities that have perpetuated conflict and poverty, and that work strategically toward a model of development that is truly inclusive for all.

Notes

1. The official name of the province is Nanggroe Aceh Darussalam (literally, the State of Aceh, Abode of Peace). It is often abbreviated as NAD.

2. The Government of Indonesia's Rehabilitation and Reconstruction Agency for Aceh and Nias (*Badan Rehabilitasi dan Rekonstruksi NAD-Nias*, or BRR NAD-Nias) estimates that there are 35,000 households that owned land and houses before the tsunami and at least 15,000 families that did not own housing or land before the disaster. Unpublished data from BRR Housing and Settlements Unit, 2006.

3. When the tsunami struck, Aceh had been under a state of civil emergency for over six months and under martial law for a year before that. Civil emergency status was officially withdrawn on May 18, 2005, almost six months after the disaster.

4. A previous peace process, facilitated by the Geneva-based Centre for Humanitarian Dialogue, broke down in May 2003, and martial law was declared in Aceh. Under martial law Aceh was virtually closed to the outside world, with severe restrictions imposed on humanitarian organizations and media in the province. Human rights organizations reported extrajudicial killings, arbitrary arrests, torture, and widespread intimidation of villagers suspected of being separatist sympathizers (Human Rights Watch 2003).

5. For empirical research on the economic impact of postdisaster shelter provision, see Shepard and Hill (2005).

6. Robin Palmer, "Oxfam GB and Land Rights: Why Does Land Matter and What Is Oxfam Doing about It? A Concept Paper," unpublished memo. Oxford: Oxfam GB/I, May 2005.

7. See also Oxfam (2005).

8. Figures from the BRR Special Unit on Barracks, interview September 2006. See subsequent discussion on landless tsunami victims.

9. Food and Agriculture Organization, "After the Tsunami" (www.fao.org/ag/magazine/0502sp2.htm [February 1, 2005]).

10. The network consists of KKTGA, Aceh Gender Transformation Working Group; SULOH, a farmer's network; WALHI, Friends of the Earth Indonesia; Koalisi NGO HAM, the human rights NGO coalition; and Forum LSM, a large NGO forum.

11. Figures from the BRR Resettlement Unit, interview October 2006.

12. Government of Indonesia, BRR Regulation 20/2006 and BRR Regulation 21/2006.

13. At the time of writing, the U.S. Agency for International Development had offered to assist the BRR in developing a subsidized credit program.

14. The BRR now estimates that of the approximately 70,000 people who remain in barracks, as many as 20,000 are pretsunami renters and squatters (the majority of whom do not have housing commitments). BRR Director of Special Unit on Barracks, presentation at the Second Extraordinary Meeting on Barracks and Shelter/Settlements in Aceh and Nias, September 29, 2006; also, personal communication from the BRR Director of Land, September 2006. At the time of writing, the BRR had just completed a census of IDPs in barracks. However, the new figures had yet to be published.

15. In Calang, as many as ninety newly constructed houses will have to be dismantled. In Aceh Besar eight houses built by Oxfam and food stalls set up by beneficiaries as livelihoods projects will have to be taken down. The BRR has said that it will compensate in kind, but there has so far been little public information on the overall compensation plan.

16. See "Memorandum of Understanding between the Government of the Republic of Indonesia and the Free Aceh Movement," *Jakarta Post*, August 15, 2005 (www.thejakarta-post.com/RI_GAM_MOU.pdf [November 2006]).

17. These include GAM ex-combatants, GAM noncombatants, amnestied political prisoners, and a broad category of "conflict victims," including civil servants, community leaders, villagers, IDPs, transmigrants, and, most contentiously, members of antiseparatist groups.

18. See "Memorandum of Understanding between the Government of the Republic of Indonesia and the Free Aceh Movement," *Jakarta Post*, August 15, 2005 (www.thejakarta-post.com/RI_GAM_MOU.pdf [November 2006]).

19. These included article 67 on political parties, article 121 on the economy, article 163 on education, article 175 on health, and article 179 on human rights.

20. Interviews with Desa Meunasah Kulam village leaders and residents, October–December 2006.

References

Asian Development Bank. 2005. "An Initial Assessment of the Impact of the Earthquake and Tsunami of December 26, 2004 on South and Southeast Asia." Manila (January).

Brown, Graham. 2005. "Horizontal Inequalities, Ethnic Separatism, and Violent Conflict: The Case of Aceh." Human Development Report Occasional Paper 28. New York: United Nations Development Program.

BRR NAD-Nias. 2005. "Aceh and Nias One Year after the Tsunami: The Recovery Effort and Way Forward." Jakarta: Government of Indonesia (December).

Decentralization Support Facility. 2006a. "Aceh Conflict Monitoring Update, 1st–31st January, 2006." Jakarta.

———. 2006b. "Aceh Conflict Monitoring Update, 1st June–31st July 31, 2006." Jakarta.

Down to Earth. 1998. "Mobil Oil and Human Rights Abuse in Aceh." *Down to Earth Newsletter*, no. 39 (November).

———. 2000. "Aceh Ecological War Zone." *Down to Earth Newsletter*, no. 47 (November).

Fitzpatrick, Daniel. 2005. "Restoring and Confirming Rights to Land in Tsunami-Affected Aceh." United Nations Development Program–Oxfam Report. Banda Aceh (July).

Foley, Conor. 2005. "Land and Property Rights in Aceh. Part I: Challenges for the Return, Reintegration, and Recovery Process." Unpublished briefing paper, prepared for International Rescue Committee (November).

Human Rights Watch. 2003. "Aceh under Martial Law: Inside the Secret War." Report C1510. New York (December).

International Crisis Group. 2005. "Aceh: A New Chance for Peace." Asia Briefing 40. Brussels (August).

International Labour Organization. 2005. "ILO Response to Support the Recovery and Reconstruction Efforts in Crisis-Affected Areas in Indonesia. Special Edition on Indonesia Earthquake and Tsunamis." Updated version. Jakarta (April).

Moser, Caroline. 2006. "Asset-Based Approaches to Poverty Reduction in a Globalized Context." Background paper presented at the Brookings Institution–Ford Foundation Workshop on Asset-Based Approaches to Poverty in a Globalized Context. Washington, June 27–28.

Multi-Donor Fund for Aceh and Nias. 2006. "The First Year of the Multi-Donor Fund: Results, Challenges, and Opportunities." Progress Report 2. Jakarta (June).

National Development Planning Board (BAPPENAS). 2005. "The Master Plan for the Rehabilitation and Reconstruction of the Regions and Communities of the Province of Nanggroe Aceh Darussalam and the Islands of Nias, Province of North Sumatra." Jakarta: Government of Indonesia (April).

Oxfam. 2005. "The Tsunami's Impact on Women." Briefing Note. Oxford (March).

Shepard, Stephen, and Richard Hill. 2005. "The Economic Assessment of Shelter Assistance in Post-Disaster Settings." Silver Spring, Md.: Cooperative Housing Foundation (CHF) International (August).

United Nations Development Program. 2004. *Indonesia Human Development Report. The Economics of Democracy. Financing Human Development in Indonesia.* New York.

United Nations Office of the Special Envoy for Tsunami Recovery. 2005. "Tsunami Recovery: Taking Stock after 12 Months." New York: United Nations (December 22).

Williams, Shaun. 2005. "Getting Back Home." Report commissioned by Oxfam. Geneva: United Nations High Commissioner for Refugees.

World Bank. 2006a. "Aceh Public Expenditure Analysis. Spending for Reconstruction and Poverty Reduction." Washington (September).

———. 2006b. "GAM Reintegration Needs Assessment: Enhancing Peace through Community-Level Development Planning." Washington (March).

10

Hurricane Katrina: Impact on Assets and Asset-Building Approaches to Poverty Reduction

AMY LIU

With a death toll of more than 1,700, Hurricane Katrina was the deadliest natural disaster in the United States since a hurricane struck Galveston, Texas, in 1900.[1] In late August 2005, Katrina's category-four winds destroyed or severely damaged approximately 160,000 homes and rental units in the New Orleans area (Department of Homeland Security 2006). Over 1 million people from the Gulf Coast were displaced, and approximately $81.2 billion in total damages were generated (National Weather Service 2006).

More than one year later, the long-term recovery of the New Orleans region remains a steep climb. Many hard-hit neighborhoods look essentially unchanged while the region's population is only slowly returning. The return and resilience of the city and its residents depend upon the restoration of a range of political, financial, human, and social capital as well as other assets that existed before the storm. This chapter reviews the patterns of household assets in New Orleans before Katrina, discusses how those assets were affected by the hurricane, and explores what lessons the storm and its aftermath may provide for leaders in postdisaster contexts, both as the Katrina recovery effort evolves and in dealing with future catastrophes.

Asset Patterns in New Orleans before Hurricane Katrina

It is impossible to assess the recovery potential of the New Orleans region and its people without first understanding the asset status in New Orleans before the hurricane. Even before the devastation wrought in August 2005, New Orleans was a struggling city and region. The metropolitan area suffered from high levels of racial and economic segregation, unsafe and unsustainable development patterns, and a weak economy, much of which was fueled by historic developments and ill-informed federal, state, and local policies (Metropolitan Policy Program 2005). These trends set the context for the quality of household and community assets before the storm, and determined the extent to which families and the region were armed with adequate resources to recover after the disaster.

Racial Segregation and Growing Concentrations of Poverty

Pre-Katrina New Orleans was afflicted by stark racial and class divides. First, pockets of severe poverty existed in the urban core. In 2000, among the fifty largest cities, New Orleans had the second highest concentration of poverty in the country. Approximately 38 percent of the city's poor residents—50,000 people—lived in extremely poor neighborhoods (Berube and Katz 2005).

Second, the city had become more segregated. New Orleans—once a racially integrated community in the 1950s—had become by 2000 a place divided by race, with the typical African American living in a neighborhood that was 82 percent black (Lewis 1976; Bureau of the Census 2000; Metropolitan Policy Program 2005).

Together, the racial and economic divisions emerged in other important indicators of economic success and self-sufficiency. The median household income for African Americans in the city was just $21,461, almost half that of whites, and only 13 percent of black adults possessed a college degree or higher, while 48 percent of whites did (Bureau of the Census 2000). This racial and economic gap was present in household ownership as well, with 15 percent more whites than blacks owning their homes (Metropolitan Policy Program 2005). Finally, more than one third of African Americans lacked access to a car, compared with only 15 percent of whites, which partly explains the difficulties some households had in evacuating the city before the storm.

Suburban Growth and Decentralization

Like many of America's cities, New Orleans underwent rapid suburbanization, losing both people and jobs from the core over the last two decades. This further isolated low-income people and African Americans in the city and relocated job growth away from low-skilled workers.

As poverty hardened over the years in the heart of the city, middle-class families, including black households, moved out, especially to the surrounding parishes. For instance, the New Orleans region saw a net out-migration of African Americans in the 1990s, topping off a four-decade trend (Frey 2004). But the city's "white flight" was more dramatic. According to the 2000 census, New Orleans lost more than half of its white residents between 1970 and 2000 while its share of African Americans grew by 27 percent (Bureau of the Census 2000). Thus New Orleans transitioned from being 45 percent African American in 1970 to being more than two-thirds black by 2000.

As a result of these trends, the city's share of the region's population shrank by 18 percent between 1970 and 2000. In 1970, 54 percent of the region's population lived in the central city; 30 years later, only 36 percent did.[2] Meanwhile, suburban Jefferson Parish doubled in population size to match that of its neighboring central city. Furthermore, much of the new development occurred in the region's wetlands, further eroding the area's natural protections from hurricanes (Metropolitan Policy Program 2005).

During this same period, jobs also suburbanized. In 1970 New Orleans was home to two-thirds of the region's jobs, but by 2000 that share had dropped to less than half at 42 percent.

Weak Economy

The New Orleans metropolitan area was struggling economically before Hurricane Katrina. The region's core industries, such as oil and gas extraction and port-related employment, had been losing jobs since 2000 (Bureau of Labor Statistics 2005). The sectors that were growing, mostly in tourism and hospitality, were generating jobs that often paid below the national average. Average earnings from jobs in the accommodations sector, for example, paid $19,000 annually (Metropolitan Policy Program 2005). Furthermore, the region's dependence on the service sector meant that fewer well paying jobs were open to individuals without a college degree. The New Orleans region ranked 96th out of the 100 largest metropolitan areas in median household income at $35,317, in part reflecting the composition of the jobs in the economy and the skills and education levels of the workers (Bureau of the Census 2000). Average annual pay in the New Orleans area grew just 7 percent between 2000 and 2004, lagging far behind the national growth rate of 16 percent (Metropolitan Policy Program 2005).

The bottom line is that Hurricane Katrina struck a city that was already facing economic and social distress. The vast disparities in household assets and overall modest assets in the economy ensured that the storm would hit the poorest groups hardest and complicate the ability of the region as a whole to rebound.

Hurricane Katrina's Effect on Assets and the Capacity to Rebuild Them

Federal, state, local, and community leaders as well as relief workers can look to past natural disasters to learn how best to help families rebuild their lives after major catastrophes. Like other natural disasters before it, Hurricane Katrina reminds us that such large-scale events often disproportionately affect families with few resources, a situation that impedes their ability to recover quickly. This hurricane splintered the financial, social, and human capital assets of low-income families, making recovery and family stability one year later still quite difficult.

Impact on Financial Capital

The most widespread asset struck was housing—approximately 160,000 homes and rental units were damaged or destroyed—and blacks were disproportionately affected in this regard. While neighborhoods of all incomes in the city of New Orleans were not spared from the effects of the storm, those living in the flooded zone were 80.3 percent minority and earned approximately $20,000 less in average household income than those in the dry areas of the city (Metropolitan Policy Program 2005). The most well-known, hard-hit neighborhood was the Lower Ninth Ward, home to nearly 14,000 African Americans, of whom 36.4 percent were poor and 59 percent were homeowners. While the Lower Ninth Ward is not the lowest-lying neighborhood in New Orleans, it suffered the worst damage among neighborhoods in the storm's path. Nearly all of the affordable homes were literally flattened and blown off their foundations because they were built at lower quality. Consequently, many of the residents of the Lower Ninth Ward were rendered homeless and assetless.[3]

The loss of a home, particularly for lower-income homeowners, raises a whole set of challenges. First, many black homeowners in the city were elderly (Metropolitan Policy Program 2005). These households were often house-rich but cash-poor. Furthermore, many homeowners were long-time residents of the city, having paid off their mortgages years ago. With mortgages paid they often dropped the mandatory home insurance. Thus, not only did many long-time homeowners lose their primary or only asset, they did not have the resources or the insurance coverage to recoup their losses.

Second, many low-income, working-class, and elderly homeowners had very little income with which to repair and rebuild their damaged properties. This is in sharp contrast to middle-class or wealthier homeowners in New Orleans who had the capacity to buy a second residence while rebuilding their damaged home, or at least had the resources to clean and gut their flooded home, preparing it for sale if desired.

Finally, 54 percent of the households in the city's flood area were renters and approximately 48,000 units of rental housing were severely damaged by the hurricane (Metropolitan Policy Program 2005).[4] One year after the storm, renter households are having a difficult time returning to the city because available apartments are few, and rent levels are rising due to limited supply. According to the latest 2006 data from the U.S. Department of Housing and Urban Development, fair market rents in the New Orleans metropolitan area have jumped 39 percent in just one year. For instance, the typical rent for a two-bedroom apartment in the region is now $940 a month, up from $676 in 2005 (Liu, Fellowes, and Mabanta 2006). This situation is exacerbated by increased competition for rental housing as former homeowners, still displaced from their homes or pushed out by the increasing costs of homeownership (from spikes in insurance and utility bills), look to rent for awhile. In addition, former public housing residents who have not been able to return to still-damaged homes are also now forced to find alternative homes in the private rental market.[5] The need for families to have a secure home to regain an economic footing is critical, yet limited rental housing supply and increasing rent prices are making it difficult for all returning families to make such an important transition to stability and eventual wealth accumulation.

Beyond the hurricane's impact on housing, damage to other financial assets may have much more severe repercussions. Many experts are concerned that the rash of bankruptcies and the longer-term damage to the financial status of low-income and working-class families could jeopardize the creditworthiness of the population at large. This is likely given the unstable economic and employment conditions that many families face after a major catastrophe. By August 2006 unemployment in the New Orleans region rose to 7.2 percent, far higher than the national rate of 4.6 percent (Liu, Fellowes, and Mabanta 2006).[6] Thus many low-income and working-class families remain without jobs, making it difficult for them to pay monthly bills and make credit card payments. Lending institutions may not be able to suspend mortgage payments much longer, requiring borrowers to make payments on severely damaged homes that remain uninhabitable. In the immediate term, any major deterioration of credit scores as a result of missed financial obligations would likely affect the ability of low- and moderate-income homeowners to qualify for additional loans to renovate their damaged properties. In the longer term, the worsening of credit scores will weaken the overall financial worthiness and purchasing power of low-income families, forcing them to face higher interest rates and overall higher costs of living in the future.

Impact on Social Capital

The damage to social capital wrought by Hurricane Katrina is more difficult to measure but no less important. Before the storm generations of African American families lived on the same block in the same neighborhood. Over generations this proximity created a great deal of social capital as families and neighbors developed support networks with one another. These systems were completely thrown into disarray by Katrina.

One unique aspect of Hurricane Katrina compared to past U.S. natural disasters is the scale of the human displacement. Over 1 million people were displaced from the Gulf Coast by the storm. As of this writing, nearly 400,000 persons from the New Orleans area still remain displaced.

Louisianans are proud of the fact that they have the highest nativity rate in the country: 80 percent of Louisianans were born and raised in the state. For many families, including African American families in New Orleans, whole generations lived near each other. Sisters would own separate homes on the same block, just down the block from their parents, while grandma lived alone just a few streets over. Beyond the family, overall neighborhood ties were strong.

When Hurricane Katrina struck, many of these long-time neighborhood and family ties were fractured, hurting the ability for whole neighborhoods to come together and rebuild and for families to turn to a support network they need to reconstruct their lives. When many low-income families were evacuated, they were often split up as they were shuttled to different emergency shelters. Emergency housing set up in response to the hurricane was dispersed and isolated, often in trailer parks, making it impossible to rebuild previous social networks even for those that have been resettled. The end result is that neighborhoods like the Lower Ninth Ward appear like ghost towns more than one year out whereas upper-middle-class neighborhoods such as Lakeview, where social networks were retained (via the Internet or face-to-face organizing since many had resources to stay), have been buzzing with activities as neighbors launch their own neighborhood planning process.

Impact on Human Capital

Katrina also dealt a heavy blow to human capital assets, both to those households returning and those still displaced by the storm.[7] As of August of 2006, the labor force in greater New Orleans was 30 percent smaller than it had been a year before. Although the loss of almost 190,000 workers in the past year was felt by all major industries across the region, the health and education sectors were affected the most. Ironically, those latter industries—representing day care workers, pediatricians, and other primary care doctors, and teachers and staff from prekindergarten to higher education institutions—are the backbone of services needed to support the return to work and the building of human capital after a storm. Also, as mentioned earlier, the loss of jobs in the area coincided with an increase in the unemployment rate, which as of August of 2006 had reached 7.2 percent, much higher than the rate before Katrina.

Furthermore, according to the U.S. Department of Labor, at the storm's one-year anniversary, it was estimated that 278,000 workers were still displaced. Out of those evacuees, 23 percent remain unemployed, leading to further concern about their emotional well-being and overall ability to accumulate other assets and regain their financial and economic footing.

Lessons Learned and Policy Implications

The U.S. government has the opportunity not only to help rebuild New Orleans but to do so in a way that makes the city and region better than it was before, strengthening assets and opportunities there and perhaps even in cities throughout the country. Katrina offers a number of lessons for the process of restoring family and community assets immediately after a disaster and as part of a longer-term recovery.[8]

Build Healthy, Mixed-Income Neighborhoods That Provide Better Opportunities for Families

As leaders consider ways to restore lost housing units and damaged neighborhoods, they must aim to rebuild neighborhoods in ways that ensure that asset-building opportunities are available. Specifically, leaders must replace neighborhoods of poverty with healthy, mixed-income neighborhoods that provide good schools and opportunities for families.

There is plenty of academic evidence cautioning that any attempts to merely replicate economically isolated or high-poverty neighborhoods in the city would recreate a host of socioeconomic problems for returning families and the city as a whole. Residents who live in such neighborhoods are exposed to high crime rates, have access to low-quality schools, and are often cut off from employment opportunities and rich job networks. With few private sector investments, extremely poor neighborhoods often have no access to grocery stores, and their properties hold little market value for their homeowners. The stress of living in neighborhoods of concentrated poverty has also been shown to exact a huge toll on residents' mental and physical health. Finally, there are also taxpayer costs to high levels of poverty. Taxpayers pay when local governments are burdened with public services associated with poverty, such as public safety and social services; when such costs are passed on to taxpayers, many middle-class families choose to leave, further weakening local tax bases.

It is understandable that many low-income residents in New Orleans have apprehensions about the goal of mixed-income communities due to a distrust of the government as well as a distrust of developers' true intentions to retain affordable housing or a portion of new development as low income. But when done well, including strong resident engagement in the planning process, mixed-income developments provide quality, permanent, affordable housing in neighborhoods that are integrated with schools, jobs, amenities, transportation access, and social services. Successful examples of mixed-income communities do exist, such as Murphy Park in St. Louis, and residents of New Orleans should look to these models as ones to replicate in their own communities.

Support the Development of Rental Housing

Leaders must embrace rental housing as a priority and see it as a stepping-stone to asset building and recovery. As mentioned earlier, the need for affordable rental housing is increasingly critical in a postdisaster context as many returning families may still be displaced from their homes, experience unemployment, or face increasing rent prices and limited housing options. Furthermore, employers of service and entry-level workers have asserted that the lack of affordable rental housing in the region is a major obstacle to their ability to attract and retain workers. Without safe, secure, and affordable housing, the restoration of social and economic stability for any family and worker after a disaster is hard to achieve.

In the case of Hurricane Katrina, both the federal government and its state partners (especially Louisiana and Mississippi) have made housing recovery their number one priority. However, the main concern, one year out from Katrina, is that government officials have been overly oriented toward providing aid to homeowners (and even middle-class homeowners in the case of Mississippi) and spending less resources to restore both private rental housing and housing for public- and assisted-housing residents. For instance, Louisiana's Road Home program, a comprehensive plan to restore the housing infrastructure in southern Louisiana, is a well-thought-out program that provides funds to both home-owners and developers of rental housing.[9] However, the emphasis on homeown-ers is evident. Of the federal housing funds that the state has received (not including tax credits), $6.3 billion support homeowner assistance while just $1.5 billion is targeted to rebuild rental housing. But, as this chapter has noted, over half of the households most affected by the storm in the city of New Orleans were renters. In Mississippi the emphasis on homeowners is even more pronounced. One year after the storm, the governor had launched only a housing recovery plan for homeowners outside of the flood-damaged areas (and thus not covering many low- and moderate-income homeowners in the cities). A plan for rental housing had yet to be developed and announced.

In short, in any postdisaster recovery effort, public leaders must place equal emphasis on restoring both homeowner and rental housing to meet the housing needs of all families. A robust rental market for households and workers of all income levels is critical if the region and its economy are to recover.

Invest in Workforce Development

In general, investment in skills and job opportunities is critical to any asset-building strategy. As the trends demonstrate, before Katrina the New Orleans region was beset with a low-quality workforce, marked by limited educational attainment levels, poor literacy rates, and low participation in the labor force. Thus leaders need to invest in a robust regional workforce development system, training in construction and other growing trades, and creation of new jobs with career ladders, not only to ensure that returnees have an opportunity to grow their incomes and assets in the short term but also to support the advancement of a human capital infrastructure in the region for the long term.

To accomplish this, public and private sector leaders need to collaborate to identify and build on key and growing industry clusters that are driven by the immediate needs of the rebuilding effort and also to leverage the move toward services and innovation that can help the region create quality jobs for residents. Identifying these key industry clusters will assist the local job training system in tailoring its efforts toward the jobs that are actually available or projected, therefore allowing workers, especially returning evacuees, to be better connected to the job market. Furthermore, these leaders should work on creating a coordinated, regional workforce development system that transcends parochial jurisdictional boundaries to streamline education, training, and other social service delivery systems in order to better meet the immediate needs of workers and employers in the regional economy.

Engage Citizens in the Rebuilding Process and Restore Social Networks

All rebuilding efforts must engage the full citizenry in the future of the region so that they can provide input into the plans that are being formed about their city or neighborhood. This includes engaging residents fully in neighborhood, city-wide, and even regional planning processes about the recovery and long-term redevelopment goals regarding the economy, equity, the environment, and quality of life and basic services. No doubt doing this has been especially difficult for government and nonprofit leaders working in the most affected neighborhoods, where limited family and economic resources have fractured important social networks.

Concerted efforts must be made to establish a communications and networking infrastructure to rebuild broken social networks and connect displaced families to key information—such as available housing assistance, mental health and social services, and employment opportunities—that will help them make decisions about their future. To that end the state of Louisiana, with community and philanthropic partners, created a toll-free number and web portal called Louisiana Rebuilds to connect Louisiana residents displaced by hurricanes Katrina and Rita to reliable information about the status of rebuilding efforts, availability of resources and support networks, and other economic, social, and public assistance.[10] The information is also made available in several languages, including English, Spanish, Vietnamese, and several Chinese dialects. Efforts like these to rebuild social networks and reconnect returning and displaced residents would also allow for the active and quality participation of residents in their own rebuilding process.

Conclusion

Over the last few decades, there has been growing recognition of the importance of asset accumulation strategies to help improve the life outcomes of disadvantaged households. But in a postdisaster context, the whirl of emergency responders and the introduction of new actors in a rebuilding context often set the value of household asset building aside as other short-term needs are catapulted to the forefront.

Yet the impact of Hurricane Katrina provides a powerful reminder that the structural barriers to asset accumulation before the storm may slow down or hamper a full recovery of a city and its people. New Orleans and its economy, with its multicultural diversity and distinctiveness, cannot make a full comeback as a favored, historic destination for visitors and families if many of its original residents and workers do not return. Many of those residents had few assets before the storm, and those that they did have were lost, making them even more vulnerable. They will need targeted assistance and resources if they are to make their way home and be productive citizens of the Crescent City.

Public, private, and nonprofit leaders must remain committed at all times to ensuring that disadvantaged families have the opportunity to accumulate assets and capital, even in the aftermath of a major natural disaster. But most fundamentally, the United States must not lose sight of the fact that Katrina exposed the stark reality that many structural challenges still remain in our cities that limit asset accumulation and opportunities for families. Leaders need to make it a priority to help lift families out of poverty, promote wealth creation, and ensure that our cities and regions are inclusive and prosperous.

Notes

1. See "Hurricane Katrina Death Toll by Locality" (en.wikipedia.org/wiki/Hurricane_Katrina_death_toll_by_locality [December 2006]). For other estimates, see "Deaths of Evacuees Push Toll to 1,577," *New Orleans Times-Picayune*, May 19, 2006; Gary Younge, "Gone with the Wind," *Guardian*, July 29, 2006.

2. Based on decennial census figures readjusted to consistent geography. See Bureau of the Census, "Census of Population and Housing" (www.census.gov/prod/www/abs/decennial/index.htm), years 1970–2000.

3. See Metropolitan Policy Program (2005). Calculations used data from Census 2000 and the FEMA flood-extent shapefiles generated shortly after the storm.

4. Renter household data based on calculations using data from Census 2000 and the FEMA flood-extent shapefile. For damage estimates for rental housing, see Department of Homeland Security (2006).

5. The federal government's announced intention to demolish several public housing developments further intensifies the pressure on former public housing residents to find private sector housing. See Department of Housing and Urban Development, "HUD Outlines Aggressive Plan to Bring Families Back to New Orleans' Public Housing," press release, June 14, 2006 (www.hud.gov/news/release.cfm?content=pr06-066.cfm [December 2006]).

6. Note, at the time of the one-year anniversary of Katrina, only June 2006 unemployment rate data were available.

7. The figures in this section are from Liu, Fellowes, and Mabanta (2006).

8. For more comprehensive coverage of the lessons discussed in this section, see Liu (2006).

9. For more information about the program, see "The Road Home" (www.road2la.org [December 2006]).

10. See "Louisiana Rebuilds" (www.louisianarebuilds.info [December 2006]).

References

Berube, Alan, and Bruce Katz. 2005. "Katrina's Window: Confronting Concentrated Poverty across America." Special Analysis in Metropolitan Policy. Brookings (October).

Bureau of Labor Statistics. 2005. "Quarterly Census of Employment and Wages: First Quarter." Department of Labor.

Bureau of the Census. 2000. *Census 2000*. Department of Commerce.

Department of Homeland Security. 2006. "Current Housing Units Damage Estimates: Hurricane Katrina, Rita, and Wilma." Report (February).

Frey, William H. 2004. "The New Great Migration: Black Americans' Return to the South, 1965–2000." Living Cities Census Series. Brookings (May).

Lewis, Peirce F. 1976. *New Orleans: The Making of an Urban Landscape.* Cambridge: Ballinger.

Liu, Amy. 2006. "Building a Better New Orleans: A Review of and Plan for Progress One Year after Hurricane Katrina." Special Analysis in Metropolitan Policy. Brookings (August).

Liu, Amy, Matt Fellowes, and Mia Mabanta. 2006. "Special Edition of the Katrina Index: A One-Year Review of Key Indicators of Recovery in Post-Storm New Orleans." Special Analysis in Metropolitan Policy. Brookings (August).

Metropolitan Policy Program. 2005. "New Orleans after the Storm: Lessons from the Past, a Plan for the Future." Special Analysis. Brookings (October).

National Weather Service. 2006. "Service Assessment Hurricane Katrina August 23–32." Report. Silver Spring, Md.

11

Gangs, Violence, and Asset Building

DENNIS RODGERS

The past decade has seen an increasing interest in policy interventions concerned with the promotion of sustainable asset-building strategies for the
poor. Building on Amartya Sen's seminal work (1981) on entitlements, such
approaches identify assets as the foundation upon which social agents build sustainable livelihoods, thereby suggesting that poverty and vulnerability are closely
linked to deficient asset endowment and constrained possibilities for asset accumulation. The processes by which assets are both obtained initially and then
fructified are complex, however, and ultimately determined by "an iterative
asset-institutions-opportunities nexus" (Moser 2006, p. 8). In other words, a
combination of factors including the nature of the assets involved, formal and
informal rules, norms and practices that govern social life, and contingent
opportunities that emerge for social agents all articulate together in ways that
can either promote or impede the accumulation and consolidation of asset
bases. These interrelationships clearly require further elaboration, and this chapter proposes to unpack some of the potential underlying dynamics of this nexus,
drawing on recent empirical research on gangs in postconflict Central America.
In doing so, it will highlight the fact that asset-building and accumulation
processes need to be conceptualized in a much more nuanced manner than is
generally the case if we are to properly understand their highly variable nature

and the reasons for their potential mutability. This has critical implications for the determination of appropriate asset-based policy initiatives aimed at sustained poverty reduction, particularly in postconflict situations.

The chapter begins by briefly exploring salient features of postconflict Central America, followed by a characterization of youth gangs as potential forms of asset building and accumulation. It then traces their shifting evolution as such in the postconflict Nicaraguan context. This specific focus is especially appropriate to exploring the underlying nature of asset-building processes because gangs in contemporary Nicaragua have emerged as a primary institutional means through which impoverished social agents attempt to generate and accumulate assets, but at the same time, they have done so in a way that underlines the potential mutability of such processes in postconflict situations.

The evolutionary trajectory of these gangs is then analyzed for what it has to say about asset building from a theoretical perspective. This analysis draws on ideas from the American economist Mancur Olson, as well as from the French regulation school of political economy, to suggest that such processes ought to be conceived in terms of "regimes of asset accumulation" that can be either "narrow" or "encompassing," depending on a wider "mode of regulation" that changes in response to both endogenous and exogenous factors. Rethinking asset-building processes in this way has important implications for sustainable asset-based policy interventions—particularly in volatile postconflict situations—as it highlights how the nature of any given regime of asset accumulation can potentially mutate as a result of wider structural factors. Any asset-based intervention must therefore take such factors into account in their own right and not simply regard them as contextual backdrop.

Violence, Gangs, and Assets in Postconflict Central America

As Cathy McIlwaine (1999, p. 454) has pointed out "violence [is] now on the 'development map' . . . as . . . [an] increasing concern." Although wars—whether between or within states—are perhaps the most paradigmatic manifestations of violence, they are by no means the only ones, and they are certainly not the only ones to have critical implications for development. What might be termed more "prosaic" forms of violence, such as domestic violence or crime, also pose critical development problems. Criminal violence, in particular, has been increasingly recognized as a major development concern since the end of the cold war (Ayres 1998; UN Research Institute for Social Development 1995). This is the case in contemporary postconflict Central America, where "rising crime is threatening democratic development and slowing economic growth," according to a recent report by the U.S. Agency for International Development (USAID 2006, p. 6). Although the last of the civil wars that plagued the region during the 1970s and 1980s was formally ended in 1996, violence has continued to affect Central America unabated into the twenty-first century in the form of rampant criminality, with brutality in many instances reaching greater levels of intensity than during the previous decades of formal warfare (Call 2000; Londoño, Gaviria, and Guerrero 2000; Moser and Winton 2002).

To a large extent, this situation is actually due to what might be termed the "compounded interest" of these past conflicts, which has critically weakened Central American states, either directly, through destruction of capacity and infrastructure or exhaustion of resources, or indirectly, as uneasy peace agreements between opposing factions have led to tension and polarization (Pearce 1998). The contemporary criminal "savage wars of peace" are particularly indicative of this weakness, reflecting the inability of postwar Central American states to establish "a certain order . . . over a given territory," and to back this up with "a centralized coercive guarantee," which as Guillermo O'Donnell (1999, p. 135) points out—following Max Weber—is perhaps the most basic institutional characteristic of a state. This inability has crucial ramifications for the coherent accumulation of assets by social agents since it is the state's coercive guarantee that allows for predictability in social exchanges. Because this coercive guarantee clearly extends irregularly across the territory of contemporary Central American states, the viable composition, consolidation, and management of asset portfolios by social agents is much harder. This difficulty is exacerbated by widespread corruption, high levels of poverty, and entrenched inequality, as well as the fundamentally constrained nature of the Central American economies due to their lack of resources and their asymmetric integration into a hemispheric economic system that William Robinson (1998) has described as constituting a form of "maldevelopment."

The 2006 USAID report mentioned above specifically identifies youth gangs as the predominant form of criminal violence in Central America, estimating for example that 60 percent of total crime in El Salvador is attributable to gang activity (USAID 2006, p. 21). Certainly there is no doubt that gangs are a particularly virulent form of criminal violence in contemporary Central America (Arana 2001; Liebel 2004; Rodgers 1999). They clearly contribute to asset erosion in a variety of ways, most obviously through theft and other delinquent activities that dispossess individuals, enterprises, and sometimes whole communities of financial capital. More broadly, gangs can also disrupt the operation of markets and lead to weak investor confidence, as is evidenced by Central America's high business risk ratings.[1] Gangs can negatively impact physical capital in ways that range from minor acts of vandalism, such as the painting of graffiti, to the wholesale destruction of infrastructure, both public and private. The widespread presence of gangs can also affect human capital, both directly, through injury and loss of life, and indirectly, through the diversion of scarce resources to criminal justice and incarceration. Finally, gangs can lead to a deterioration of social capital, as their violent social practices precipitate a climate of fear and insecurity that replaces collective norms of trust and reciprocity with a Hobbesian "warre of every man against every man" (Hobbes [1651] 1996, p. 90).

However, Martín Sánchez-Jankowski (1991, pp. 21–22) takes Thomas Hobbes's description of this state of "warre" as the starting point for an alternative analysis of U.S. gangs, contending that instead of creating such circumstances, they primarily constitute attempts to mitigate them. In particular, he argues that gangs emerge in "low-income areas of American cities [that] are . . . organized around an intense competition for, and conflict over, the scarce resources that exist in these areas. . . . In this Hobbesian world, the gang emerges as [an] organizational response . . . seeking to improve the competitive advantage of its members in obtaining an increase in material resources." In other words, Sánchez-Jankowski characterizes gangs as forms of organized collective economic enterprise that can potentially significantly increase the asset bases of their members in contexts of impoverishment and material constraint. The parallels between his admittedly rather Darwinian vision of life in low-income areas in American cities and postconflict situations such as those that characterize contemporary Central America are obvious—indeed, the latter probably fit the Hobbesian descriptor better—and it is thus perhaps not surprising that gangs in the region are widely reported to be heavily involved in a range of illegal economic activities, including especially drug trafficking (see USAID 2006). From an asset-based perspective, this can be conceived as a form of financial capital asset accumulation.

At the same time, gangs are rarely solely about economics. As numerous classic studies of U.S. gangs— including Whyte's *Street Corner Society* (1943) or Suttles's *The Social Order of the Slum* (1968)—have pointed out, they are also often about social construction. This particularly holds true in contexts where more traditional vehicles for social organization—such as the state—have either been significantly weakened or are absent, as is the case in both inner city America and in postwar Central America (albeit not to the same degree). The means through which gangs can positively contribute to processes of social construction are both direct, through imposition of rules and predictable patterns of regularized behavior on both gang members and their wider local communities, as well as indirect, by becoming the symbolic embodiment of a localized "social imaginary" through which "people imagine their social existence, how they fit together with others, [and] how things go on between them and their fellows" (Taylor 2002, p. 106).[2] From an asset-based perspective, such gangs clearly constitute vehicles for the creation and accumulation of social capital, both at an individual and a collective level.

Gangs as Variable Forms of Asset Building in Postconflict Nicaragua

During the past decade in postconflict Nicaragua, gangs have acted as examples of first social and then economic asset accumulation. The following discussion is based on empirical material from longitudinal ethnographic research carried out in 1996–97 and 2002–03 in a poor Managua neighborhood called *barrio* Luis Fanor Hernández.[3]

Contemporary Nicaragua arguably represents a paradigmatic example of a postconflict context. It is the poorest country in Central America, as "approximately 70 percent of the Nicaraguan population lives in extreme poverty (less than U.S.$1 per day), and unemployment hovers around 60–65 percent" (USAID 2006, p. 124). The postwar state has undergone a profound process of institutional debilitation. Nicaragua is not the most violent country in the region—although historically it is probably the one most associated with conflict in the global public imagination—but it has nevertheless experienced a massive generalized crime surge since the early 1990s that is unmatched in the Western hemisphere. According to Nicaraguan police statistics, crime levels rose steadily by an annual average of 10 percent during the 1990s, compared to just 2 percent in the 1980s, with the absolute number of crimes almost quadrupling between 1990 and 2004. In particular, crimes against persons—including homicides, rapes, and assaults—rose by over 460 percent.[4]

While the overall trend of increasing crime is undoubtedly accurate, it should be noted that official figures are highly problematic. The national homicide rate—the international benchmark for measuring violence—is particularly unreliable and stands at an average of fifteen deaths per 100,000 persons between 1990 and 2003, compared to almost three times that many in Honduras and over six times that in Guatemala and El Salvador (Moser and Winton 2002, p. 47).[5] More qualitative indicators, such as crime victimization surveys, suggest that levels of violence are extremely high, however. For example, a survey carried out in 1997 reported that one in six Nicaraguans claimed to have been the victim of a criminal attack at least once in the previous four months, a proportion that rose to one in four in the capital city, Managua.[6] Similarly, a

1999 survey found that crime was considered the principal problem affecting the country by a margin of over 30 percent (United Nations Development Program 2000, p. 130).

This same survey also found that over 50 percent of respondents considered gangs to be the most likely perpetrators of crime (Cajina 2000, p. 177). Although the gang phenomenon in Nicaragua has roots that can be traced back to the 1940s, it came to the fore as a major social concern after the end of the civil war that affected Nicaragua during the 1980s. In part this was due to the mass demobilization of young Sandinista army conscripts and Contra guerrillas—the age of conscription in Nicaragua was sixteen years—as well as the high levels of sociopolitical instability that followed the change of regime in 1990. Gangs rapidly established themselves as a feature of Nicaraguan urban life, robbing, beating, terrorizing, and frequently murdering in the streets of the country's cities. As I have described in more detail elsewhere (Rodgers 2000, 2006a, 2006b), these contemporary gangs—known as *pandillas*—basically consist of variably sized groups of generally male youths between seven and twenty-three years old, who engage in illicit and violent behavior—although not all their activities are illicit or violent.[7] The pandillas have a particular territorial dynamic, being associated with a specific poor urban neighborhood or slum. They are found in all of the larger Nicaraguan urban centers but are most prominent in Managua, the capital city, where according to the Nicaraguan Police there were 184 gangs involving 2,614 gang members in 2004 (USAID 2006, p. 125).[8] Even though not all acts of urban brutality in Nicaragua are perpetrated by gangs, a significant number are. Over half of all those arrested in Nicaragua in 1997 were young males between thirteen and twenty-five years old, which corresponds to the typical gang member age and gender profile and can therefore be taken as indirectly indicative of a high level of gang-related criminality—although obviously not all were gang members (Rocha 2000).

However, although gang violence in Nicaragua undoubtedly has a range of detrimental social consequences, it can also be argued that it has a number of more positive facets. This was clearly the case in the gang warfare of the mid-1990s, for example. Conflicts revolved around attacking and defending neighborhoods and often had dramatic consequences for local communities. At the same time, the gangs engaged each other in a prescribed manner that arguably limited the scope of violence. Gang wars were quasi-ritualized and followed set patterns: the first battle of a gang war typically involved fighting with fists and stones, but each new battle involved an escalation of weaponry, first to knives and broken bottles, then to hand guns and mortars, and eventually to AK-47s and fragmentation grenades. Although the rate of escalation varied, its sequence never did: gangs did not begin their wars immediately with firearms. This fixed nature arguably acted as a mechanism for restraining both the intensity and scope of violence, insofar as escalation is a positive constitutive process in which each stage calls for the application of greater but definite force, meaning that it is always under the actors' control. In a wider context of chronic, unpredictable brutality and insecurity, this was often recognized as something positive by local neighborhood populations, and community members never called the police during gang wars, nor did they ever denounce gang members.[9]

Indeed, gangs arguably went beyond just providing neighborhood inhabitants with a concrete sense of physical security. They arguably constituted a tangible institutional medium through which to think and enact otherwise absent forms of community. In barrio Luis Fanor Hernández, for example, neighborhood inhabitants were usually suspicious of each other and avoided interaction to evade entanglement in webs of reciprocity in a context of ever-increasing impoverishment and material constraint. Yet they would actively seek each other out to avidly swap stories about their local gang's exploits, exchanging eyewitness accounts, spreading rumors, and retelling incidents, thereby converting the gang into a primary symbolic index of community in a socially atomized collectivity. To this extent gangs in mid-1990s Nicaragua can arguably be said to have contributed to the creation and accumulation—as well as the practical operationalization—of stocks of bridging social capital that brought fragmented local communities together in poor urban neighborhoods.

On revisiting Nicaragua in 2002, however, it rapidly became apparent that this gang violence–based form of asset building and accumulation had completely transformed. Ritualized gang warfare had almost completely disappeared. The principal activity was now drug trafficking, and gangs were widely considered critical sources of danger within local communities.[10] Underpinning these transformations was the evolution of gangs from vehicles for production and accumulation of social capital to agents of financial capital accretion. Although this accumulation of a different type of asset was still based on violence, it was a significantly different sort of violence from that of the past. Gangs no longer engaged in conflicts with other gangs but rather directed their brutality against the local community, imposing regimes of terror intended to ensure the unimpeded functioning of the local drug economy. The barrio Luis Fanor Hernández gang, for example, made certain that drug transactions in the neighborhood proceeded smoothly by enforcing contracts, roughing up recalcitrant clients or untrustworthy neighbors, and guarding drug shipments as they were moved both within and outside the neighborhood. In stark contrast to the gang wars of the past, which had generated forms of bridging social capital, these new practices of violence were highly limited in the scope of what might be termed their asset "profitability," effectively constituting very parochial means of accumulation that benefited only a restricted minority.

Theorizing Asset-Building Processes and Asset-Building Gangs

In a pioneering article on the "asset vulnerability framework," Caroline Moser (1998) argues that it is not just the fact of having assets that is important but also having "the *right mix*," as certain combinations of assets can lead to negative developmental outcomes. She highlights, for example, that "while marital separation, or a difficult youth leaving home, can reduce domestic violence, it can also mean that households have less labor to call on. Similarly, large 'stocks' of social capital may be of little use, if the household lacks a house, friends or education" (p.16). Moser thus points to the importance of considering the interrelations between different types of assets systemically and clearly suggests that this involves coherently theorizing asset building and accumulation in a way that does not fall into the trap of either considering different types of assets as necessarily fungible or else seeing assets as being regulated by intrinsic and naturally self-compounding processes. This is something that the empirical material presented above on the transformation of Nicaraguan gangs also highlights, in that the asset-building and accumulation processes that they arguably represent emerge as both highly variable and seemingly very volatile. Not only was there a critical shift in the nature of the assets created and accumulated as a result of gang activity, from social to financial forms of capital, but there was also a fundamental change in how these assets were accumulated, from an "encompassing" basis to a much more "narrow" one.

I borrow these labels from the American economist Mancur Olson (2000), who uses them to describe the potentially distinct types of underpinnings different forms of economic activity can have. Fittingly in relation to this chapter, Olson explains this idea through the example of banditry, drawing on the real-life example of the early twentieth-century Chinese warlord Feng Yu-hsiang, who used his troops to suppress bands of roving bandits within his domain of Tientsin, thereby earning the support and affection of its inhabitants despite relentlessly taxing them himself. Olson (2000, p. 7) asks the question, "Why should warlords, who were simply stationary bandits continuously stealing from a given group of victims be preferred, by those victims, to roving bandits who soon departed?" To answer this query, he suggests that a crucial distinction has to be made between "roving" and "stationary" banditry. Roving bandits are intrinsically detrimental to society because they have parochially "narrow" interests and therefore engage in "uncoordinated competitive theft" that is economically both inefficient and unsustainable. Stationary bandits, on the other hand, set themselves up as permanent fixtures within a given territorial domain and end up institutionalizing their theft in the form of taxation because it is a more efficient means of systematically plundering under conditions of monopoly. However, they thereby unavoidably develop an "encompassing" interest for their domain because they will inexorably seek to promote the most sustainable and efficient forms of economic development possible in order to maximize their profits, and this leads them to providing various public goods to those falling under their rule.

While Olson's distinction between narrow and encompassing is useful for conceptualizing the evolving basis upon which gangs in Nicaragua build and accumulate assets, it tells us little about the actual shift that occurred between the 1990s and 2000s in terms of the actual assets produced and accumulated as a result of gang activity. Moreover, Olson effectively contends that there is a natural evolutionary trajectory from roving to stationary banditry—implicitly grounded in an efficiency criterion—but the barrio Luis Fanor Hernández gang's mutation as presented above constitutes almost precisely the opposite path. Part of the problem is that Olson's general framework—implicitly based on mainstream neoclassical economic theory—sees asset building and accumulation as intrinsically bounded, self-regulating universal processes that will always tend toward efficiency maximization. The empirical material presented above on Nicaraguan gangs suggests instead that different dynamics will apply to the production and accumulation of different types of assets. This is something that is at the core of a body of theoretical work known as the French regulation school of political economy. This framework—which is especially associated with the work of the French economists Michel Aglietta (1976), Robert Boyer (1986), and Alain Lipietz (1985)—rests upon two key notions: the idea of a "regime of accumulation" and the concept of the "mode of regulation." The regime of accumulation refers to the systemic distribution of a given asset in terms of the articulation of processes of production, accumulation, and consumption. The mode of regulation is the set of rules, procedures, norms, and institutions through which the accumulation regime is secured—in other words, what creates orderly arrangements or patterns of social practice that allow for the emergence of particular systems of asset building and accumulation.

As David Harvey (1990, p. 122) has pointed out, this kind of theoretical distinction is useful "as a heuristic device" because it focuses attention on the fact that the systems of asset production, accumulation, and distribution are not naturally functioning and self-regulating processes but are instead dependent on "complex interrelations, habits, political practices, and cultural forms that allow [these] . . . system[s] to acquire sufficient semblance of order to function coherently at least for a certain period of time." At the same time, however, this configuration of sociocultural, economic, and political practices is "a necessarily imperfect and improbable outcome of dispersed human efforts," and despite "the possibility that a given set of arrangements may be able to promote accumulation for a given period of time, every regulatory framework inevitably loses that ability, becoming a fetter on profitability" (Steinmetz 2003, p. 327–28). Regulation theory is therefore inherently concerned with both change and stability, and allows for a more nuanced analysis of asset production, accumulation, and consumption processes that is applicable to the evolution of Nicaraguan gang-based asset building, which can be viewed in terms of two longitudinally different "regimes of (asset) accumulation." Although Nicaraguan gang activities in the 1990s and the 2000s are clearly very different, both in the assets they involve and their underlying dynamics, they are both concerned with the production, accumulation, distribution, and consumption of capital resources— what regulation theory ultimately defines as a "regime of accumulation." Seen in this way, and recovering Olson's terms discussed above, gangs in the 1990s can be said to have constituted encompassing regimes of asset accumulation that were organized around the management of social capital resources, principally through gang warfare, while gangs in the 2000s were narrow regimes of asset accumulation based on the management of financial capital assets through drug trafficking.

The emergence of these specific regimes of accumulation at these particular moments in time is related to wider contextual factors—what regulation theory calls the "mode of regulation." A number of factors explain the fact that gangs in the 1990s emerged as an institutional vehicle for asset building and that the asset they produced, consolidated, and accumulated was social. These include historical, demographic, and sociopolitical reasons, some of which were well summarized for me by gang members who emerged from the mass of Sandinista army and Contra guerilla conscript youths demobilized after the end of the civil war in 1990, and whom I interviewed during the course of my 1996–97 fieldwork. All told me the same things in interviews, irrespective of the side they had originated from: the change of government in 1990 led to a devaluation of their social status that, as conscripts "defending the nation" or as "freedom fighters," had been high within their respective social contexts, and becoming gang members had been a means of reaffirming themselves, particularly vis-à-vis a wider society that seemed to very rapidly "forget" them. Becoming a gang member had also been a way of recapturing some of the dramatic, yet marking and almost addictive, adrenaline-charged experiences of war, danger, and death, as well as of comradeship and solidarity, that they had lived through as conscripts or guerrillas and which were rapidly becoming scarce commodities in postconflict Nicaragua. Finally, to many becoming a gang member had actually seemed a natural continuation of their previous roles as conscripts or guerrillas. The early 1990s had been highly uncertain times, marked by political polarization, violence, and spiraling insecurity, and by joining a gang, these youths felt they could "serve" their friends and families by "protecting" them more effectively than as individuals.

Ultimately, though, gangs can be said to have emerged in the early 1990s primarily in response to wider structural processes: what the social anthropologist Ghassan Hage (2003, p. 78) has called a condition of "social death," a state of being whereby traditional channels for becoming "socially recognized beings" are closed off, thus reducing the "possibilities of a worthy life" (see Rodgers, 2006b). Seen in this way, the emergence of gangs as an institutionalized regime of collective asset accumulation principally organized in relation to social capital makes perfect functional sense. The nature of the transformation of Nicaraguan gangs by the early 2000s demonstrates, however, that the encompassing nature of their gang-based regime of social capital asset accumulation—which derived from gang members' previous experiences of solidarity and comradeship, and their pride in having "defended the nation"— was ultimately a nonviable adaptation to the confusion of postconflict Nicaragua. Once again, the reasons for this are complex and also relate to a mixture of both endogenous and exogenous factors. Endogenously, the means by which gangs in the 1990s initially attempted to maintain and accumulate both collective and individual social capital stocks can be said to have failed, due in part to the unsustainability of the violent social practices they entailed. Similarly, the emergence of a new opportunity in the form of drug dealing inevitably meant that gangs had to become more parochial once they succumbed to its attraction since the management of an illegal economic activity such as drug trafficking must inherently be secretive and therefore necessarily restrictive in terms of those involved.

However, the development of a narrow regime of economic asset accumulation such as the one characterizing Nicaraguan gangs in the 2000s is perhaps better considered in more exogenous terms, as an end result of the failure of the previous incarnation of gangs to detain the shrinking of the sociological basis of collective social life in postconflict Nicaragua, which contracted initially from the nation-state to the local neighborhood (see Núñez 1996), and then arguably from the neighborhood to the gang group. While the first shift is linked to the polarizing legacy of civil war, the second is related to particular contemporary processes of social exclusion and patterns of sociospatial reorganization that have particularly affected the Nicaraguan poor. As I have described in more detail elsewhere (Rodgers, 2004a), a veritable "revolt of the elites"—to use Christopher Lasch's (1995) expression—has occurred in Nicaragua. This is most evident in the transformation of the country's principal city, Managua, where a process of "disembedding" has splintered the city through construction of a "fortified network" of work and leisure "safe havens" for the rich, which exclude the poor by high walls, private security, sophisticated technology, construction of an inequitable road network, and a changed urban governmentality (see Rodgers 2006c). The urban slums and poor neighborhoods of the city have thereby become "dumping grounds" for the poor, or as Mike Davis (2004, p. 28) dramatically puts it, "a fully franchised solution to the problem of warehousing the twenty-first century's surplus humanity."

It is in relation to this emergent pattern of sociospatial exclusion that the transformation of Nicaraguan gangs from encompassing regimes of social asset accumulation to narrow regimes of economic asset accumulation must arguably primarily be considered. Davis (2004, p. 28) suggests that urban slums and poor neighborhoods are becoming increasingly disconnected from large-scale economic activity, which is increasingly global and technological in scope and nature. As a result, he contends, slums and poor neighborhoods will progressively be characterized by "ruthless Darwinian competition, as increasing numbers of poor people compete for the same informal scraps, ensur[ing] self-consuming communal violence as the highest form of urban involution." This evolving urban dystopia provides the context for the gangs' mutation into narrow regimes of financial capital accumulation through drug trafficking practices underpinned by extreme forms of violence. Thus the recourse to drug dealing by gangs needs to be understood not so much in terms of Nicaragua's emergence as a drug route during the late 1990s, as conventionally thought, but more in terms of the conjunction of that phenomenon with the shrinking basis of collective social life in postconflict Nicaragua, on the one hand, and the country's changing urban political economy, on the other.

Conclusion and Policy Implications

This chapter has proposed that asset-building processes should be conceived in more nuanced terms than is conventionally the case, as variable "regimes of asset accumulation" that can be either "narrow" or "encompassing" depending on a wider "mode of regulation" that can change significantly in response to both endogenous and exogenous factors. This is particularly the case for asset-based socioeconomic practices in postconflict situations, including gangs, which this chapter has shown have been vehicles for important forms of asset building in postconflict Nicaragua. The case study presented highlights both the variability and volatility of gang-based forms of asset building and accumulation, tracing the evolution of Nicaraguan gangs from encompassing regimes of social capital accumulation based on practices of gang warfare to narrow regimes of financial capital accumulation based on drug dealing. This mutation underlines the way in which asset building and accumulation are neither intrinsically self-regulating nor bounded processes that always tend toward efficiency maximization. Instead, an alternative interpretation has been proposed that draws on elements from the work of the American economist Mancur Olson as well as from the so-called French regulation school and its concepts of "regime of accumulation" and "mode of regulation." In arriving at this interpretation, the chapter explicitly follows Gerry Stoker's suggestion that "studies need to move from theory through empirical application and back to theory. [A] . . . regime approach does not need a stack of case studies which discover regimes to bolster its position. . . . It rather needs to be able to substantiate the claim that its framework . . . is robust and flexible enough to both describe and explain the variety of power distributions in different localities" (1995, p. 66).

Ultimately, as George Steinmetz (2003, p. 331) remarked, "Regulation theory [is] useful descriptively for characterizing the contingent articulations among an array of seemingly unrelated practices and tracing the ways in which these partial regularities are cobbled together into a structure that can temporarily promote capital accumulation." Seen in this way, the variable and volatile nature of gang-based asset building emerges mainly as a function of contingency and accident rather as an outcome of any intrinsic self-regulating or natural process. This is important because it allows an understanding of asset-building processes in "figurational" terms, eschewing the positivist compulsion to seek "constant conjunctions of events" in favor of a more general theoretical understanding of particular constellations of structures and practices that jointly produce effects that are not necessarily repeatable but can be broadly generalized (see Steinmetz 2003, p. 328). In social policy terms, what this means is that it is not just asset accumulation per se that counts but also the nature of the regime of asset accumulation and in particular whether it is "narrow" or "encompassing" in its underlying dynamics. This, in turn, depends largely on the wider "mode of regulation." The gangs of Central America that are considered so detrimental to the region's development (see USAID 2006) are in fact a desperate epiphenomenon of wider structural circumstances that asset-building policies must explicitly take into account in order to identify sustainable asset-based poverty reduction strategies. In other words, it is critical that the mode of regulation—which can variably shape regimes of asset accumulation in often highly volatile ways, particularly in postconflict situations—be understood as a factor in its own right rather than simply as a context.

Notes

1. See "Criminal Gangs in Central America," *The Economist*, January 5, 2006, p. 26.

2. The fact that gangs are violent is no bar to this; as the German sociologist Georg Simmel (1955, p. 16) pointed out, conflict is as significant an element of the dynamics that create and maintain social relationships as "unity" (*einheit*).

3. This name is a pseudonym, as are the names of all the informants mentioned in this chapter. The first period of fieldwork was carried out from July 1996 to July 1997 as part of a social anthropology Ph.D. program at the University of Cambridge (Rodgers 2000). The second period of fieldwork was conducted from February through March 2002 as part of the London School of Economics Crisis States Programme (phase 1), which also sponsored another visit from December 2002 to January 2003.

4. Calculated on the basis of Serbin and Ferreyra (2000, 185-87); Policía Nacional de Nicaragua, "Comparativo" (www.policia.gob.ni/AD_tabla2.htm [November 2006]).

5. As Godnick, Muggah, and Waszink (2002, p. 26) note, "Given the anecdotal information on violence as portrayed in the Nicaraguan press and the general perception of violence in Nicaraguan society, these figures are suspiciously low." There are several likely reasons for this, the most important being the inefficiency and weakness of Nicaraguan state institutions. The Pan-American Health Organization (1998, p. 384) has estimated that over 50 percent of all mortalities in Nicaragua in 1995 were not registered due to deficient record-keeping by hospitals and morgues, for example. Moreover, since the change of regime in 1990, a painstakingly slow process of depoliticization and reductions in both size and funding—partly related to stringent budget-cutting efforts by the Nicaraguan state—have severely affected the operational capacity of the National Police, which has only limited patrolling capacities in urban areas and is completely absent in 21 percent of the country's 146 municipalities (Cajina 2000, p. 174). It should also be noted that both Presidents Arnoldo Alemán (1997–2001) and Enrique Bolaños (2002–06) made fighting crime a key element of their government program and "preferred" positive—this is, low—crime statistics.

6. *La Tribuna*, May 2, 1997, p. 4.

7. Female gang members are not unknown but are extremely rare. See Rodgers (2006b, p. 285–87) for a discussion of this gender bias.

8. These statistics undoubtedly err on the low side (see footnote 5).

9. At the same time, it should be said that the police were not a very visible presence in poor neighborhoods during the 1990s, partly because gangs generally outgunned them. This obviously made effective patrolling and control rather difficult, as the Nicaraguan police commissioner admitted frankly in an interview in 2001. See "Population Out-Guns Police," *Nicaragua Network Newsletter* 9, no. 6, February 5–11, 2001 (www.tulane.edu/~libweb/RESTRICTED/NICANEWS/2001_0205.txt [November 2006]).

10. For an account of the growth of the cocaine trade in Nicaragua, see Rodgers (2004b).

References

Aglietta, Michel. 1976. *Régulation et crisis du capitalisme*. Paris: Calmann Levy.

Arana, Ana. 2001. "The New Battle for Central America." *Foreign Affairs* 89, no. 6: 88–101.

Ayres, Robert L. 1998. *Crime and Violence as Development Issues in Latin America and the Caribbean*. Washington: World Bank.

Boyer, Robert. 1986. *La théorie de la regulation: Une analyse critique*. Paris: La Découverte.

Cajina, Roberto. J. 2000. "Nicaragua: De la seguridad del Estado a la inseguridad ciudadana." In *Gobernabilidad democrática y seguridad ciudadana en Centroamérica: El caso de Nicaragua*, edited by Andrés Serbin and Diego Ferreyra, pp. 157–83. Managua: Coordinadora Regional de Investigaciones Económicas y Sociales (CRIES).

Call, Charles. 2000. "Sustainable Development in Central America: The Challenges of Violence, Injustice and Insecurity." CA 2020 Working Paper 8. Hamburg: Institut für Iberoamerika-Kunde.

Davis, Mike. 2004. "Planet of Slums: Urban Involution and the Informal Proletariat." *New Left Review* 26: 5–34.

Godnick, William, Robert Muggah, and Camilla Waszink. 2002. "Stray Bullets: The Impact of Small Arms Misuse in Central America." Occasional Paper 5. Geneva: Small Arms Survey.

Hage, Ghassan. 2003. "'Comes a Time We Are All Enthusiasm': Understanding Palestinian Suicide Bombers in Times of Exighophobia." *Public Culture* 15, no. 1: 65–89.

Harvey, David. 1990. *The Condition of Postmodernity: An Inquiry into the Origins of Cultural Change*. Oxford: Blackwell.

Hobbes, Thomas. [1651]1996. *Leviathan*. Cambridge University Press.

Lasch, Christopher. 1995. *The Revolt of the Elites and the Betrayal of Democracy*. New York: Norton.

Liebel, Manfred. 2004. "Pandillas juveniles en Centroamérica o la difícil búsqueda de justicia en una sociedad violenta." *Desacatos* 14 (Spring-Summer): 85–104.

Lipietz, Alain. 1985. *Mirages et miracles: Problèmes de l'industrialisation dans le tiers monde*. Paris: La Découverte.

Londoño, Juan-Luis, Alejandro Gaviria, and Roberto Guerrero, eds. 2000. *Asalto al desarrollo: Violencia en América Latina*. Washington: Inter-American Development Bank.

McIlwaine, Cathy 1999. "Geography and Development: Crime and Violence as Development Issues." *Progress in Human Geography* 23, no. 3: 453–63.

Moser, Caroline. 1998. "The Asset Vulnerability Framework: Reassessing Urban Poverty Reduction Strategies." *World Development* 26, no. 1: 1–19.

———. 2006. "Asset-Based Approaches to Poverty Reduction in a Globalized Context." Background paper prepared for the Brookings Institution–Ford Foundation workshop on Asset-Based Approaches to Poverty Reduction in a Globalized Context. Washington, June 27–28.

Moser, Caroline, and Ailsa Winton. 2002. "Violence in the Central American Region: Towards an Integrated Framework for Violence Reduction." Working Paper 171. London: Overseas Development Institute.

Núñez, Juan-Carlos. 1996. *De la ciudad al barrio: Redes y tejidos urbanos en Guatemala, El Salvador y Nicaragua*. Ciudad de Guatemala: Universidad Rafael Landívar, Programa de Fortalecimiento de las Sedes Regionales.

O'Donnell, Guillermo. 1999. *Counterpoints: Selected Essays on Authoritarianism and Democratization.* University of Notre Dame Press.

Olson, Mancur. 2000. *Power and Prosperity: Outgrowing Communist and Capitalist Dictatorships.* New York: Basic Books.

Pan-American Health Organization. 1998. *Health in the Americas.* Vol. 2. Washington.

Pearce, Jenny. 1998. "From Civil War to 'Civil Society': Has the End of the Cold War Brought Peace to Central America?" *International Affairs* 74, no. 3: 587–615.

Robinson, William I. 1998. "(Mal)development in Central America: Globalization and Social Change." *Development and Change* 29, no. 3: 467–97.

Rocha, J. L. 2000. "Pandillero: La mano que empuña el mortero." *Envío* 216 (March): 19–25.

Rodgers, Dennis. 1999. "Youth Gangs and Violence in Latin America and the Caribbean: A Literature Survey." Latin America and Caribbean Region Sustainable Development Working Paper 4. Washington: World Bank.

———. 2000. "Living in the Shadow of Death: Violence, Pandillas, and Social Disintegration in Contemporary Urban Nicaragua." Unpublished Ph.D. dissertation. University of Cambridge, Department of Social Anthropology.

———. 2004a. "Disembedding the City: Crime, Insecurity, and Spatial Organization in Managua, Nicaragua." *Environment and Urbanization* 16, no. 2: 113–24.

———. 2004b. "La globalización de un barrio desde abajo: Emigrantes, remesas, taxis, y drogas." *Envío* 264, March: 23–30.

———. 2006a. "Cuando la pandilla se pone mala: Violencia juvenil y cambio social en Nicaragua." *Etnografías Contemporáneas* 2, no. 2: 75–98.

———. 2006b. "Living in the shadow of death: Gangs, violence, and social order in urban Nicaragua, 1996–2002." *Journal of Latin American Studies* 38, no. 2: 267–92.

———. 2006c. "The State as a Gang: Conceptualizing the Governmentality of Violence in Contemporary Nicaragua." *Critique of Anthropology* 26, no. 3: 315–30.

Sánchez-Jankowski, Martín. 1991. *Islands in the Street: Gangs and American Urban Society.* University of California Press.

Sen, Amartya. 1981. *Poverty and Famines: An Essay on Entitlement and Deprivation.* Oxford: Clarendon Press.

Serbin, Andrés, and Diego Ferreyra, eds. 2000. *Gobernabilidad democrática y seguridad ciudadana en Centroamérica: El caso de Nicaragua.* Managua: CRIES.

Simmel, Georg. 1955. *Conflict and the Web of Group Affiliations.* Translated by Kurt H. Wolff and Reinhard Bendix. Glencoe, Ill.: Free Press.

Steinmetz, George. 2003. "The State of Emergency and the Revival of American Imperialism: Toward an Authoritarian Post-Fordism." *Public Culture* 15, no. 2: 323–45.

Stoker, Gerry. 1995. "Regime Theory and Urban Politics." In *Theories of Urban Politics*, edited by David Judge, Gerry Stoker, and Hal Wolman. London: Sage.

Suttles, Gerald D. 1968. *The Social Order of the Slum: Ethnicity and Territory in the Inner City.* University of Chicago Press.

Taylor, Charles. 2002. "Modern Social Imaginaries." *Public Culture* 14, no. 1: 91–124.

United Nations Development Program. 2000. *El desarrollo humano en Nicaragua.* Managua.

UN Research Institute for Social Development. 1995. *States of Disarray: The Social Effects of Globalization.* Geneva.

USAID. 2006. "Central America and Mexico Gang Assessment." Report prepared for the USAID Bureau for Latin American and Caribbean Affairs, Office for Regional Sustainable Development (April).

Whyte, William F. 1943. *Street Corner Society: The Structure of an Italian Slum.* University of Chicago Press.

12

Beyond Microfinance

VIJAY MAHAJAN

Economists of all hues, from Adam Smith to Karl Marx, have emphasized the centrality of capital to enhancing incomes and wealth. The classical view about the role of capital in the economic growth of nations is equally applicable to households. Poverty begins with low investment, which leads, in succession, to low productivity, low income, and low or no savings, thus leaving no scope for investment and continuing the vicious cycle.

One remedy for this situation is thought to be an injection of capital (if possible by borrowing it from someone with a surplus). This breaks the vicious cycle by increasing the level of investment, thereby enhancing productivity and eventually income. Additional income leads to enhanced savings, which then can be used to service the loan and still invest in the next cycle. This chain of "virtuous" events is based on several assumptions, including the absence of risk and the magnitude of surpluses generated. But how simplistic these assumptions are can be understood by looking at a real life example: the Jawaja leather workers.

Limits of Capital

In 1976 Ravi Matthai, the founder-director of the Indian Institute of Management, Ahmedabad (IIMA), led a group of faculty members and business school graduates to work with rural poor communities in what came to be called the

Jawaja Rural University Project. Among the people they worked with were the *raigars*, a traditional community of leather workers engaged in that activity through caste. Though the raigars had a great deal of skill in all aspects of leatherwork, from flaying dead cattle to tanning the hides to making shoes and other leather goods, they continued to be poor over generations. In addition, due to the nature of their work, they were treated as "untouchables" by upper-caste people.

A study by the IIMA group found that, in their quest for social acceptability, the raigars had stopped flaying cattle (considered menial); instead, they bought tanned hides from traders in the nearby town (Matthai 1979). The raigars bought the hides on credit and made rough leather shoes, which they sold back to the traders. The traders charged no apparent interest, but the traders' payment to the raigars for the shoes and the prices they charged for the shoes on the market meant a doubling of the traders' money. To release the raigars from their debts to the traders, the IIMA volunteers got them cheap bank loans to purchase the hides. The raigars found, however, that they were not able to sell to retailers directly, as these retailers wanted the shoes on credit. The raigars then tried selling directly to customers in weekly markets but found that, for this, they had to go from place to place and did not have enough time to make the shoes. With the encouragement of the IIMA volunteers, the raigars formed an association, with most of them making shoes and a few of them selling shoes.

The IIMA volunteers then introduced the raigars to an ethnic shop in Delhi, which was willing to buy shoes from them and to pay cash, but the shop wanted softer shoes and bags and purses with ethnic designs. The volunteers arranged for the raigars to learn both a method of tanning to produce soft leather hides and a shoemaking method to produce traditional looking shoes. They also brought in designers from the National Institute of Design in Ahmedabad. After several years of support from the IIMA volunteers, the Jawaja Leather Workers' Association stabilized to an extent where about fifty raigars were getting a steady livelihood making products for the Delhi ethnic market. It took several person-months of work by IIMA volunteers and the designers to get this number of raigars to this level.

This story is one of several score from the personal experience of the author that shows that access to capital is not a sufficient condition to improve the livelihoods of the poor. Yet policymakers and development practitioners are increasingly being made to believe in this simple-minded solution to poverty: microcredit. The idea began to find currency in the early 1990s, in a world tired of the complexity of the poverty problem and the lack of success in resolving it. Interest rose to a crescendo in 2005. This is not to deny that microcredit by itself does often work—and when it does, it alleviates poverty to some extent—but such situations are possible mainly among the enterprising poor and in dynamic, high-density (even if poor) economies. Microcredit does not work by itself for the less-enterprising poor and in low-density economies. Such situations do require capital—but not the kind that microcredit is geared to provide.

Furthermore, financial capital is just one of five forms of capital, the others being natural, physical, social, and human capital. Natural capital includes land, water, forests, livestock, and weather. Physical capital includes buildings, industrial plants and machinery, and infrastructure. Social capital is composed of kinship groups, associations, institutions, and trust and norms. Human capital includes nutrition, health education, skills, and competencies. All these are interlinked through financial capital, which is central. Financial capital includes savings, credit, and other financial instruments.

The example of the Jawaja leather workers shows that merely focusing on financial capital was an inadequate solution to a complex problem. The raigars had ceded their traditional entitlement to their natural capital—dead cattle—in their quest for social acceptance, but as a result they became dependent on traders for the supply of this critical resource. Consequently they had to build up both human capital, in terms of new skills for soft leather tanning and product design, and social capital, in the form of an association to sell their goods together. Only then could the additional financial capital be used effectively.

Natural, human, and social capital are usually endowments (something one is born with or inherits) or entitlements (something that society confers on a person due to his status, and this may be for the rich as well as the poor). For example, the raigars were entitled to natural capital in the form of all the by-products they could derive out of anyone's dead animal: flesh, bones, hides, hooves, horns, teeth, tail, hair, and entrails. Over the past few centuries, even these forms of capital have become financialized, that is, they have prices and titles permitting exchange and thus have become tradable.

Land, which was communally owned at one time, has become titled and tradable. Forests, which were communal or state property, are being privatized and sold for sustainable exploitation. Human capital is increasingly being financialized, with schooling and health care being charged for in most economies. At a more crass level, slavery in the olden times and human trafficking and bonded labor today are other examples of the financialization of human capital. Even the enormous sums paid to football players and screen stars are examples of the financialization of human capital. Social capital, too, is being financialized. One can now buy memberships and access to social clubs and networks, which was earlier not possible in kinship groups—one had to be born into them. A raigar can drink tea in a tearoom, at least in a big town, if he can pay for it, and he can socialize with others sitting there, whereas earlier his caste made him "untouchable." Physical capital, even public goods, has always been financialized. The most remarkable example of the financialization of a public good is pollution credits, which make clean air tradable.

In short, the dominance of financial capital over all other forms of capital is an abiding feature of human history, and this trend adversely affects the poor in the globalized context. Thus enhancing access to financial assets is a key to helping the poor realize economic opportunity.

The financial capital of the poor tends to be slim or negative. When borrowing from others is lower than savings plus loans to others, financial net worth is positive. But when borrowing exceeds savings and loans to others, financial net worth is negative. High rates of interest on borrowing add to the debt burden, lowering net worth over the years. This is the classic debt trap.

In the category of natural capital, land is highly prized among the poor, whether it is just a plot for a house, land for a homestead, or a marginal farm. Even encroached land or land without title is valued. The availability of irrigation, for even part of the year, greatly enhances the value of land. With livestock, as with human capital, numbers matter, because the pigs, sheep, goats, and cattle are left unfenced for free grazing, so whatever they produce is net income.

Like their financial capital, the physical capital of the poor tends to be low. They own little housing, productive assets, equipment, or access to utilities and infrastructure.

Social capital, however, is prevalent among the poor. This capital is in the form of kinship groups, whether family, clan, tribe, caste, neighborhood, language group, or religion. The poor invest a lot in maintaining their social capital because it serves as a form of insurance in adversity. That is the reason behind such paradoxes as very poor households spending a large amount of money—even taking out loans—for community ceremonies such as marriages and funerals.

The primary capital of the very poor is their own bodies, which they use for generating their livelihoods. Next most important are family members. Everyone can be a source of income, even though that person has to be fed and clothed. This explains why fertility rates among the poor are high: a child becomes a part of the labor supply fairly early—and without much investment.

When the family finds itself in overwhelming debt, it may liquidate such natural capital as cattle or land. The family also may use their social capital, borrowing from their extended families and other social networks—enough at least for everyday needs. In extreme cases, their human capital—their bodies—

becomes the only way to repay. This leads to extreme actions such as working as bonded labor or being involved in child trafficking, organ sale, or prostitution.

Protecting Capital

There is an assumption that credit is the main financial service needed by the poor. Actually, it is not. The poor want to save much more than they want to borrow. There are six times as many savers as borrowers in Bank Rakyat Indonesia's village banking program. And the Self-Employed Women's Association Bank in India has discovered that women value a safe place to keep their savings. The poor also want to protect themselves against risks. However, the microfinance field in general focuses on credit and does not emphasize other financial services, such as savings and insurance. Savings are particularly important since they act as self-insurance in case of small emergencies or sudden demands for cash, as well as providing equity for borrowing and collateral for repayment of loans.

Economists tell us that at low levels of income, the marginal propensity to save is low due to spending on everyday necessities. As income rises the propensity to save rises, as people strive to save for their future. The question is whether at incomes below the poverty line this propensity is positive or negative. Table 12-1 shows data from a survey in 2003 in Jharkhand, a poor state in India. As can be seen, the lower the income level, the less the saving, with saving becoming negative below a certain level. Thus the economists' view seems to be correct.

But does this mean that the poor do not save at all? In practice, they do. Dividing the year into just three seasons—summer, rainy, and winter—we found that the poor saved money in the winter, broke even during the rainy season, and borrowed in the summer (Mahajan 2003, pp. 37–45). If they did not have adequate savings from the winter season, they suffered extreme distress in the other seasons. (Saving food grains at harvest could reduce their dependence on high-interest loans for buying food grains later at high prices, making way for grain banks. But in an increasingly financialized world, it is not always possible to have such arrangements, and saving in the form of money becomes necessary.)

Surveys done by BASIX India (a microfinance institution) show that the poor are willing to save money as long as they are reasonably sure of the safety of their savings and of their ability to draw from their savings at short notice. The interest rate is not as important to the poor as is the safety and liquidity of their savings. Also of importance is being able to deposit into their savings accounts frequently and in small amounts. In its Krishna Bhima Samruddi Bank, BASIX runs a daily deposit service, in which street vendors and petty shopkeepers can

Table 12-1. *Savings According to Income, Jharkhand, 2003*
Units as indicated

| Community | Amount in rupees[a] | | Saving or deficit as percent of income |
	Average annual income	Average annual expenditure	
Bhuiya	10,758	14,496	−35
Chamar	14,414	16,754	−16
Khairwar	22,099	18,728	15
Oraon	25,582	23,506	8
Koiri	34,978	29,755	15
Upper castes	53,270	50,422	5

Source: Household survey by BASIX–Jharkhand Livelihood Enhancement Action Platform (Mahajan 2003, p. 39).
a. 45 rupees = U.S.$1.

deposit as little as 10 rupees (U.S.$0.22) a day, without moving from their workplace. This service entitles the savers to life insurance worth 10,000 rupees and to a loan. This kind of composite financial service, not just microfinance, enables the poor to build financial assets.

Borrowing has been looked down upon in many cultures, and borrowing beyond one's ability to repay has been reviled. The phenomenon of encouraging people to take out loans to buy consumer goods is relatively recent; it is a private sector version of Keynesian thinking, where the aggregate demand in the economy can be boosted by enhancing government spending based on borrowed money. Here, demand is boosted by enhancing consumer spending based on borrowed money. This kind of credit is and will always be a liability.

However, credit that is used to enhance income through starting or improving an economic activity is an example of a liability that can be converted into an asset over a period of time and under certain favorable conditions. The favorable conditions are linked to conversion efficiency, or the ratio between input prices and output prices. If there is a net profit, then the loan can be repaid over time. The fact that these assumptions do not always hold true makes the credit-based activity risky, both for the lender and the borrower. Microenterprises with fairly high conversion efficiency, however, will retire the liability in time, converting it to an asset. Table 12-2 shows examples of such high-return activities.

However, it takes 25,000 rupees of capital (U.S.$550, or about the annual per capita income in India) to generate enough surplus to move a poor household out of the vicious cycle described at the beginning of this chapter. Microcredit at the lower end is therefore not really an asset-building strategy. (Com-

Table 12-2. *Return on Investment in Microenterprises*
Units as indicated

Sr. no.	Microentrepreneur	Capital employed (rupees)	Earnings (rupees per day)	Opportunity cost of labor (rupees per day)	Interest paid (rupees per day)[a]	Net return (rupees per day)	Financial rate of return (percent per day)	Annual return on investment (percent per year)	Annual income (rupees per year)[b]
1	Fish trader lady (mornings)	500	100	30	50.00	20.00	4.0	1,000	5,000
2	Bangle trader lady	3,000	150	30	10.00	110.00	3.7	917	27,500
3	Grocery shop man	5,000	150	50	15.00	85.00	1.7	425	21,250
4	Tea shop man	7,500	150	50	12.50	87.50	1.16	292	21,875
5	Fruit and vegetable shop (self + 1 employee)	15,000	250	100	25.00	125.00	0.8	208	31,250
6	Food vending (self + 2 employees)	20,000	325	150	33.33	141.67	0.7	177	40,625

Source: Author's calculations based on field data collected for NIBM–MCRIL Workshop on MFI Guarantees, Pune, India, December 2000, conducted by Malcolm Harper.

a. Interest rates are 10 percent per day for sr. no. 1 from wholesalers, 10 percent per month for sr. nos. 2 and 3, and 5 percent per month for sr. nos. 4 through 6.

b. Annual income based on 250 days per year.

modity derivatives can act as a hedging mechanism for input and output prices, but no microfinance institution is yet working on this strategy.) In addition to credit and saving accounts, another important financial service for the poor, given their vulnerability to livelihood risks, is insurance: life insurance, health insurance, crop insurance, and insurance for such income-earning assets as livestock and irrigation pumps. Though insurance (except endowment life insurance) is by itself not an asset-building strategy, it is fundamental to protecting whatever assets the poor may own.

Microfinance and Capital

Microfinance, as the name implies, starts small. And in most cases, microfinance initially means microcredit, so loans as small as U.S.$10 are made. In India, for example, over two million self-help groups, with a membership exceeding 30 million, mostly women, meet periodically, usually once a month, to save sums as little as 10 rupees (U.S.$0.22). The savings of all members are pooled for a few months, and then the members start giving tiny loans to each other: U.S.$5 for buying medicines for a sick child, U.S.$10 to start roadside vegetable vending, or U.S.$20 to buy a goat, for example.

In the Indian model, after a year or two of such internal lending the group gets linked to a bank. This means, based on appraisal of the group quality (which is assessed through records of meetings, regularity of attendance and saving by members, extent of internal lending, the regularity of its repayment, and general group awareness and cohesion), the bank gives a bulk loan to the group, usually two to four times their accumulated savings (which may be mostly lent out).

The group's funds thus augmented, members accept proposals for more ambitious projects. The choice of project is left to the borrower, and while her fellow members approve the loan amount and repayment terms, unlike in some government loan programs, no one pushes a particular activity on a reluctant borrower. The woman who borrowed U.S.$10 for vegetable vending, for example, may want to become a bangle trader instead and so needs U.S.$25 for a buying trip to the nearby town.

Perhaps the woman who borrowed U.S.$20 for a goat wants to buy a scrub cow, an expenditure that requires $100. Her request may be refused: she may be lent only U.S.$50, which is not enough for a scrub cow but is enough for two more goats. Loan refusals may also mean that seasonal trading opportunities cannot be acted upon. These refusals partly arise from an overall funds constraint but may also be due to the conservatism (and perhaps envy) of fellow members and to the rule-bound nature of direct lending institutions, which cannot appraise each borrower because of cost considerations.

The step-by-step feature of microcredit, starting small with successive loans increasing in size, reduces risk for the borrower and the lender. The step-by-step approach also acts as an excellent teacher of the poor regarding self-employment and, eventually, microentrepreneurship. But a subset of borrowers, often the most enterprising, are held back by this approach.

Microcredit has thus enhanced financial inclusion, but there is a long way to go. As per the Microcredit Summit 2005 estimates, considered to be optimistic, nearly 100 million households have gained access to microfinance (Daley-Harris 2005). This is a remarkable achievement. In contrast, the Microfinance Information eXchange (MIX), which mainly focuses on the top few hundred microfinance institutions, estimates that number at 27 million households.[1] In either case, the number, compared to about 500 million poor households around the world who need access to financial services, is still small. A survey of microfinance in South Asia by Sanjay Sinha and others (2006), done for the World Bank, shows that in India only about 8 percent of the estimated 200 million who needed microcredit had been linked to microfinance.

Although microcredit has reached several million poor people who would not be served by banks or formal financial institutions, there is enough evidence to show that outreach is limited and that the poorest tend to be left out. There are methodological variations, and in general those programs that follow the Grameen Bank (Bangladesh) methodology tend to have greater outreach to the poor because of the exclusion of anyone owning more than a half-acre of land or equivalent asset.

In contrast, between a quarter to a half of the members of Indian self-help groups tend to be above the official poverty line (still quite a low income). More important, the poorest households tend to exclude themselves due to requirements to meet and save regularly in the initial year or so before they can get a loan. The Bangladesh Rural Advancement Committee, which runs specialized programs for the very poor using a combination of food aid and microcredit, does not place such conditions on loans. But it is an exception. For most microfinance institutions, their own sustainability must be a priority.

Microfinance institutions are in fact barely financially sustainable, so how can they build assets for the poor? While the author supports, and has worked for, the financial self-sustainability of such institutions, the assumption that this can be possible for all microcredit institutions and quickly needs to be examined. Even the best cases took a long time to get there (Grameen Bank, Bangladesh, took twenty years) or got there by shedding their nongovernmental organization status.² India's self-help group program has grown big on the basis of external support for the one-time costs of group formation and for the ongoing group support costs. With political pressure to lower interest rates on loans to self-help groups, even variable costs are not being met in most places. Only about a hundred of the thousands of microfinance institutions around the world are financially self-sufficient according to the Consultative Group to Assist the Poor (2004), a consortium of public and private development agencies. The experience of BASIX indicates that it is difficult to stay focused on the mission and simultaneously fulfill investors' expectations and regulatory requirements. The trade-off between enhancing access and maintaining institutional sustainability remains an abiding challenge.³

Thus using microfinance institutions as the primary agencies for building the financial assets of the poor is a doubtful strategy. This is a job for the mainstream financial sector. The role of microfinance is to continue to explore how to offer credit to the poor and to do so in a sustainable way, but mainstream banks and insurance companies need to enter the scene and scale it up.

From Microcredit to Livelihood Finance

In 2002, six years after the inception of its microcredit program, BASIX performed an impact assessment study (Indian Market Research Bureau 2002). It found that only 52 percent of its three-year-plus microcredit customers reported an increase in income; 23 percent reported no change, while another 25 percent actually reported a decline. What was the reason for this? The analysis shows that the reasons were poorly managed risk, low productivity in crop cultivation and livestock rearing, and inability to get good prices from the input and output markets. Based on this study, BASIX revised its strategy and now offers microcredit along with a suite of insurance products covering life, health, crops, and livestock. For enhancing productivity, a range of agricultural and business development services are offered to borrowers. For ensuring better prices, alternate market linkages are being facilitated on both the input and output sides. Producers are encouraged to form groups and cooperatives, which are then given institutional development services to become more effective.

To enable the poor to realize economic opportunities in the globalized context, the paradigm must be broadened from microcredit to livelihood finance, which is a comprehensive approach to promoting sustainable livelihoods for the poor that provides financial services, agricultural and business development services, and institutional development services. Financial services include savings; credit for investment in natural resources; insurance on health, crops, and livestock; infrastructure finance for roads, power, marketplaces, and telecommunications; and investment in human development, that is, nutrition, health, education, and vocational training. Agricultural and business development services include productivity enhancement, risk mitigation other than insurance (such as vaccination of livestock), local-value addition, and alternate market linkages. Institutional development services focus on forming and strengthening producer organizations—such as self-help groups, water users' associations, and credit and commodity cooperatives—and establishing systems for accounting, performance, incentives, and the like.

Microcredit, by definition, is a single intervention: small loans, given for short durations, with repayments beginning as quickly and as frequently as possible. Moreover, whether given through groups or directly to individuals, microcredit loans go to individuals, not to collectives. In contrast, livelihood finance requires larger amounts of money; it may entail more than just loans (including equity or risk funds and indeed some public subsidies). Furthermore, livelihood finance covers longer durations, at least five and maybe twenty years, and it almost always would be used for collective purposes. Thus microcredit and livelihood finance are fundamentally different (Mahajan 2005).

Livelihood finance would begin by organizing the poor, as was done in Jawaja, not for disbursing credit but for encouraging savings (financial assets), learning new skills (human capital), and building a sense of solidarity (social capital). Credit would also be given for investing in natural and human capital, not just for physical capital. Business development services—product design and market linkages, for example—would be integrated with financial services, as was done in Jawaja. Finally, to enable the rural poor to work together effectively, institutional development services would be provided. Only then would the poor be able to realize economic opportunity (or at least survive in the face of adversity) in this globalizing world.

Notes

1. See Microfinance Information eXchange, *The MicroBanking Bulletin* (www.mixmbb.org/en/index.html [December 2006]).

2. An example of the latter is PRODEM (Promotion and Development of Microenterprises), a Bolivian nonprofit that established BancoSol, a commercial bank that offers financial services to the microentreprenurial sector.

3. The author has dealt with this issue in detail elsewhere and has not found a single exception to this trade-off in the twenty years he has participated in the development finance world. See Mahajan and Ramola (1996).

References

Consultative Group to Assist the Poor. 2004. "Financial Institutions with a Double Bottom Line: Implications for the Future of Microfinance." Occasional Paper 8. Washington (July).

Daley-Harris, Sam. 2005. "State of the Microcredit Summit Campaign Report 2005." Washington: Microcredit Summit Campaign.

Development Finance Forum. 2004. *Capital Plus: The Challenge of Development in Development Finance Institutions.* Chicago.

Indian Market Research Bureau. 2002. "An Impact Assessment Study of Microcredit." Hyderabad: BASIX.

Mahajan, Vijay, ed. 2003. "A Study of Livelihoods in Jharkhan—Status and Strategy." Mimeo. Hyderabad: BASIX.

———. 2005. "From Microcredit to Livelihood Finance." *Economic and Political Weekly* 40, no. 41: 4416–19.

Mahajan, Vijay, and Bharti Gupta Ramola. 1996. "Financial Services for the Rural Poor and Women in India—Access and Sustainability." *Journal of International Development* 8, no. 2: 211–24.

Matthai, Ravi. 1979. *The Rural University: The Jawaja Experiment in Educational Innovation.* Ahmedabad: Indian Institute of Management.

Sinha, Sanjay, and others. 2006. "Microfinance in South Asia: Poverty Lending to Financial Inclusion in the 21st Century." Washington: World Bank, South Asia Financial Sector Division. (March).

13

Using Microinsurance and Financial Education to Protect and Accumulate Assets

MONIQUE COHEN AND PAMELA YOUNG

Erick, a Ugandan living in a village fifty kilometers north of Kampala, was not what one would consider destitute.[1] He ran a small business and owned a small plot of land. His children went to school and his wife took care of the few animals that they had. Though far from rich, Erick and his family survived without too many worries. Then one day Erick fell sick. He wasn't too concerned at first and figured the illness would subside within a few days. It did not. He stopped working, and so did his wife, who now had to take care of him. Unable to pay for school fees, he withdrew his children from school. To cover medical costs, he sold his cow for a fraction of the price it would normally fetch. By the time he recovered, he and his family were far worse off than they had been before. Just like that, all of the hard-earned gains that Erick and his wife had worked for disappeared.

Over the last two decades, microfinance has captured the attention of the international development and business communities as a "silver bullet" for poverty alleviation. Stories abound of village women in Asia, Africa, and Latin America who, upon receiving a series of small loans from a microfinance institution (MFI), were able to use their entrepreneurial skills to lift themselves out of poverty. The reality, however, is much more complicated. While small loans have helped many of the poor worldwide by allowing them to start small businesses or buy assets, the road out of poverty is hardly smooth. Frequent financial pressures and unexpected shocks often erode hard-earned gains, such that households like Erick's can suddenly find themselves back to square one. The mobilization of savings can mitigate some of the losses, but seldom are savings of the poor enough to cover the full cost of a shock like a death in the family or illness. What the poor need is a way to protect their assets from unforeseen risks.

Microinsurance is one possible solution. Like regular insurance, it involves the pooling of risks across individuals who make small, regular payments in exchange for the promise of future compensation in the event of a financial loss. The "micro" refers to the fact that it targets the low-income market through innovative cost structures, premium payment systems, terms of coverage, and delivery modes.

Many MFIs are experimenting in microinsurance, and while these experiments show a lot of promise, the rates of adoption and usage are often lower than the MFIs' projections. Even when the product is well designed, the uptake is often lower than desired. The problem, it appears, lies in people's understanding of insurance. The experience of the MFI Tau Yeu May (TYM) in Vietnam is typical. In 1996 it introduced to its members a "mutual assistance fund" that is similar to a life insurance policy. All members were required to contribute to the mutual assistance fund, so adoption was not an issue; but most clients were not aware of its benefits and did not know how to make a claim until a TYM staff member contacted them (Tran and Yun 2004). Case studies of other microinsurance schemes reveal the same finding: the poor generally do not understand (and hence do not use) microinsurance.

This chapter examines the need to protect the assets of the poor through microinsurance. Using evidence drawn largely (though not exclusively) from East Africa and India, it looks at the most common strategies used by the poor to cope with risk and identifies their shortcomings. It then presents microinsurance as a possible solution and proposes financial education as a way to increase the poor's understanding and adoption of microinsurance.

Vulnerability

Vulnerability is based on a probability: the more likely one is to fall below a certain threshold (say, the poverty line) as a result of a shock or stress event, the more vulnerable that individual is. Shocks are unexpected occurrences such as death, illness, or accidents; stress events refer to anticipated events requiring large expenditures, such as weddings, payment of school fees, or purchase of a house. Everyone faces the risk of suffering a financial loss or carrying a large financial burden due to a shock or stress event. Not everyone, however, is equally vulnerable. Some individuals—generally the more wealthy—are better able to cope, either because they have savings from which they could draw, assets that they could sell, or insurance coverage that could compensate for their losses. In contrast, others—especially the poor and even some of the nonpoor who live near the poverty line—have a much harder time.

A major reason why the poor and the "vulnerable nonpoor" (those who live near the poverty line and are at high risk of falling below it) struggle more with shocks and stress events than the nonpoor is because they simply have less. They generally lack the financial reserves and a mechanism like insurance that can help to cushion the blow. Their income flows may also be seasonal or erratic, such that they may go for months at a time without earning income, which can further inhibit their ability to manage cash flow during a crisis.

The amount of assets that one has is not the only factor that affects how a shock has an impact on a household. The quality of the assets also matters. When a record-breaking monsoon hit Mumbai in July 2005, it flooded large sections of the city, including some of the more affluent neighborhoods as well as many of the slums that surrounded the airport.[2] Many people suffered property damage, but those who suffered most were the slum dwellers who lost their homes entirely. Overnight, thousands became homeless. In this case everyone—poor and nonpoor—faced the same risk of encountering a shock, but the impact of the shock was far more devastating on the poor because they had poorer quality housing that was easily destroyed in the flood.

Coping Strategies

Low-income households use a variety of strategies to cope with financial burdens that result from shocks and stress events. These strategies can be divided into ex ante (or precautionary) measures taken before a shock or stress event occurs and ex post ones taken afterward. Ex ante measures may seek to mitigate a risk, such as putting bars on a window to reduce the chance of theft, or they may seek to mitigate losses in the event of a shock, such as insurance. Lending to friends and neighbors can also be an ex ante coping mechanism if the money is lent with the expectation that the borrower will reciprocate the favor to the lender in the event that the latter experiences a similar shock in the future. In contrast, ex post strategies try to manage losses after they have already occurred. Borrowing money from friends and relatives and reducing consumption are examples of ex post strategies.

Within each of these categories are both formal and informal mechanisms. Informal mechanisms fall outside the purview of regulated financial systems.

Table 13-1. *Coping Strategies*

Strategy	Ex ante	Ex post
Informal		
Self-insurance	Accumulate savings	Borrow from friends and family, moneylenders, MFIs, or banks
	Purchase assets (for example, gold)	Liquidate assets
	Diversify income sources by starting side business	
	Engage in reciprocal lending	
	Pay for preventive health care	
	Put bars on windows	
Group-based insurance	Join groups like ROSCAs, ASCAs, and other types of welfare associations[a]	Borrow from church groups
		Hold fundraisers
Formal		
Social protection	Preventive public health services (for example, vaccinations)	Public clinics
	Agricultural research	Government handouts such as disability compensation
	Commodity price stabilization	Food aid
Insurance	Purchase insurance from MFIs or formal insurers	. . .

a. ROSCAs, accumulating savings and credit associations; ASCAs, rotating savings and credit associations.

For example, in some parts of India, a popular, informal way for women to "save for a rainy day" (an ex ante strategy) is to buy gold. A formal equivalent of savings in gold is cash deposits in a bank account. Table 13-1 presents some of the more common coping strategies based on these categories. The following subsections describe them in greater detail.

Self-Insurance

Self-insurance refers to measures that do not involve the sharing or pooling of risk in any way. Rather, an individual (or household) simply manages the risk (or the loss) by him- or herself. For example, a household may create small, home-based businesses to supplement income from existing microenterprises or earnings from casual labor and salaried employment. In this way, even if the household loses its primary source of income (due to, say, a bad season resulting in a poor harvest or the breadwinner of a family losing a job), it would still have some means of earning a living. A household may also build assets by investing in housing or purchasing livestock, or it may strengthen its social networks by participating in reciprocal borrowing and lending systems. Even paying for preventive health care may be considered a form of self-insurance: for many who depend on physical labor for work, their health is their most valuable asset, and taking care of it becomes a form of self-insurance.

Self-insuring measures are common among people of all income levels, even though by themselves they offer only limited protection. Borrowing is especially popular. In Tanzania and Uganda, people prefer to borrow when faced with an unexpected need for cash, even if they could draw down their savings, which would be cheaper (Cohen and Sebstad 2005). Similarly, in Bolivia borrowing is a frequently used response to a crisis (Velasco and Granado 2004). In part this preference for borrowing reflects the fact that few people have the capacity to accumulate enough savings for more than one emergency. It also indicates the fact that people tend to earmark their savings for buying assets and are therefore reluctant to use them for other purposes.

Another risk management strategy is the sale of productive assets, such as livestock, household items, and land. Liquidating assets can provide short-term relief to a cash-strapped household. However, once depleted, an asset base is extremely difficult to build up again. As a result, selling assets is generally a measure of last resort that is rarely preferred.

Informal Group-Based Mechanisms

In some parts of the world, low-income households form community-based savings clubs or welfare associations as a way to share risk.[3] Though considered to be "informal" in that they are not part of any regulated financial systems, many have well-defined charters and rules regarding the obligations and rights of members. Savings clubs include so-called rotating savings and credit associations (ROSCAs), whose members make regular contributions to a savings fund. The fund is then given to a different member every week or month, such that everyone in a ROSCA can expect to receive a large lump sum periodically. A group-based mechanism that is similar to ROSCAs is the accumulating savings and credit associations (ASCAs), which also involve members contributing regularly to a central fund, but do not rotate it to different members on a regular schedule. Other welfare associations include groups whose funds are distributed only in cases of emergency. Burial societies, which pool together money for the purpose of paying funeral expenses, are particularly common. In some East African countries, even rich people join these types of welfare associations, in part due to tradition and in part to the high cost of burial ceremonies.[4] In Uganda, the popular *munno mukabi* or "friends in need" system helps to cover the costs of social functions, which can include food for guests and embalming of the body at funerals (Wright and others 1999).

One reason why group-based mechanisms are popular is that they are generally very flexible, allowing members to access funds quickly and easily. In Indonesia a member faced with an emergency can apply to draw his or her turn in a ROSCA early, so long as the individual takes the money at a discount.[5] As for burial societies, many will disburse funds without a death certificate and instead depend on oral verification by family members (Cohen and Sebstad 2005).

Another reason for their popularity is the fact that belonging to such a group strengthens an individual's ties to the community. In India self-help groups—which consist of ten to thirty individuals who come together for some purpose, whether to save, borrow, or simply share experiences and build camaraderie—are nearly ubiquitous. They provide many MFIs and other organizations with an entry point for reaching the poor.

Social Protection

The poor have few formal mechanisms for coping with shocks and stress events. One is social protection: government-backed programs and services that seek to protect the poor from risks. It includes both ex ante and ex post measures. An example of ex ante social protection is India's Integrated Child Development Services scheme, which provides nutrition, health, and early development services to mothers and their young children (World Bank 2001). Such preventive services reduce the levels of risk that households face. An example of an ex post social protection service is food aid provided by the United Nations World Food Program, which helps households to cope with malnutrition and starvation. Because social protection is highly dependent on national budgetary constraints and institutional capacity, the kind and level of protection that it provides vary significantly by country.

In general, government services offer only very limited protection to the poor because they are often inadequate and of inferior quality. In terms of health care in India, for example, even those without the financial means to pay for private care often opt to borrow and pay more rather than use public facilities for free. Public clinics usually have long lines, few or no available doctors on call, and not enough medicine in stock. As a result as much as 80 percent of health costs in the country are paid out of pocket (Peters and others 2002).

Formal Insurance

Formal insurance generally refers to insurance schemes provided by regulated financial institutions. Among the poor, formal insurance is very rare, although in a few countries some of the previously "uncovered" sector now have access to some types of formal insurance through MFIs. The most popular is the credit-life policy, which covers the death of the insured (a borrower) for the life of a loan. A borrower pays a premium (usually a percentage of the loan amount) at the begin-

Table 13-2. *Savings Portfolio of Prudence from Karatina, Kenya*

Savings source	Contribution	Payout
ROSCA 1	Daily, $0.29 (4 members)	$26.60 a month
ROSCA 2	Weekly, $2.90 (4 members)	$11.60 a week
ASCA	Weekly, $1 (40 members)	Can borrow anytime
Informal funeral insurance fund	Monthly, $11.40 (100 members)	Covers funeral costs for immediate family
Cash at home	$3–5	When needed
Savings in livestock	Cow in village	Provision for old age

Source: Wright (2005).

ning of a loan cycle. In the event that he or she dies, the insurance company covers the outstanding balance of the loan and, in some cases, provides the family with a lump sum payment to compensate for funeral costs. Another type of formal insurance that is being offered to the low-income population in some countries is health insurance. In Uganda MicroCare Ltd. offers health insurance to low-income households through its partnership with several MFIs. Its policy allows insured families to use health services at select health care providers. A few MFIs are also looking into ways of providing other types of insurance, such as crop insurance, but these efforts are still in their infancy. Generally speaking, formal insurance remains outside the reach of many of the poor.

Combining Strategies

While some strategies are more popular than others, no single strategy by itself is sufficient. Rather, poor people commonly rely on a combination of self-insurance, informal group-based insurance, and social protection mechanisms (and in some rare cases, formal insurance). Prudence, a woman from Kenya, is a case in point (see table 13-2). Her savings alone took several forms, including informal group-based mechanisms like ROSCAs, a "mattress account" consisting of cash stored at home, and livestock.

Several factors appear to influence the choice of strategies. One is wealth. Because certain strategies cost more than others, some are simply not affordable to the poor. In general, the wealthier one is, the more able one is to take precautionary measures and to manage a crisis, sometimes without the help of others. Putting up bars on shop windows, hiring security guards, paying for preventive health care, or even participating in a ROSCA requires some ability to pay or contribute up front. Some people may also have formal insurance or simply more resources at hand to self-insure such that they can handle small expenses like basic outpatient services, prescription drugs, and transportation to a clinic.

In contrast, poorer households have less access to these types of strategies because they cannot afford them. Perception may also play a role in preventing people from using some strategies. In many countries, formal insurance is viewed as only for the rich. In Kenya, Tanzania, and Uganda, it is seen as affordable by only the top 10 percent of the population (Cohen and Sebstad 2003).

Another factor is gender. Women and men generally face different types of risks, and in many developing countries where men tend to be the breadwinners of households, women-headed households are generally the most vulnerable type of household and have the least access to protective mechanisms, whether formal or informal. Widows are especially vulnerable due to disadvantages in the labor market and, in some countries, inheritance or property rights laws that offer no protection. Lea, a Muslim client of the Youth Self-Employment Foundation in Tanzania, is typical of women-headed households in East Africa (Cohen, McCord, and Sebstad 2003). When Lea's husband was murdered by bandits in 1993, she followed the Muslim tradition of *edda,* which required her to stay in isolation for three months. During this time her brother-in-law sold all of the household's property, including a car and a house that was under construction. He also took all of the household's savings. Even though Lea had used income from her own microenterprise to help build the household's assets before her husband's death, she and her children were left with nothing. Her business did not generate enough income to feed her four children, pay the rent, and cover health bills and school fees (Millinga 2002).

Women also face some health risks that men do not, such as rape or domestic violence and maternal health issues. Women who do not engage in risky sexual behaviors may nonetheless contract HIV/AIDS if their husbands are not faithful (particularly common in areas where men often migrate to cities to find work), especially when they are unable to say no to sex or don't insist on the use of condoms.

Finally, men and women also may not have the same access to various coping mechanisms. Among the informal group-based insurance options, some welfare societies are gender specific, such that female-headed households may be excluded from some groups. They may also be more socially excluded and less able to contribute regularly to a group because they are more likely to be poor. For these women self-insurance may be the only feasible option.

Because women generally have fewer assets, less control over assets, and fewer legal rights or ways to exercise their legal rights to own assets, they often develop complex risk management behaviors that consist of several strategies. For example, women may belong to more than one informal insurance scheme. In addition, they may borrow from one or more MFIs as a strategy to protect themselves against future risks or to have timely access to lump sums of cash when an

Table 13-3. *Payouts Available to Dorothy through Membership in Several Welfare Associations*
Tanzanian shillings

Welfare association	Amount of payout
Victoria (burial society)	90,000
DAMOPWA (burial society)	80,000
CDA (burial society)	100,000
Teachers 1 (health insurance)	35,000
Teachers 2 (health insurance)	80,000
Total	385,000

Source: Millinga (2002).

emergency demands it. The case of Dorothy, a woman in Tanzania, is typical (Millinga 2002). She was a member of five Funeral and Friends in Need societies, which included two health insurance plans to which she belonged as a teacher. Her total monthly premium was TZS 9,500, or roughly U.S.$13.[6] She also made monthly deposits of TZS 4,000 (U.S.$5.40) at one MFI and weekly deposits at another. Explaining why she joined multiple societies, she said, "I come originally from Kagera region, where my parents and relatives live. In case of death of one of them, I need at least TZS 300,000 for travel and other costs. One burial society is not enough." Table 13-3 presents a list of payouts from each of the welfare associations to which she belonged.

Limitations of Current Coping Strategies

While most of the informal and formal coping mechanisms discussed above have been around for many years (or even generations), they have many short-comings. In terms of borrowing and other self-insurance mechanisms, the costs can increase significantly the financial burden on a household, thereby exacerbating the impact of the shock. Loans at low or no interest from family and friends are an option, but the amount of money available from these sources is usually small or even nonexistent. Furthermore, they can come with obligations of reciprocity when the lender is in need. As for selling assets, the seller generally loses money on the sale because she or he is almost always selling in a hurry and at a discount. If the asset is a productive one, such as farming equipment, the seller also forgoes future revenue that the asset could have generated. In essence, selling assets deals a double blow to a household faced with a financial crisis: selling at a loss and losing future income (Szubert 2004).

Informal group-based mechanisms also fall short of meeting the needs of the poor. As the case of Dorothy illustrates, burial societies and welfare associations generally have very limited coverage. Funds available from a single group may not even cover the cost of transportation for the body of the deceased to return to its home village, which these days can be quite high due to an increasing number of workers migrating significant distances from rural to urban areas. Shortfalls in cash reserves often result when contributions by members are erratic, and sequential shocks can deplete reserves. Consequently, households are under pressure to belong to multiple associations as a way to guarantee access to funds. In doing so, a household can have one membership to cover the funeral costs, a second one to provide food for the children, and a third one to pay for other necessary expenses that are not tied directly to the funeral, such as food and school fees (Bester and others 2004). Because each membership incurs transaction costs in the form of time, fees, and in-kind contributions, relying on informal group-based mechanisms can be a very costly strategy for coping with risks and shocks.

Even some of the better-off who generally have more access to different kinds of mechanisms are beginning to feel greater financial pressure. Elimination of drug subsidies and imposition of user fees for health services in some countries are eroding the affordability of basic health care. Repeated stresses from chronic diseases like HIV/AIDS and diabetes or having multiple members of a household fall sick at the same time can be financially overwhelming.

Finally, the strategies themselves can often compound the impact of a shock or stress event (see figure 13-1). The case of Eumeri, a member of a microfinance institution in Uganda, illustrates this compounding effect.[7] She and three generations of her family (she, her husband, their children, and grandchildren) lived together and were relatively well-off until her husband, a lawyer, suffered a stroke. With the chief breadwinner of the household unable to work, Eumeri started a baking business with a loan from the MFI. When that failed, she borrowed more money to open a food stall inside the canteen of a school. To make ends meet, she withdrew her children from university and school and relied on small contributions from friends and family. She also withdrew her savings—and with it, her membership—from a savings club to which she belonged in order to pay off her first loan. Two years after her husband's stroke, she was still struggling to get back on her feet: she was in debt, some of her children were no longer in school, and she could not borrow from her savings club anymore.

Because the coping strategies that poor households use often lead to secondary expenses (such as paying off debt) or further losses of income (due to the depletion of productive assets), they lose the ability to take control of their situ-

Figure 13-1. *Compounding Effects of Common Coping Strategies*

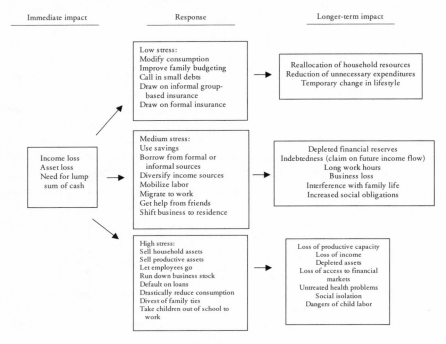

Source: Cohen and Sebstad (2005).

ation. Instead, they are forced into an increasingly reactive mode, responding to crisis after crisis and using increasingly stressful coping mechanisms. Such strategies inhibit a household's ability to recover in the short and long run. As a result the downward spiral toward even greater poverty continues.

In the end the effectiveness of any single coping strategy depends largely on the size, nature, and frequency of the loss in relation to the income level and resource endowment of the household. The relationship between assets and risk management is complex. The occurrence of shocks and stress events can deplete reserves that took years to accumulate and push a person back into poverty. The next section looks at microinsurance and how this new area within microfinance shows promise of reducing the vulnerability of the poor and increasing their chances of moving out of poverty traps.

Reducing Vulnerability with Microinsurance

Microinsurance provides financial protection to the poor for certain risks in a way that reflects their cash constraints and coverage requirements. It is a risk management system in which individuals, businesses, or other organizations pay a certain sum of money (a premium) in exchange for guaranteed compensation for losses resulting from certain shocks and stress events. No one size fits all, and many of the products incorporate innovative features designed specifically for their target population. For example, in Bangladesh the insurance company Delta Life found that its client group was less homogeneous than expected and not everyone could pay weekly premiums. In response, Delta Life responded by offering a range of premium payment options (McCord and Churchill 2005). In East Africa some health microinsurance schemes have special arrangements with rural hospitals and clinics that allow for direct payment of service, without requiring patients to file claims, and a few are experimenting with biometrics for identification and payment purposes. Such attempts at tailoring the product to the needs of the poor make microinsurance more than just a downscaled version of conventional insurance; rather, it represents an uncharted frontier within the fields of microfinance and insurance.

A handful of MFIs are now testing microinsurance products covering loans, life, and health in different countries. Some are also offering property insurance in combination with credit-life insurance. These products reflect the priority of risks according to the poor: the loss of a household income earner, sickness of a family member, and theft and fire (see table 13-4).

The demand for microinsurance varies depending on a person's position in her or his life cycle. For MFIs whose clientele consists of large numbers of older women and women with older husbands, life insurance can take on tremendous importance. Originally, Vimo SEWA—the insurance arm of SEWA Bank, a women's bank in Ahmedabad, India—offered a life insurance policy covering only its female members and not their husbands because SEWA Bank management did not believe a broad life insurance policy covering both spouses was affordable. The bank's management met with such opposition, however, that it ultimately relented and created a life insurance product that covers both husband and wife. The vocal demand from SEWA members shows how these women understood the need for insurance in case their husbands pass away.[8]

So far, microinsurance has met with varying degrees of success. Evidence from some health insurance schemes provides valuable insights into how insurance can change behaviors. Exploratory interviews in Uganda indicated that as a result of accessing health insurance, policyholders are more likely to go to a

Table 13-4. *Priority of Risks in Selected Countries*

Country	Risks in order of priority
Uganda	Health, death, disability, property loss, risk of loan
Malawi	Fear of early death
Philippines	Death, old age, ill health
Vietnam	Illness, natural disaster, accidents, illness or death of livestock
Georgia	Health, business losses, theft, death of family member, income continuation or pensions
Bolivia	Illness, death, property loss including crop loss in rural areas

Source: Cohen and Sebstad (2005).

physician and follow a course of treatment than to wait and attempt to treat the symptoms themselves or just take no action. In addition, policyholders observed that access to health insurance lessened asset depletion and lowered their level of business losses as a result of sickness (Young 2006).

Credit-life policies that cover outstanding microfinance loan balances of deceased clients have been among the most successful types of microinsurance in terms of profitability. Customers' understanding of these policies varies, however. Many policyholders are not aware of the fees they must pay to have this insurance (since the fees are tacked onto loan repayments), and many do not even know that they have insurance. Because very few clients actually die during the life of a loan, savvier borrowers question the value of a product that appears to protect the MFI more than the clients, especially since clients have no coverage when they are not borrowing. Some members are aware of the risks that they face, but they nonetheless have negative views of insurance because their claims were never honored (Sebageni 2003). There are also gaps in coverage: some MFIs set age ceilings on borrowers, and those most likely to die usually do not qualify. The result is mixed reception for formal insurance schemes among low-income households.

Financial Education to Link Client and Product

With growing numbers of financial service providers and new products and services in the microfinance field, low-income people in many countries now have more choices for financial services than ever before. However, having greater access does not always translate into actual use. This is especially true of microinsurance. Many of the poor have misconceptions about it. The insurance company COLUMNA in Guatemala, which offers life and other insurance products through a partnership with cooperatives, learned that the main reason for nonrenewal of policies among its clients is a lack of understanding (Herrera and Miranda 2004). Similarly, in Uganda people who understand health insurance are much more willing to buy it while those who don't understand it generally do not buy it. Some think insurance is only for the rich. Others think having insurance will bring bad luck.[9] Such negative perceptions of insurance contribute to the high dropout rates of many microinsurance schemes (Enarsson, Wirén, and Almeyda 2006).

The relatively low rates of adoption and usage suggest that many people stick to their current coping strategies, whether formal or informal, even when a better or more appropriate service is available. Those who have access to formal insurance rarely give up using self-insurance or informal group-based mechanisms. They simply restructure and add to their mix of strategies for risk management.

Such behaviors are more than just a risk diversification strategy; they also appear to reflect people's lack of understanding about microinsurance. The new microinsurance products incorporate a range of features, benefits, costs, and obligations that are not familiar to most people. Many of them are reluctant to pay in advance for services they may not receive. Those who have had bad experiences in the past with insurance—be it through government-backed insurance programs from long ago or microinsurance—tend to avoid it.

To truly benefit from the expanded range of risk management options, the poor need to be able to effectively compare product features and make informed decisions about which products would best serve their needs. Just because clients have successfully used formal financial services before does not mean they will use new products, especially ones like microinsurance that are more complicated. Promotional materials may help to explain some of the features of a policy, but their utility is limited if clients lack the literacy level, skills, or knowledge to understand them. Designing the right product is essential, but it is not enough.

Financial education offers a way to address this gap in consumer knowledge. Financial education is teaching the knowledge, skills, and attitudes required to adopt good money-management practices for earning, spending, saving, borrowing, and investing. Participants who receive financial education acquire the information and tools to make better financial choices and work toward their financial goals. The goal of financial education is more than just transferring the know-how; it is about changing behaviors.

Financial education can be a useful tool in promoting the adoption of microinsurance because it links the product to the policyholder. Low-income households that receive financial education are better able to understand the risk-pooling concepts as they apply to life and health insurance. Such education would also help overcome the low level of trust among potential policyholders.

Financial education on insurance helps both consumer and provider. On the consumer side, it allows prospective policyholders to assess the financial marketplace and overcome common current financial behaviors such as reactive response to shocks, lack of planning for expected life events, limited saving for emergencies or large expected expenditures, and lack of skills to plan cash flow (Cohen and others 2006). It also helps them to plan for the future. One misunderstanding among current microinsurance clients concerns beneficiaries. Women who are clients of MFIs may not understand the term "beneficiary" and end up naming people as beneficiaries who may not be able or willing to take care of their families. Taking the time to explain the concept can help prevent such unwanted occurrences. On the provider side, insurers and MFIs would benefit from having informed consumers who are more likely to stay with the product (and the institution), thereby improving the financial viability of the financial service provider.

Because financial education focuses on the clients' understanding and use of different financial products, it also has a significant impact on asset protection and accumulation. It helps prospective clients to target the assets that they need to protect through formal microinsurance and those that need to be protected through savings or other methods. It can also help clients to mobilize more effectively the assets that they are protecting.

Microinsurance provides a vehicle for asset protection, mobilization, and accumulation. In general, people who have received payouts from an insurance policy—and hence have some understanding of its benefits —are satisfied with the product, in part because it covered costs such as funeral expenses and in part because the payout allowed them to purchase assets that they otherwise would not have.

Conclusion

Risk and vulnerability are an everyday reality for the poor. Over time, they have developed strategies for managing both expected and unexpected risks by combining current income, savings, credit, informal insurance mechanisms, and the accumulation of assets to meet the financial challenges of risks. Current risk management strategies being used by the poor do not adequately protect them against repeated risk events, however. When economic shocks begin to add up, the risk management strategies of the poor often fail because they do not have enough assets to sustain large or repeated shocks. Formal insurance mechanisms in the form of microinsurance can fill this gap. Microinsurance not only protects the assets of the poor from economic shocks, it also allows the poor to mobilize those assets and increase their income because they are not required to save as much for a rainy day.

Clients who understand how microinsurance works and how they should use microinsurance are more able to take advantage of opportunities as they present themselves. Financial education can bridge the gap between microinsurance implementation and program adoption on the part of microinsurance clients. It can change clients' attitudes and behaviors toward microinsurance, ensuring uptake and persistence.

Poor people know how to build and use assets and increase their incomes. Persistent shocks can easily erode hard-won gains, making it difficult to hold on to them. The result is that assets are prevented from becoming a base for the creation of new wealth. Financial education provides a link between financial services and clients, enabling them not only to use microinsurance well but also to manage money more effectively. Because simply designing the right product is seldom enough to lure customers, financial education may prove to be a crucial piece of the puzzle.

Notes

1. Pamela Young, field notes from Uganda, June 2006.

2. See "Heavy Rains Paralyse Mumbai," July 26, 2005 (in.rediff.com/news/2005/jul/26mumbai.htm [December 2006]).

3. Informal group-based mechanisms have not been observed extensively in the transition countries of Eastern Europe and the Newly Independent States. Exceptions include Romania and Uzbekistan, where this is a middle-class phenomenon. Personal communication from Michal Matul, Microfinance Centre, Warsaw, 2006.

4. For more information on burial societies and other types of welfare associations, see Rutherford (2000).

5. See Michael McCord, Gaby Ramm, and Elizabeth McGuinness, "Microinsurance: Demand and Market Prospects—Indonesia" (www.microfinanceopportunities.org/pubs MI.html [December 2006]).

6. The U.S. dollar equivalent is calculated using the 2002 exchange rate of roughly TZS 740 to U.S.$1.

7. Monique Cohen, personal field notes from Uganda, 1999.

8. Monique Cohen, field notes from Ahmedabad, India, 1999.

9. McCord, Ramm, and McGuinness, "Microinsurance: Demand and Market Prospects—Indonesia."

References

Bester, Hennie, and others. 2004. "Making Insurance Markets Work for the Poor in South Africa—Scoping Study." Final report. Johannesburg: Genesis Analytics.

Cohen, Monique, Michael McCord, and Jennefer Sebstad. 2003. "Reducing Vulnerability: Demand for and Supply of Microinsurance in East Africa." Nairobi: MicroSave (December).

Cohen, Monique, and Jennefer Sebstad. 2005. "Reducing Vulnerability: The Demand for Microinsurance." *Journal for International Development* 17, no. 3: 397–474.

Enarsson, Sven, Kjell Wirén, and Gloria Almeyda. 2006. "Savings- and Credit-Linked Insurance." In *Protecting the Poor: A Microinsurance Compendium*, edited by Craig Churchill. Geneva: International Labour Organization.

Herrera, Carlos, and Bernardo Miranda. 2004. "COLUMNA Guatemala." Working Group on Microinsurance, Good and Bad Practices, Case Study 5. Washington: Consultative Group to Assist the Poor (CGAP).

McCord, Michael, and Craig Churchill. 2005. "Delta Life Bangladesh." Working Group on Microinsurance, Good and Bad Practices, Case Study 7. Washington: CGAP.

McCord, Michael, and Sylvia Osinde. 2003. "Reducing Vulnerability: The Supply of Health Microinsurance in East Africa—A Synthesis Report." Nairobi: MicroSave (July).

Millinga, Altemius. 2002. "Assessing the Demand for Microinsurance in Tanzania." Nairobi: MicroSave.

Peters, David, and others. 2002. *Better Health Systems for India's Poor: Findings, Analysis and Options.* Washington: World Bank.

Rutherford, Stuart. 2000. *The Poor and Their Money.* New Delhi: Oxford University Press.

Sebageni, Grace. 2003. "Assessing the Demand for Microinsurance in Uganda." Nairobi: MicroSave.

Szubert, Dorota. 2004. "Understanding the Demand for Microinsurance in Albania: Results of Exploratory Qualitative Study." Mimeo. Warsaw: Microfinance Centre for Central and Eastern Europe and the Newly Independent States.

Tran, Nhu-An, and Tan See Yun. 2004. "TYM's Mutual Assistance Fund Vietnam." Working Group on Microinsurance, Good and Bad Practices, Case Study 3. Washington: CGAP.

Velasco, Carmen, and Andrea del Granado. 2004. "Resultados del market research para la programa financiera." Bolivia: Pro Mujer (June).

World Bank. 2001. *India: Improving Household Food and Nutrition Security,* vol.1. Washington: World Bank.

Wright, Graham. 2005. "Understanding and Assessing the Demand for Microfinance." Paper presented at the conference on Expanding Access to Microfinance: Challenges and Actors (www.microsave.org). Paris, June 20.

Wright, Graham, Deborah Kasente, Germina Ssemogerere, and Leonard Mutesasira. 1999. "Vulnerability, Risks, and Assets, and Empowerment—The Impact of Microfinance on Poverty Alleviation." MicroSave Africa. September.

Young, Pamela. 2006. "Microinsurance: Exploring Ways to Assess Its Impact." Working Paper. Washington: Microfinance Opportunities (June).

14

Migrant Foreign Savings and Asset Accumulation

MANUEL OROZCO

This chapter explores the relationship between migrant foreign savings and financial asset accumulation.[1] Primarily, it distinguishes between different types of transnational economic activities that migrants engage in and demonstrates that not all of them are equally conducive to asset accumulation. Moreover, remittances in particular offer the dual function of livelihood survival and asset building, depending on the communities and families sending and receiving money. Empirical data demonstrate that savings and investments—and consequently, asset accumulation—are only rarely possible, and few people devote resources to them. In the cases where these assets are present, however, they are strongly related to inflows of remittances, as well as to additional factors such as income or the constancy of the remittance flow.

This chapter also analyzes the factors that make asset accumulation possible in cases where it is the result of remittances. For example, the ability of the local economy to absorb migrant savings determines the extent to which the kind of financial mobilization that can enable asset accumulation and wealth generation is present. Furthermore, there are a number of important development initiatives that leverage migrant savings for asset accumulation and development. This chapter offers policy recommendations for improving these and future development interventions.

Understanding Development and Asset Accumulation

More than three quarters of the world's population are reported to be poor; they are unable to address their basic needs and live under perpetually precarious and marginal conditions. It is therefore no surprise that the promotion of economic and social (or human) development has become an increasingly poignant topic, not only for the development community but for the general public as well. Although the imperative for action is clear, it is nonetheless crucial to define the term "development" before determining how best to pursue it. Some experts and analysts find it problematic or even irrelevant to define development or developing nations (Ray 1998, p. 3), but this author nonetheless finds it useful to do so.

Development is generally associated with a condition that ensures a better standard of living for people. The United Nations Development Program (UNDP) takes a rather normative view of the subject, stating that development "is about creating an environment in which people can develop their full potential and lead productive, creative lives in accord with their needs and interests. People are the real wealth of nations. Development is thus about expanding the choices people have to lead lives that they value" (UNDP 2006).

Development is often strongly associated with education, health, and material asset accumulation. In fact, the UNDP's measurement of the human development index considers these three particular factors: a long and healthy life, as measured by life expectancy at birth; education, as measured by the adult literacy rate (with two-thirds weight) and the combined primary, secondary, and tertiary gross enrollment ratio (with one-third weight); and a decent standard of living, as measured by GDP per capita (UNDP 2005, p. 341). Economic development can be defined as a condition by which individuals and society at large enjoy a healthy quality of life, are free, have opportunities for upward mobility, and are able to improve their material circumstances.

This chapter focuses on the steps the poor take in order to improve their own circumstances, specifically by accumulating assets. Caroline Moser's analysis of asset accumulation as a differentiated practice from livelihood strategies and social protection is an important consideration when thinking about the ways in which "a stock of financial, human, natural or social resources can be acquired, developed, improved and transferred across generations" (Ford Foundation 2004, as cited by Moser 2006) enables people to have a better quality of life. An asset-based approach in turn provides clues about people's capabilities to strengthen or expand their resources (Moser 2006).

Finance and access to financial resources are cornerstone components of material asset accumulation. Together they provide the means to strengthen or enhance a person's and society's material base by mobilizing existent assets in order to generate new resources and wealth, including education, health, real estate, and business. As in other contexts, finance provides opportunities to build wealth. An adequate stock of capital therefore ensures the positive capital output ratio necessary to generate additional wealth. Research has shown that lower cash-to-deposit ratios and higher deposit-to-GDP ratios are linked to higher per capita GDP levels (Peachy and Roe 2006, p. 14). In addition, such resources are more efficient when made available for credit and investment in local economies, and are efficiently distributed when such credit is made universally accessible and affordable to anyone seeking to expand his or her capacities.

Migrant Foreign Savings and Asset Accumulation

In today's globalized economies, the resources or stocks that migrants raise in their efforts to support their families constitute a large portion of their families' financial assets. Migrant foreign savings, the stock of predominantly economic and financial resources, then become an important economic base for remittances to recipient households that may constitute the foundation for asset accumulation and poverty reduction.

However, to understand the relationship between migrant foreign savings and asset accumulation, it is first important to distinguish between the various types of transnational economic activities that migrants engage in. Trends in international migration over the past thirty years have shown that migrants have become substantively and more directly involved in different economic and social activities in their countries of origin. This is due in part to the dynamics of globalization and to new opportunities resulting from political and economic opening in their home societies. One of the most important outcomes of globalization and migration has been the formation of transnational families and communities, which can be characterized as groups or families that maintain relations and connections that encompass both the home and host societies.[2]

In practical terms, a typical immigrant's economic linkage with his or her home country extends to at least four practices that involve spending or investment: family remittance transfers; demand for services such as telecommunication, consumer goods, or travel; capital investment; and charitable donations to philanthropic organizations raising funds for the migrant's home community.

Remittances are the most widespread and important migrant economic activity. While the determinants of sending do not vary between nationalities, the frequencies and quantities of money sent fluctuate across groups. For example, Latinos and Filipinos in the United States send an average of U.S.$300 a month, whereas Southeast Asians in Japan send U.S.$671, Filipinos in Japan send U.S.$600, and Ghanaians in Europe send U.S.$400 every six weeks (Orozco and Fedewa 2005; Orozco 2005a).

Migrants also maintain links with their home countries by staying in touch, calling and visiting their homeland. They purchase and consume foodstuffs from their home country such as tortillas, beef jerky, cheese, rum, and coffee, and spend money on phone cards to call their families. Eighty percent of Latinos buy phone cards and speak to their relatives by phone for an average of two hours a month (Orozco, 2005b).

Finally, migrants establish economic linkages with their home countries by donating and investing. In the case of donations, migrants raise funds to help their hometown through organized civil society groups. Belonging to a hometown association (HTA) is an important migrant activity that can provide substantial economic resources for the communities of origin. These donations may amount to U.S.$100 to $200 a year per individual, and in some countries, like Mexico, donations on aggregate may translate to more than U.S.$50 million. Migrants often also invest in property and small businesses, devoting on average between U.S.$5,000 and $10,000 annually.

Although these are predominantly concrete, financially driven activities, they also represent a source of social capital and strongly express migrants' transnational identity through symbolic and material commitments to the homeland. The implications of these activities have raised interest in and questions about their effect on development and the ways in which these interactions can be leveraged to further promote development.

These practices generate significant revenue and benefits for many. For example, Salvadoran and Ghanaian communities have been established for more than thirty years in the United States and have maintained their associations with their homeland to varying degrees. Tables 14-1 and 14-2 show estimates of the number of transnational activities that keep migrants connected with their home country. The plurality of money spent is on remittances, which earn the intermediary companies revenues of 10 percent. Nevertheless, other activities such as phone calls also have substantial impacts on the two economies.

Transnational financial practices are not fungible between different diaspora communities but rather reflect specific needs and priorities among migrants and together do not necessarily represent assets in themselves. In other words, the

Table 14-1. *Transnational Financial Activities of Salvadoran Migrants in the United States, 2005*[a]

Units as indicated

Activity	Percent	Number	Amount (U.S.$) Annual cost or expense	Volume
Call on average 120 minutes	41	340,300	288	98,006,400
Send over $300	32	265,600	4,200	1,115,520,000
Buy home-country goods	66	547,800	200	109,560,000
Travel once a year	24	199,200	700	139,440,000
And spend over U.S.$1,000	61	506,300	1,000	506,300,000
Have a mortgage loan	13	107,900	7,000	755,300,000
Own a small business	3	24,900	7,500	186,750,000
Help family with mortgage	13	107,900	2,000	215,800,000
Belong to an HTA	5	41,500	200	1,500,000

Source: Orozco and others (2005b).
a. Based on a total of 830,000 Salvadorans remitting from the United States.

Table 14-2. *Transnational Financial Activities of Ghanaian Migrants in the United States, 2005*[a]

Units as indicated

Activity	Percent	Number	Amount (U.S.$) Annual cost or expense	Volume
Call on average 80 minutes	50	100,000	432	43,200,000
Send over $300	60	120,000	4,800	576,000,000
Buy home-country goods	80	160,000	200	32,000,000
Travel once a year	50	100,000	1,200	120,000,000
And spend over U.S.$1,000	80	160,000	1,000	160,000,000
Have a mortgage loan	20	40,000	7,500	300,000,000
Belong to an HTA	20	40,000	200	8,000,000

Source: Orozco and others (2005a).
a. Based on a total of 200,000 Ghanaians remitting from the United States.

various transnational financial activities are not equally conducive to asset accumulation. The consumption of goods and services (such as phone calls), for example, is rather attributed to daily livelihood realities.

Remittances, on the other hand, are both a combination of social protection and stock accumulation. Studies show that, depending on the groups and families, migrants may see a portion of their remittance as an asset in itself because

Table 14-3. *Asset-Building Practices among Senders and Recipients from Twelve Latin American Countries, 2004*[a]

Percent

Asset-building activity	Sender	Recipient
Have a bank account	27	50
Have a mortgage loan	10	10
Operate a small business	3	17
Have a small business loan	1	4
Have a student loan	1	3
Pay for insurance policies	2	6
Lend money to family to invest	2	2
Do not have financial obligations	n.a.	32

Source: Orozco and others (2005b).

a. Senders and recipients from the following twelve countries: Bolivia, Colombia, Cuba, Dominican Republic, Ecuador, El Salvador, Guatemala, Guyana, Honduras, Jamaica, Mexico, and Nicaragua.

Table 14-4. *Proportion of Senders and Recipients Helping with Other Economic Obligations, 2004*[a]

Percent

Obligation	Sender	Recipient
Pay mortgage loan	12	28
Pay loans to take care of a small business	2	27
Pay for a student loan	2	8
Help pay for health insurance	2	16
Other financial obligations	22	26

Source: Orozco and others (2005b).

a. Senders and recipients from the following twelve countries: Bolivia, Colombia, Cuba, Dominican Republic, Ecuador, El Salvador, Guatemala, Guyana, Honduras, Jamaica, Mexico, and Nicaragua.

they then use it to invest in their families' material circumstances to transform their lives (Pozo and Amuedo-Dorantes 2006). Remittances sent to address educational needs, for example, create a basis for asset building.

Like remittances, investment in business and real estate and migrant donations to local communities represent unambiguously concrete forms of asset accumulation at the individual and community levels. Between 10 and 20 percent of migrants invest in their home country, and nearly 30 percent build savings at home (Orozco 2005b). Tables 14-3 and 14-4 show the kind of asset-building practices that were found among migrants from twelve different Latin American countries.

This analysis is based on surveys of 3,000 remittance senders that were used to ascertain the determinants of remittance sending as well as the factors affecting financial asset-building activities. Statistical analysis showed that females remit about 9 percent less money than do males, that the amount of funds remitted increases by about 5 percent for each year of age, and that the longer an individual has lived in the United States, the less they remit. Also, senders giving to a spouse are 2.4 times more likely than those not sending to a spouse to give money to pay off loans (Orozco 2005b). The longer a person has been remitting, the more money they tend to remit. Eventually, however, as the duration of remitting increases, the likelihood that monies will be sent to pay off loans decreases.

Ownership of a savings account in the home country is the single most important factor in determining whether money is sent to pay off preexisting loans. When an immigrant has a bank account, the amount remitted increases by an average of 9 percent. If that account is in the home country, the migrant will remit nearly 25 percent more dollars. This may reflect the fact that savings are often part of small investment ventures migrants keep in the home country. Indeed, senders with savings accounts in the home country are 3.3 times more likely to send money to support a business abroad than those without savings accounts (Orozco 2005b). Aside from being indicative of remittance likelihood, monies sent to help pay off a loan abroad behave similarly to standard remittances.

These results suggest that migrants to the United States that have formal financial commitments—in the form of savings accounts or loans—are more likely to send money. In these two cases, the monies are targeted for what can only be considered investment purposes in the home country, for example, running a business or paying off loans. Once again, this suggests that financial diversification is associated with making productive monetary contributions back to the country of origin.

Limits of Migrant Asset Accumulation

The findings presented above point to two important factors associated with migrants. First, investment of resources for asset building is limited only to a small proportion of migrants due to the prevalence of low income and education levels. There is no single, homogeneous migrant group, and these diverse groups have varying degrees of access to the resources that facilitate asset accumulation. In the case of Latinos in the United States, three broad groups can be identified that in turn are distributed by country of origin. Important factors distinguishing these groups are bank account ownership and legal status. The

Table 14-5. *Distribution of Migrants with and without Bank Accounts, by Legal Status, United States, 2004*

Percent

	Legal status		
Banking status	Documented	Undocumented	Total
Has bank account	26[a]	13[b]	39
No bank account	22[b]	39[c]	61

Source: Vasconcelos (2004).
a. Average annual income greater than $30,000.
b. Average annual income less than or equal to $30,000.
c. Average annual income less than or equal to $20,000.

three groups are undocumented individuals, some of whom may have a bank account but who overall live on less than U.S.$25,000 a year; people with legal status and no bank account; and people with legal status and bank accounts whose annual income is above U.S.$30,000. (See table 14-5.)

Second, when such low levels of investment occur, they reflect rational financial calculations about the future and an effort to build assets associated with remitting and finances. The productivity of the local economy will determine the leveraging impact of remittances and therefore factors directly into these calculations. Low levels of investment—either through remittances or other methods of international finance—often reflect an unprofitable productive base in the home economy. The social and productive base of an economy significantly defines the ways in which remittances will effectively function in that economy. In other words, if migrants understand that the situation in their community of origin is such that their remittances will have little impact, they will naturally be less likely to remit.

The extent to which economic and social structures in the home country absorb migrant savings is the first issue development practitioners should investigate. It is important to analyze the productive forces in the economy of destination for remittances, including efficiency, diversification and concentration of production within the various sectors, prevalence of entrepreneurship, technological development, and the extent to which government policies are conducive to investment and production. Such analysis will highlight the importance of creating development strategies that link the local economies with diaspora or migrant foreign savings.

A recent comparative study of four semirural communities in Latin America showed that the local economies were unable to fully absorb the remittance funds that they were receiving; clearly there was a need for strategies and policies

Table 14-6. *Economic Profile of Four Latin American Cities, 2006*
Units as indicated

Factor	Jerez, Zacatecas, Mexico	Salcaja, Quetzaltenango, Guatemala	Suchitoto, El Salvador	Catamayo, Loja, Ecuador
Basic profile				
Population	37,558	14,829	17,869	27,000
Labor force (percent)	41	37	34	31
Population under 20 years of age (percent)	34.7[a]	36.81[b]	34[c]	30[b]
Main economic activities (percent)				
Commerce and services	35	42	15.5	39
Agriculture	19	4[d]	52.2	20[e]
Manufacturing	13	6	7.6	8
Construction	11	n.a.	n.a.	n.a.
Proximity to major urban center (km)	45 (to Zacatecas)	9 (to Quetzaltenango)	45 (to San Salvador)	45 (to Loja)
Cost of living (U.S.$)				
Food	219	228	209	201
Services (utilities)	60	44	40	43
Education	13	32	29	56
Health	40	41	34	68
Entertainment	27	3	40	35
Income				
Wages	323	303	125	162
Monthly remittances amount received	637	331	515	181
Total earnings, remittances included	960	634	640	343

Source: Orozco (2006).
a. Ages <1–14.
b. Ages 5–19.
c. Ages 7–18.
d. Excludes subsistence farming.
e. Estimate.

such as those outlined above (Orozco 2006). (See table 14-6.) The study also exposed the relative fragilities of the local economies, which suffered from high costs of living that made it difficult for remittance recipients to save and mobilize their savings.

In each community examined as part of this study, the entrepreneurial class was ill suited to meet the economic demands of remittance recipients, and modes of operation were relatively primitive. Moreover, governments and civil society did not provide recipient families with adequate support networks to help them cope with the impacts of out-migration. As a result nearly one-third of recipients reported that they were considering leaving their communities in the near future and migrating abroad. With few exceptions, financial institutions, which are critical to asset accumulation, were not addressing the demand by supplying financial products to remittance senders and recipients.

If an economy is unable to supply the necessary financial infrastructure, the labor force will shrink and eventually a portion will migrate in order to provide for their families. Yet when these migrants send money home, their beneficiaries may be limited in how effectively they can use these funds unless the local economy provides an effective supply for the demand for services and products. This indicates that the need for significant policy change among development practitioners is more urgent than previously perceived.

Policies on Transnational Migrant Asset Accumulation

Leveraging policies that encourage asset accumulation among migrants and their families requires creativity. Moser (2006) argues that asset accumulation policy should focus on "creating opportunities for the poor to accumulate and consolidate their assets in a sustainable way." These policies should address issues relating to institutions, opportunities, and strategies. Moreover, Moser stresses the consideration of two sets of policies, first and second generation. First-generation policy focuses on laying out a social and economic infrastructure, while second-generation policy attempts to "strengthen accumulated assets, to ensure their further consolidation and to prevent erosion."

Within the context of transnational migration, and specifically among remittance senders and recipients, first-generation policies should center on ways to accelerate the process of educational attainment by increasing the average amount of schooling and improving student academic performance. This means that educational services must respond to the purchasing power of remittance senders and recipients by offering better-quality education. First-generation policies should also concentrate on increasing the percentage of migrants and families that have access to financial institutions.

Second-generation policies should focus on designing financial products that build assets for individuals, families, and communities. While a country's resources are critical for economic growth, it is even more imperative that they are used effectively. Resources must be made available in the form of credit that can then be tapped for investment. The challenge for policymakers is to ensure that such credit is sufficiently accessible and is in fact being used. According to Beck and Torre (2006), there are three possible problems with credit access that countries might face: first, potential borrowers (for noneconomic reasons) cannot or do not tap into credit; second, creditors are not fully exploiting their outreach capabilities and hence are inefficient; and third, creditors are operating at an unsustainable level when granting excess credit. They further suggest that both government and financial institutions have a role to play in addressing these three challenges, separately and collaboratively (Beck and Torre 2006, p. 48).

Access to microfinance and banking institutions is critical for development. Savings and credit must go hand in hand to first stabilize vulnerable households and then provide them with opportunities for upward mobility. This can be inhibited by factors such as financial illiteracy, sparse coverage of institutions in rural areas, high costs for formal banking services, or institutions' unwillingness to work with low-income or rural customers. The World Savings Banks Institute recommends that approaches to improving access both strengthen nonbank alternatives for those without access and increase the role of savings banks in improving access for those who have been neglected by the formal banking system (Peachy and Roe 2006, p. 83).

Development policy is critically important to promoting asset accumulation by leveraging remittance funds and migrant capital investment. Financial intermediation projects run by credit unions and microfinance institutions often make the investing climate in the home country much more hospitable for incoming remittances. It is also important for policymakers—both internationally and within the home country—to engage banking institutions more actively by identifying their opportunity costs in rural areas. These funds then can be used to support projects based on their feasibility as well as to provide advice on business consolidation where microenterprise is ineffective or inefficient. These projects should develop education and health services in cooperation with schools, public or private. Essential to the success of such educational projects are clearly defined goals and standards among community leaders, financial institutions, and local governments to raise educational attainment from sixth to twelfth grade levels.

The local economies and governments in the countries where emigration occurs are constrained by unwillingness to leverage foreign savings, uncertainty as to how to proceed, and by struggling economies that are barely growing, thus limiting the options for asset building or accumulation. Given the reality of continued transnational migration, the demand for and supply of foreign labor, and the increasing interest among donors in leveraging these flows, it is critically important to manage migration through guest worker programs and legalization of undocumented workers. A guest worker program based on country quota allocations is one such possibility. This kind of initiative should include two important components linked by a conditionality framework. First, the guest worker program should be accompanied by a foreign assistance package aimed at supporting a local financial and economic base that will encourage immigrants to eventually return. Second, local governments should commit to adopting policies aimed at leveraging remittance flows while strengthening their ties to diaspora populations. In turn, quotas should be conditioned on the economic performance of these countries, including their ability to adopt leveraging policies.

One of the pioneering institutions addressing the link between remittances and development has been the Multilateral Investment Fund (MIF) of the Inter-American Development Bank. The MIF has addressed this issue from a research, advocacy, and operational perspective. Since 1999 it has engaged in a series of discussions and studies on the impact of remittances in Latin America and the policy problems posed by high transaction costs. The MIF encouraged movement on this front by taking the initiative to fund projects aimed at modernizing a financial infrastructure that could attract money transfers at a lower cost while addressing the financial needs of unbanked remittance-receiving households.

To that effect, the MIF has funded over $70 million in projects in several countries in Latin America (Brazil, Colombia, Dominican Republic, Ecuador, El Salvador, Mexico, and Nicaragua), many of which go to microfinance institutions or alternative savings and credit institutions. The MIF has also partnered with other donors and institutions. For example, it now has an alliance with the United Nations International Fund for Agricultural Development. In April 2004 the two organizations announced the creation of a $7.6 million program to fund remittance-related projects that addressed microfinance and investment. Under this agreement, to which MIF provided $4 million, local counterpart organizations such as microfinance institutions and credit unions are expected to commit $1.6 million to the projects that they propose.[3]

Conclusion

Transnational financial interactions are multifaceted, and due to a variety of factors, certain migrants are able to successfully engage in such transactions and others are not. Family remittances—as well as the transfer of goods and services, capital investment, and participation in hometown associations—are financial activities not pursued to the same degree among different groups of remitters. Furthermore the ability of these activities to promote asset accumulation is frequently determined by the financial infrastructure in the country of origin. It is therefore clear that one size does not fit all, and aid organizations must pursue tailored strategies based on the state of the financial infrastructure in the home community and the makeup of the remitting group.

Any analysis and recommendation about leveraging migrant foreign savings as sources for asset accumulation cannot ignore the broader context of migration. Specifically, migration from Latin America to the United States is a product of a market for foreign labor and inefficient government migration management. Consequently, foreign laborers work under precarious conditions, living on low wages and struggling to turn their resources into assets.

By carrying out successful development interventions, organizations such as the Inter-American Development Bank have demonstrated that this bleak scenario need not be the fate of all migrants and those dependent on them. By encouraging the migration of targeted groups likely to pursue financial interaction in a manner that promotes asset accumulation, while simultaneously supporting and developing the financial infrastructure in the home country, development organizations can enhance an already powerful catalyst for development.

Notes

1. I agree with Moser that asset accumulation includes a wide source of stock, including education, health, and finances. Here the focus is on financial assets.

2. There are a range of definitions; for example, one is "groupings of migrants who participate on a routine basis in a field of relationships, practices and norms that include both places of origin and destination" (Roberts, Frank, and Lozano-Ascencio 1999).

3. Inter-American Development Bank, MIF, "RG-M1019: MIF-IFAD Partnership Facility for Rural Private Sector Dev-LAC" (www.iadb.org/projects/Project.cfm?project=RG-M1019&Language=English [December 2006]).

References

Beck, Thorsten, and Augusto de la Torre. 2006. "The Basic Analytics of Access to Financial Services." Draft of working paper. Washington: World Bank (March).

Ford Foundation. 2004. *Building Assets to Reduce Poverty and Injustice*. New York.

Moser, Caroline. 2006. "Asset-Based Approaches to Poverty Reduction in a Globalized Context." Paper prepared for the Brookings Institution–Ford Foundation workshop on Asset-Based Approaches to Poverty Reduction in a Globalized Context. Washington, June 27–28.

Orozco, Manuel. 2006. "Remittances and the Local Economy in Latin America: Between Hardship and Hope." Washington: Inter-American Development Bank.

Orozco, Manuel, and Rachel Fedewa. 2005. "Regional Integration? Trends and Patterns of Remittance Flows within South East Asia." TA 6212-REG Southeast Asia Workers Remittance Study. Manila: Asian Development Bank.

Orozco, Manuel, and others. 2005a. "Diasporas, Development and Transnational Integration: Ghanaians in the U.S., U.K., and Germany." Washington: Institute for the Study of International Migration and Inter-American Dialogue.

Orozco, Manuel, and others. 2005b. "Transnational Engagement, Remittances and their Relationship to Development in Latin America and the Caribbean." Georgetown University, Institute for the Study of International Migration.

Peachy, Stephen, and Alan Roe. 2006. *Access to Finance—What Does It Mean and How Do Savings Banks Foster Access?* Brussels: World Savings Banks Institute and European Savings Banks Group.

Pozo, Susan, and Catalina Amuedo-Dorantes. 2006. "Remittances as Insurance: Evidence from Mexican Migrants." *Journal of Population Economics* 19, no. 2: 227–54.

Ray, Debraj. 1998. *Development Economics*. Princeton University Press.

Roberts, Bryan R., Reanne Frank, and Fernando Lozano-Ascencio. 1999. "Transnational Migrant Communities and Mexican Migration to the U.S." *Ethnic and Racial Studies* 22, no. 2: 238–66.

UNDP. 2006. "Human Development Report." New York.

UNDP. 2005. *Human Development Report 2005: International Cooperation at a Crossroads.* New York.

Vasconcelos, Pedro de. 2004. "Sending Money Home: Remittances to Latin America from the United States." Washington: Inter-American Development Bank.

15

Transnational Communities of the United States and Latin America

HÉCTOR CORDERO-GUZMÁN AND VICTORIA QUIROZ-BECERRA

One of the most moving scenes in Alex Rivera's documentary film, *The Sixth Section*, shows how the members of Grupo Union (Unity Group), based in Newburgh, New York, participate in the inauguration of a nearly U.S.$50,000 sports stadium that was to become the symbol of the group's presence and visibility back in their community of origin, San Vicente de Boquerón, Puebla, Mexico.[1] Grupo Union eventually invested in several other projects, including an ambulance, materials for the local school, renovation of the church, and a basketball court, and was embarking on an ambitious water project. As the group discusses the project, one member says, "This is our most ambitious project to date. If we had water in the town, we could return to work the land." In the film the state governor is heard praising the work of the group as he meets with representatives from many other similar Poblano communities

The Ford Foundation and the Rockefeller Foundation provided invaluable support, and we have benefited from the comments of Miguel Corona, James DeFilippis, Pablo Farias, Miguel Garcia, George MacCarthy, Katherine McFate, Caroline Moser, David Myhre, Erika Neumaier, James Pickett, Ruben Puentes, and Liliana Rivera Sanchez. We are also grateful for the assistance received from Ana Calero, Myrna Chase, Tracy Chimelis, Jessica Conzo, Wendy Garcia, Christine Hernandez, Maritza Hernandez, Michelle Khromov, Migi Lee, Joyce Marotta, Argelis Morel, Wilneida Negron, Ben Rhodin, Antonio Ribeiro, Marina Rivera, and Anyiseli Rodriguez.

scattered throughout New York. He announces the construction of a paved road to better connect the town to the outside world. Members of the group remark that were it not for their resources and pressure, the government would never have proposed or built the road.

The multiplicity of practices and initiatives developed over the last two decades by Grupo Union and hundreds of similar migrant groups is forcing the reconsideration of existing models of community economic development. The community is now transnational. Migrants have developed many ways to continue their involvement in—and expand the boundaries of—their communities of origin: sending money home; exchanging resources, goods, services, and visits; and having a continuing interest in local events and politics (Smith, Cordero-Guzmán, and Grosfoguel 2001). Although these practices are not a new phenomenon, they are increasingly more important and more varied (Foner 2001). At the macroeconomic level, the fluidity and mobility of capital and production, the development of communication technologies, the advances in transportation, the globalization of the media, and the dispersion of trade have contributed to shaping transnational structures within which migrant communities operate.

Adding a cross-border lens to the study of local community economic development is necessary to understand the relevant actors and the specific practices and strategies that transnational communities have developed in the past few decades to remain connected and improve the economic structure in their communities of origin. At the same time, a transnational lens is also needed to understand levels of immigrant participation in civil society, community life, and other aspects of local economic development and politics in both their communities of settlement and destination (Smith, Cordero-Guzmán, and Grosfoguel 2001).

This chapter explores the transnational character of communities and their membership, the effects of the expansion of migrant hometown associations and other community-based organizations that link families and households, the challenges that these organizations face, and their impact on community economic development.[2]

Three Approaches to Community Economic Development

The number of approaches to or perspectives on community economic development has grown in the last decades, reflecting the increasing complexity and sophistication of local practices and the evolution of a substantial academic and practitioner literature. Implicit in definitions of community economic development is the idea that it is a process that involves the development and use of economic practices, structures, and resources fundamentally focused on the local community level. Peter Boothroyd and H. Craig Davis (1993) suggest that community economic development is divided into three broad approaches, each emphasizing one of the defining aspects of the process.[3]

The first approach focuses on the community, emphasizing the active involvement of residents in gaining access to and ownership of economic activities that contribute to economic development. The main purposes of community economic development in this approach are to enhance community solidarity and cohesion, distributive justice, and the overall quality of life in poor communities.

The second approach emphasizes the economic dimensions, focusing mainly on job creation and income growth as the ways to measure community economic development. This approach assumes that increases in employment will increase the income of community members and improve the local economy. Thus, creating locally owned enterprises and attracting outside business and investments are given priority as the most effective ways to increase employment and boost the local economy.

The third approach emphasizes institutional change and focuses on the formation of the structures, organizations, and networks that lead to development. In this approach, the goal is to provide a mechanism to manage the economic decisions of the various actors that affect the community and to develop structures that can manage and sustain the investments.

One common emphasis in all three approaches is the focus on local ownership, local control over resources, and the diversification of local economic activities as a way to stabilize production and increase income flows. These traditional approaches to community economic development make certain assumptions about the nature of the community and the linkages between "the community" and other economic actors. First, the community is conceived as geographically bounded. That is, economic activities, infrastructure, and institutions—as well as the people who make up the community—operate within the confines of a physically marked area (a neighborhood or a part of town). Second, while it is recognized that the community does not live in isolation, most approaches seek to benefit the residents, businesses, and infrastructure in a geographically designated area. As a result the various strategies for development focus on the role of local actors and institutions and their linkages to broader markets. Even when it is acknowledged that most economic transactions are connected to the larger economy, community economic development continues to be thought of as a localized enterprise. In addition, many of the approaches that emphasize the involvement of the community assume that participation involves face-to-face interaction—in place—as the way to build and strengthen relationships and solidarity among members of the community.

Challenging these assumptions are transnational practices, the actors involved in these practices, and the migrants' cross-border associations with their hometowns. First, transnational communities cannot be thought of exclusively in geographic terms since their members reside in different nation-states. Therefore, when thinking of community economic development, one needs to consider the networks and linkages, both physical and economic, between various locales, within which members of the community operate. Moreover, through their knowledge, capital, organizational capacities, institutions, and resources, migrants connect themselves to the economic activities of their hometowns and their destinations—often impacting both.

Exchanges, Structures, and Institutions across Borders

Migrants have always maintained some connection to their countries and communities of origin, and these contacts have direct implications for community economic development. At the individual level, migrants send money home, communicate with people at home, visit their communities, and exchange goods, resources, and services with those still in the places of origin. At the collective level, migrants form associations and often pool money and resources for the purpose of carrying out projects that benefit both the hometown and the migrant community (Cordero-Guzmán 2001; Goldring 2003; Delgado Wise and Rodríguez Ramírez 2003). These activities allow migrants to continue involvement in their communities of origin while also changing the character of local economies to reflect their transnational structures.

Income Flows

The growth in the flow of migrant remittances to their communities of origin has received significant attention from scholars, policy analysts, banks, and governments. There is an extensive literature on the way individuals maintain linkages to their home communities of origin through money flows and the relationship between these flows and transnational economic development (Orozco 2004; Delgado Wise and Rodríguez Ramírez 2003; Goldring 2003). The amount of money sent to home countries is substantial when compared to other sources of foreign currency and involves interactions between customers and in different ways money transfer agencies, banking institutions, and governments. These actors structure the flow of remittances and shape both the use of the money and its impact on families and communities in the country of origin.

Remittances are transfers of capital that are also part of a chain of social relations and household networks, that involve social obligations sustained across borders that also stimulate local economies (Moctezuma 2004; Orozco 2000; García Zamora 2000). A recent study notes that in Latin America remittances represent between 50 and 80 percent of income for those receiving households (Vasconcelos 2004). Roberto Suro (2003) suggests that remittances "are keeping large numbers of working-class families from slipping into poverty. If remittances were suddenly cut off, already fragile domestic economies would be imperiled by the drop in internal consumption." In addition, several authors argue that remittances stimulate development when the funds are used to improve the household's standard of living through investments in education, health, and the development of other human and physical assets.

Remittances are an important source of capital in the national income accounts (Orozco 2004). Governments in Latin America have made efforts to better record transfers of capital, to facilitate flows of capital, and to redirect some of these flows in the form of matching grants to community economic development projects. Similarly, transfer agencies have partnered with governments and designed a variety of services to increasingly attract migrant clients. For instance, the government of Jalisco in Mexico supported the Raza Express and Afinidad Jalisco Banamex (debit card) programs. Under these programs the companies deposit a portion of each dollar sent to Jalisco in a fund for infrastructure projects and microenterprises (Alarcón 2002; Orozco 2000). Remittances are also leveraged to provide capital liquidity and stimulate creation of local financial institutions and intermediaries such as credit unions. In addition to providing migrants and their families with access to financial services, such as saving accounts and credit, the deposits into these institutions become the source of loan capital for microenterprise programs and community development projects (Jaramillo 2005).

Transnationalizing Hometown Economies and Consumption Patterns

The growth of transnational communities has led to the development of migration-related businesses (travel agencies, shipping companies, money transfer businesses); new markets for products, goods, and services; consumer demands for new products; and direct migrant investment in economic projects in their communities of origin. An illustration of the transnationalization of hometown economies is that of the Mixteca region in the state of Puebla, Mexico.

In the last few decades, like many other parts of Latin America, the Mixteca has experienced rapid out-migration due in part to the economic restructuring of a predominantly agricultural region, which accelerated with the 1980s Mexican economic crisis and the subsequent implementation of NAFTA-driven policies in the 1990s (Rivera-Sánchez 2004). As a result of both internal and international migration, the Mixteca Poblana region experienced rapid changes in the structure of the market economy. These changes can be seen in services and products specifically aimed at the migrant market and in enterprises set up by returning migrants. Among the first are shipping services, travel agencies, Internet cafes, and remittance exchange centers. These businesses offer services to the most common U.S. cities of destination and function to connect the community and to cater to the needs of migrants. We visited a *paquetería* (packaging and shipping service) named De Paisano a Paisano (From Townfolk to Townfolk); its straightforward motto was *conectando a nuestra gente* (connecting our people) through the movement of goods and resources.

The migration and remittances economy also affects the local market in other ways. Many migrants dream of returning to their community of origin and endeavor to build their own homes, resulting in a demand for land, construction workers, and all kinds of building materials. Throughout Mixteca and the immigrant-sending regions of Latin America, numerous towns have a number of houses under construction in styles that are reminiscent of receiving communities such as certain parts of Queens in New York.

The growing number of hotels in the region can be attributed in part to migrants who return home on visits. One of the towns we visited in the Mixteca, a town with only a little over 5,000 inhabitants, has at least three formal hotels.[4] During town holidays and festivities, visiting migrants and extended family and friends are the usual guests in these hotels. However, demand for hotels comes also from suppliers who deliver goods to the local stores. The region has also seen an increasing number of Internet cafes, cellular phone and video game stores, pizzerias, and hamburger joints. There are even stores that sell "American groceries," stocked with chips, cereals, canned goods, sodas, and everything else one would expect from a corner bodega in Manhattan just like there are stores in El Barrio (East Harlem) and elsewhere in New York stocked with Mexican and Latin American goods. The combination of continued mass migration and the globalization of consumer tastes helps create and shape local consumer demands for products (Guarnizo 2003) in both sending and receiving communities.

Many returned migrants open businesses in their hometowns, capitalized with the savings acquired during migration and taking advantage of increasing demand for new products and services due to evolving tastes in their towns of origin. Migrants use not only the capital accumulated while working abroad but also some of the skills learned while working in the United States. In the Mixteca we visited a cafeteria, opened by a returned migrant, that catered to established local tastes but also offered a juice bar, American coffee, and bagels sent fresh every week—via one of the many shipping services in town—from his friends at the New York delicatessen where he used to work. The primary demand for his bagels does not come from the rare American tourist, who in fact would much rather eat the local food, but from some locals who used to work in delis in New York and developed a taste for morning bagels.

Governments have also encouraged migrants' direct investment in their communities of origin as part of national strategies for economic development. For instance, the state government of Guanajuato, Mexico, created La Comunidad, which seeks the direct investment of migrants in projects that generate employment opportunities in communities with high migration. The program provides technical assistance and is also one of several programs that matches the financing invested by migrants. Aside from generating income for migrants, these enterprises are meant to serve and diversify the economy of the community as a whole.[5] Stimulating "productive" (employment-generating) investments in towns of origin can promote and strengthen linkages between migrants and their communities and can help improve the local economy.

Transnationalizing Collective Action

In addition to their individual economic support for their hometown economies, migrants act collectively to help their communities of origin. A migrant hometown association assists with immigration, helps migrants adapt to their new home but also to stay connected to their old one, and articulates home community needs (Cordero-Guzmán 2005; Fox and Rivera-Salgado 2004; Levitt 2001).

Establishing hometown associations is one way that migrants act transnationally and attempt to improve their communities of origin. Like other migrant-led, community-based organizations, these groups engage in four sets of broad functions: helping in the migration process; providing services and programs that assist in the adaptation and incorporation of migrants in the receiving communities; articulating community needs, raising and managing resources, and maintaining a sense of group identity; and connecting migrant diasporas to the countries and communities of origin.

The survival of these associations depends on the strength of the connections to communities of origin and the help they can accumulate, organize, and send to them. Their survival is also related to what the migrants themselves gain from participating in clubs, which is usually a sense of security, a sense of personal and group loyalty and identity, increased status, and a way to articulate a connection to their communities of origin.

Migrant hometown associations sometimes have performed the role that, when done, traditionally belongs to the state in terms of local infrastructure assessment, planning, and development. In a study of Mexican migrant hometown associations, Manuel Orozco and Michelle Lapointe (2004) found that more than a third of the projects were involved in hometown infrastructure, including the paving of streets; construction of bridges, roads, and electric plants; installation of irrigation systems and wells; maintenance of parks, cemeteries, and public gardens; and construction of recreation facilities. In addition, more than half of the projects focused on education and health and included donations of school and medical supplies, construction of clinics, and school repairs. A few associations also provided social and health services to their hometowns (Goldring 2001)and many associations participate in and help sponsor the town's religious and cultural festivities.

The work of a New York–based organization created by a group of migrants from a municipality in the state of Puebla is typical of most migrant hometown associations (Lowell and Garza 2000; Goldring 2003). This group has been involved in bringing potable water, electrification projects, sewer projects, and public lighting to the town. More recently the organization has focused on projects related to education and health, mainly through the donation of computers, school supplies, and over-the-counter medicines. The group also organizes a yearly lighting of a community Christmas tree, donates toys for the *día de reyes* (January 6), and helps with funeral and medical expenses.[6] Projects funded by this organization integrate criteria that respond to community concerns, economic realities, and development needs. While some of the projects are intended to improve the infrastructure and appearance of the town, the aims of the organization go beyond purely economic issues and extend into mutual support and sharing in communal events and celebrations.

Government officials at all levels have expressed interest in the projects that migrant hometown associations are carrying out, and many have approached these associations (Goldring 2004; García Zamora 2005). The responses of the associations are based on their history, membership, and local conditions in communities of origin and range from skepticism and fear of co-optation to active collaboration and partnerships. Many countries in Latin America with large migrant diasporas—particularly Colombia, El Salvador, Mexico, Dominican Republic, Ecuador, and Peru—have created government ministries and departments dedicated to addressing the needs of members of their communities living abroad. These agencies, consulates, and government officials have tried to manage the channels through which migrants participate in their countries of origin and have attempted to understand (and control) the incentives for collective action. The governments of El Salvador and Mexico, for example, have created programs that offer incentives and matching funds to the organizations to create local partnerships for their development projects (Zabin and Escala-Rabadán 1998; Orozco 2003). The Tres por Uno (Three for One) program in Mexico, for example, offers matching funds to associations carrying out development projects in their communities. Under this program the federal, state, and municipal governments offer to match in equal parts the funds invested by the migrant organizations.

Following the Mexican model, the Salvadoran government implemented the Programa Unidos por la Solidaridad (United for Solidarity Program), which offers funds to migrant hometown associations for implementation of their projects in El Salvador. The associations submit proposals for projects, and through a competitive process, some are selected for additional funding and support by the government. Unlike the Mexican Tres por Uno program, in the Salvadoran program the amount and proportion of government financing is determined on a project-by-project basis.

More recently, migrant hometown associations have emphasized the need to develop funding and resources for investment in economically productive projects. That is, the associations are emphasizing the creation, expansion, attraction, and preservation of businesses, collectives, and cooperatives as a way to bring about community economic development in their towns of origin. The idea behind this strategy is that improvements in the economic structure and the number of businesses will increase economic activity in the community, thereby providing employment to local residents, diversifying the goods and services offered to the community, increasing the pool of entrepreneurs, expanding the productive linkages of the local economy to external markets, and potentially reducing the leakages from the local economy (Cordero-Guzmán and Auspos, 2006). While some argue that these projects have had limited economic success, García Zamora and others have documented some innovative collaborations between local foundations, governments, and migrant organizations that have resulted in productive investment projects and stronger communities (García Zamora 2002; Delgado Wise and Rodríguez Ramírez 2003).

In many cases working with governments offers migrant hometown associations new channels through which they can participate in their communities of origin. Some associations have acquired a role in the decision-making process and have gained political influence at various levels of government. In their study on Mexican migrant hometown associations, for example, Carol Zabin and Luis Escala-Rabadán (1998) found that members of these organizations have acquired important leadership credentials and social status in their communities of origin.

Referring to the Tres por Uno program in Mexico, García Zamora (2005) observes while there are challenges one of the important results has been the encouragement of transnational organizing. He notes that the three main contributions of collective remittances have been the growth of solidarity between communities of origin and those abroad, the development of working relationships between communities of origin and the various levels of government, and the financing of social projects usually excluded from public planning and investment. Also, by developing working relations with municipal authorities, migrant associations have gained credibility in the United States, encouraged similar organizations in the hometowns of origin (demonstration effect), and helped to develop leadership and stimulate cooperation on both sides of the border. In essence, these associations are developing and shaping a transnational civil society (Cordero-Guzmán and Quiroz-Becerra 2006; Rivera-Salgado, Bada, and Escala-Rabadán 2005; Tarrow 2005).

In addition to hometown associations, we found other immigrant nonprofit organizations based in the receiving communities that are also involved in various types of cross-border community economic development exchanges. These organizations are often part of global civil society institutions and solidarity networks and are also part of transnational civil society. Among the most common types of projects and activities that these organizations engage in, we found programs that provided support for direct services, infrastructure development, learning and sharing models and best practices, providing technical assistance, and supporting the civil society organizations in the communities of origin (Cordero-Guzmán and Quiroz-Becerra 2006).

Challenges for Migrant Hometown Associations

In many ways, while the practice and promise of transnational community economic development has provided concrete benefits to many communities, there are some serious challenges that hometown associations and other civil society organizations face when engaging in cross-border community economic development and working to achieve lasting positive results.

Migrant hometown associations have been criticized for restricting input from the community of origin and few of these associations work with an organizational counterpart in the country of origin. Decisions regarding what projects to implement do not tend to be based on objective assessments of the needs of the community. Rather, the perceptions of association members, who are often abroad (though sometimes in consultation with relatives back home), constitute the basis for decisions regarding what projects to support, fund, and implement.

Thus the priorities of migrant hometown associations regarding projects are sometimes not aligned with those of the community. For instance, the members of one association told us that they had built a *jacalón* (roofed area) as a place for townspeople to sell their products but that it has hardly been used. Another association wanted to build a pedestrian bridge across a main highway in their hometown, but to the townspeople this was not a priority and in the end, the pedestrian bridge was not built.

In addition, existing divisions and rivalries in some communities have affected the development and implementation of projects. One association wanted to dig a community well, but the best place to dig was on the property of a person whom members of the association distrusted. Alternative locations were not as promising, the project became more costly, and the well-digging project simply ended up creating more conflict.

Some attempts have been made to help migrant hometown associations establish more effective consultation mechanisms and ways to allow other stakeholders to have more proportionate input in the decisionmaking process. Some governments and foundations have been prompted to create programs to provide technical assistance and planning to these organizations. Similarly, governments are being pushed to create programs that promote the involvement of a multiplicity of actors in the decisionmaking process. In Jalisco, Mexico, a program that promotes productive investments among members of the Federación de Clubes de Jalisco (a federation of hometown associations)—with technical assistance from North American Integration and Development and the Fundación de Fomento a la Productividad del Campo—attempted to coordinate efforts from various sectors to increase income and create jobs in local communities (Alarcón 2002). Similarly, in some communities in Mixteca and Valle de Atlixco, there were active attempts by local members to build civil society organizations that could serve as local counterparts and partners to the migrant hometown associations based in the US.

Another challenge faced by migrant hometown associations is their replication of clientelistic and patriarchal social structures and leadership within some organizations. Many programs depend largely on existing migrant networks and groups, which often reproduce traditional leadership and gender roles and thus limit women's roles in community economic development (Goldring 2001). This brings to mind Luis Guarnizo's cautionary remark regarding migrant transnational practices: "Paradoxically, instead of escaping the control of the state and corporate capital, migrant cross-border engagement provides opportunities for further capitalist expansion and the reproduction of old inequalities" (Guarnizo 2003).

In addition to the challenges related to project relevance, community input and participation, and local organizational capacity to carry out projects, the organizations and actors involved in cross-border community economic development face several other challenges. Migrants may leave home with concrete ideas of the projects they want to fund, but conditions back home often change. Migrants, however, might insist on following their nostalgia irrespective of whether the economics of the project are sound or viable (Cohen and Rodriguez 2005). Another challenge revolves around so-called vanity projects, in which groups in one town support a project because a neighboring town or another group has done a similar project. If the next town over built a dance hall or a stadium, there is a parochial competitive tendency to just want to do the same thing—but bigger and better.

Another concern involves the challenges of developing governance and monitoring mechanisms and supports that help migrants and their organizations simultaneously participate in the community economic development processes of both sending and receiving communities. So far, most hometown associations focus their activities on their communities of origin. Over time, however, these groups are facing increasing pressures to become involved and develop projects in the communities where the migrants settle, and look for ways to encourage simultaneous dual participation and community involvement in both sending and receiving communities.

Migrant hometown associations are going to continue to be the driving force in cross border community development (Delgado Wise and Rodríguez Ramírez 2003). This role puts pressure on them to secure the expertise, technical skills, and planning assistance that will allow them to better plan and select the projects they fund. Moving to a more formal level of organization will put pressure on the management of the associations. Pressure will also come from funders, clients and members, governments, and other constituencies to expand the mission, scope of work, and types and reach of projects. In addition, expectations that come from some successes will also have to be managed.

Working with government entities brings its own challenges, including bureaucratic paperwork and procedures, oversight of resources, lack of project continuity, and differences in goals and priorities (García Zamora 2002). The associations also need to understand political alliances and nuances in both countries, the one they live and work in and the country of origin. Furthermore, as migrant associations become more institutionalized, they need a more developed governance structure and physical infrastructure, including office space, regular staff, and other professional supports.

The Future of Transnational Community Development

Analyzing transnational practices and the actors involved in cross-border processes offers an opportunity to better understand the potential that migrant hometown associations and other organizations hold for transnational community economic development. Many aspects of the process, however, have received little or no academic attention. Most of the information from the field comes from a few cases in a handful of countries (Mexico, El Salvador, Haiti, and Dominican Republic). As migrants accumulate more and more resources and as they continue to remain connected to their communities of origin, the process of asset accumulation and movement of resources and initiatives across borders will continue. Rather than trying to find ways to co-opt and control the process, our research and experience suggest that it is best for policymakers and funders to act on the basis of concrete information and to judge each strategy as to its applicability to the particular social, political, and economic context. Comparative research would show how different structural positions and institutions affect transnational practices in specific ways. Do migrants from different countries create different organizational forms? If so, in what ways are they different or similar? What are the consequences of these differences and similarities for the evolution of projects and for local economic development?

Transnational practices are multidirectional and varied (Guarnizo 2003). Thus there is a need to reconsider our common understanding of economic development as a local, one-way process. Most of the literature on migration and even transnationalization takes a unidirectional perspective, that is, the focus is on the movements of people north and the flows of capital and remittances south. Aside from noting that immigrants are an integral part of the labor force in both countries, there is little knowledge of other practices that connect communities. This is particularly evident in the case of migrant organizations.

At the organizational level, there has been the nonprofitization of migrant organizations as they increasingly face the realities and integration needs of their constituencies in the countries where they work. Migrants and their children need a variety of services in the places where they settle, and their organizations are being asked to be more involved in the lives of migrants themselves. At the same time, there is also a transnationalization of north-based organizations, even migrant organizations, with increasing acknowledgment of the transnational realities of their members and participants. For example, a traditional housing group in Brooklyn became involved in remittance projects as its members realized the need to develop connections to programs and initiatives that link to migrants' countries of origin.

Migrant organizations understand that migrants want to remain connected to their countries of origin, to visit, and sometimes return permanently. The current migration legal regime makes frequent travel difficult, and many are forced to stay in the United States for longer periods of time than they originally intended. Paradoxically, longer stays in the United States reinforce transnational ties and encourage migrants to create deeper roots and linkages to the U.S. economy to support themselves and their families and also to their communities of origin, where they may return in twenty or so years. Because they have been involved in a hometown association and also in the life of their town of origin, once they return, it is as if they had never left.

Latin American immigrants and their organizations are at the center of two significant hemispheric trends: one is the increasing demographic change throughout the United States and the other is the increasing importance of immigrant diasporas for the economic and political development of their countries and communities of origin. Policymakers and funders need to better understand how immigrants work across borders and develop practices and institutions designed not just to advance their narrow economic interests but also to develop local economic structures, create work opportunities, and improve the quality of life in their communities of origin and in the diaspora communities where they live, work, and raise their children.

Notes

1. *The Sixth Section: A Documentary about Immigrants Organizing across Borders* was produced and directed by Alex Rivera in association with P.O.V./American Documentary, Inc. For more information, see "About the Film" (www.pbs.org/pov/pov2003/thesixthsection/about.html [December 2006]).

2. The data for this for this chapter come from organization interviews, site visits, participant observation, and conversations with key informants involved in cross-border community economic development.

3. For a discussion of the literature on community economic development, see Cordero-Guzmán and Auspos (2006).

4. Data based on the 2000 Mexican census. See Instituto Nacional de Estadística Geografía e Informática (INEGI), available at www.inegi.gob.mx (February 2007).

5. See Miguel L. Moctezuma, "Inversión social y productividad de los migrantes mexicanos en Estados Unidos," Red Internacional de Migración y Desarrollo at www.migraciony desarrollo.org (December 2006).

6. Interview with the president of a hometown association based in New York City, December 20, 2005.

References

Alarcón, Rafael. 2002. "The Development of Home Town Associations in the United States and the Use of Social Remittances in Mexico." In *Sending Money Home*, edited by Rodolfo de la Garza and B. Lindsay Lowell, pp. 101–24. New York: Rowman and Littlefield.

Boothroyd, Peter, and H. Craig Davis. 1993. "Community Economic Development: Three Approaches." *Journal of Planning Education and Research* 12, no. 3: 230–40.

Cohen, Jeffrey H., and Leila Rodriguez. 2005. "Remittance Outcomes in Rural Oaxaca, Mexico: Challenges, Options, and Opportunities for Migrant Households." *Population Space and Place* 11, no. 1: 49–63.

Cordero-Guzmán, Héctor. 2001. "Immigrant Aid Societies and Organizations." In *Encyclopedia of American Immigration*, edited by James Ciment, pp. 334–40. New York: M. E. Sharpe Publishers.

———. 2005. "Community-Based Organisations and Migration in New York City." *Journal of Ethnic and Migration Studies* 31, no. 5: 889–909.

Cordero-Guzmán, Héctor, and Patricia Auspos. 2006. "Community Economic Development and Community Change." In *Community Change: Theories, Practice, and Evidence*, edited by Karen Fulbright-Anderson and Patricia Auspos, pp. 195–265. Washington: Aspen Institute.

Cordero-Guzmán, Héctor, and Victoria Quiroz-Becerra. 2006. "The Cross-Border Activities of Community Based Organizations in New York." Paper presented at the American Sociological Association's 101st Annual Meeting. Montreal, August 11–14.

Delgado Wise, Raúl, and Héctor Rodríguez Ramírez. 2003. "The Emergence of Collective Migrants and Their Role in Mexico's Local and Regional Development." *Canadian Journal of Development Studies* 22, no. 3: 747–64.

Foner, Nancy. 2001. "Transnationalism Then and Now: New York Immigrants Today and at the Turn of the Twentieth Century." In *Migration, Transnationalization, and Race in a Changing New York*, edited by Héctor Cordero-Guzmán, Robert C. Smith, and Ramon Grosfoguel, pp. 35–57. Temple University Press.

Fox, Jonathan, and Gaspar Rivera-Salgado. 2004. "Building Civil Society among Indigenous Migrants." In *Indigenous Mexican Migrants in the United States*, edited by Jonathan Fox and Gaspar Rivera-Salgado, pp. 1–65. La Jolla, Calif.: Center for U.S.-Mexican Studies and Center for Comparative Immigration Studies.

García Zamora, Rodolfo. 2000. "Los retos actuales de la teoría del desarrollo." Zacatecas, México: Red Internacional de Migración y Desarrollo.

———. 2002. "Migración internacional y desarrollo local: una propuesta binacional para el desarrollo regional del sur de Zacatecas, México." Paper presented at Dinámicas tradicionales y emergentes de la emigración mexicana, Centro de Investigaciones y Estudios Superiores en Antropología Social Occidente, Guadalajara, Jalisco, November 21–23.

———. 2005. "Las remesas colectivas y el programa 3x1 como proceso de aprendizaje social transnacional." Paper presented at the seminar Mexican Migrant Social and Civic Participation in the United States, Woodrow Wilson International Center for Scholars. Washington, November 4–5.

Goldring, Luin. 2001. "The Gender and Geography of Citizenship in Mexico-U.S. Transnational Spaces." *Identities* 7, no. 4: 501–37.

———. 2003. "Re-thinking Remittances: Social and Political Dimensions of Individual and Collective Remittances." Working Paper. Toronto: Centre for Research on Latin America and the Caribbean (February).

———. 2004. "Family and Collective Remittances to Mexico: A Multi-Dimensional Typology." *Development and Change*, 35, no. 4: 799–840.

Guarnizo, Luis. 2003. "The Economics of Transnational Living." *International Migration Review* 37, no. 3: 666–99.

Jaramillo, Maria. 2005. "Leveraging the Impact of Remittances through Microfinance Products: Perspectives from Market Research." In *Beyond Small Change: Making Migrant Remittances Count,* edited by Donald F. Terry and Steven R. Wilson, pp. 133–56. Washington: Inter-American Development Bank.

Levitt, Peggy. 2001. *The Transnational Villagers*. University of California Press.

Lowell, B. Lindsay, and Rodolfo de la Garza. 2000. "The Developmental Role of Remittance in U.S. Latino Communities and in Latin American Countries." Final project report. Washington: Inter-American Dialogue (June).

Moctezuma, Miguel L. 2004. "La presencia migrante desde la distancia: Clubes de zacatecanos en Estados Unidos." In *Clubes de migrantes oriundos mexicanos en Estados Unidos: La politica transnacional de la nueva sociedad civil migrante*, edited by Guillaume Lanly and M. Basilia Valenzuela V., pp. 85–126. Guadalajara: Universidad de Guadalajara.

Orozco, Manuel. 2000. "Remittances and Markets: New Players and Practices." Washington: Inter-American Dialogue.

———. 2003. "Worker Remittances in an International Scope." Working Paper. Washington: Inter-American Dialogue (March).

———. 2004. "Oportunidades y estrategias para el desarrollo y el crecimiento a través de las remesas familiares a la República Dominicana." Paper presented at the conference Sending Money Home: An Analysis of the Remittance Market between the United Status and the Dominican Republic. Columbia University, November 23, pp. 2–3.

Orozco, Manuel, and Michelle Lapointe. 2004. "Mexican Hometown Association and Development Opportunities." *Journal of International Affairs* 57, no. 2: 31–49.

Rivera-Salgado, Gaspar, Xóchil Bada, and Luis Escala-Rabadán. 2005. "Mexican Migrant Civic and Political Participation in the U.S.: The Case of Hometown Associations in Los Angeles and Chicago." Paper presented at the seminar on Mexican Migrant Social and Civic Participation in the United States, Woodrow Wilson International Center for Scholars. Washington, November 4–5.

Rivera-Sánchez, Liliana. 2004. "Expressions of Identity and Belonging: Mexican Immigrants in New York." In *Indigenous Mexican Migrants in the United States*, edited by Jonathan Fox and Gaspar Rivera-Salgado, pp. 417–46. La Jolla, Calif.: Center for U.S.-Mexican Studies and the Center for Comparative Immigration Studies.

Smith, Robert C., Héctor Cordero-Guzmán, and Ramón Grosfoguel. 2001. "Introduction: Migration, Transnationalization, and Ethnic and Racial Dynamics in a Changing New York." In *Migration, Transnationalization, and Race in a Changing New York*, edited by Héctor Cordero-Guzmán, Robert C. Smith, and Ramón Grosfoguel, pp.1–34. Temple University Press.

Suro, Roberto. 2003. "Remittance Senders and Receivers: Tracking the Transnational Channels." Report. Washington: Multilateral Investment Fund and Pew Hispanic Center.

Tarrow, Sidney G. 2005. *The New Transnational Activism*. Cambridge University Press.

Vasconcelos, Pedro de. 2004. "Sending Money Home: Remittances to Latin America from the United States." Washington: Inter-American Development Bank.

Zabin, Carol, and Luis Escala-Rabadán. 1998. "Mexican Hometown Associations and Mexican Immigrant Political Empowerment in Los Angeles." Working Paper. Washington: Aspen Institute, Nonprofit Sector Research Fund.

16

Gender and Transnational Asset Accumulation in El Salvador

SARAH GAMMAGE

This chapter explores the gender dimensions of transnational asset holdings for Salvadoran migrants and their home communities. It focuses on a number of key assets built up or drawn down in the process of migration: remittances, savings, housing, and transnational social capital.[1] The data used are from a wide range of sources including the Salvadoran National Accounts; the Multi-Purpose Household Survey (Encuesta de Hogares de Propósitos Múltiples [EHPM]) for 2004, published by El Salvador's General Department of Surveys and Census (Dirección General de Estadística y Censos [DIGESTYC 2004]); and the Public Use Microdata Sample of the U.S. Census 2000 (PUMS).[2] Another important source is a micro–data set of 150 Salvadorans residing in greater Washington, D.C., in 2004 that summarizes different aspects of migration, remittances, and transnational activities.[3] The goal is to provide a snapshot of those transnational assets held, accumulated, or drawn down in the process of migration and to pose some questions for further research.

Background

El Salvador is the smallest, most densely populated, and arguably the most environmentally degraded country in Central America. With a population of almost

6.8 million, it is estimated that more than 25 percent have migrated or fled the civil war—with approximately 1.5 million people living and working in the United States.[4] As coffee, cotton, and sugar prices have declined and traditional exports have shrunk, El Salvador's most important export is increasingly people, and the primary destination is the United States.

Networks that were developed during the 1980s to enable households and individuals to flee from conflict continue to meet the needs of economic migrants searching for opportunities in the north (Stanley 1987; Hamilton and Chinchilla 1991). These same networks have subsequently become conduits for remittances of money and goods that flow from the north to the south and vice versa (Landolt 1997).

Remittances are now a critical source of national income and make up over half of all export earnings and more than 16 percent of GDP. Household survey data from the 2004 EHPM reveal that approximately 22 percent of households in both rural and urban areas are in receipt of remittances, receiving an average of U.S.$161 per month (DIGESTYC 2004). With more than fifty flights a day and an increase of almost 600 percent in the number of airline passengers arriving at San Salvador's national airport between 1980 and 2000, Salvadorans have become transnationals, routinely ferrying goods, couriering money, and making purchases and investments that span national borders.[5]

Migration is increasingly a livelihood strategy in El Salvador. Through migration a significant number of Salvadorans secure employment abroad, send remittances home, and improve their economic welfare and well-being and that of their families in their home country. Aspiring migrants have little formal education, come from households with few resources, and often enter the United States without documents. As undocumented workers they face limited prospects in the United States and are constrained to low-wage, service sector employment without contracts or benefits. They frequently occupy temporary positions, disproportionately undertake shift work, are forced to combine several jobs at once, and still earn less than the legal minimum wage (Gammage and Schmitt 2004). Despite the difficulties inherent in migrating, people continue to search for employment and stability in the United States. Table 16-1 provides some descriptive statistics that underscore the differences between El Salvador and the United States and highlight the potential benefits that can be garnered through migration.

Assets in the Transnational Sphere: A Framework for Analysis

Assets are built up and drawn down in the process of migrating. On the balance sheet of a company, everything that the company owns and that has monetary

Table 16-1. *Key Indicators for El Salvador and the United States, 2000*
Units as indicated

Indicator	El Salvador	United States
GDP per capita (U.S. dollars)	2,097	34,934
GDP per capita (ppp)[a]	4,475	34,934
Current account (millions of current U.S. dollars)	–1,955	–476,511
Current account (percent of GDP)	–14.8	–4.8
Tax revenue (percent of GDP)[b]	13.2	20.1
Access to an improved water source (percent)	74	100
Access to improved sanitation (percent)	83	100
Maternal mortality rate[c]	180	12
Health expenditure (percent of GDP)	7.2	12.9
Private health expenditure (percent of GDP)	4.6	7.1
Public health expenditure (percent of GDP)	2.6	5.7
Annual income (current U.S. dollars)	2,342	29,845
Annual income for Salvadorans (current U.S. dollars)	2,342	13,833
Headcount poverty rates (percent)	34.6	11.5
Headcount poverty rates for Salvadorans (percent)	34.6	18.5
Human development index	0.712	0.934
Human development index for Salvadorans	0.712	0.763

Source: Author's calculations from Bureau of the Census, "1-Percent Public Use Microdata Sample (PUMS) Files" (www.census.gov/Press-Release/www/2003/PUMS.html [December 2006]); the Salvadoran Multiple Purpose Household Survey (EHPM) 2000 (DIGESTYC 2000), available at www.digestyc.gob.sv [December]; and World Development Indicators (World Bank 2000), tables 2.15, 2.16, 2.17, 4.2, 4.6, 4.11, and 5.5.

a. Bilateral purchasing power parity (ppp) calculated using the Penn World Table and adjusting for inflation differences between the United States and El Salvador. See Center for International Comparisons, "Penn World Table" (pwt.econ.upenn.edu [November 2006]).

b. Central government revenue.

c. Expressed per 100,000 live births.

value is classified as an asset. In narrow accounting terms, assets fall into the following categories:

—current assets: cash, bank deposits, and other assets that can be turned into cash;

—trade investments: investments in a subsidiary or associated company or activity;

—fixed assets: land, buildings, plant machinery, vehicles, and furniture; and

—intangible assets, such as patents and copyrights or other assets referred to as "goodwill."[6]

Clearly, an individual is not a firm, but most accountants would approach an individual's asset evaluation by similarly assuming that the assets of an individual are those possessions or attributes that have monetary value, including the liabilities owed to the individual by others and net of those owed by that individual to

Box 16-1. *Individual Assets*

TYPE OF ASSETS	DEFINITION
Current assets	Cash, bank deposits
Investments	In productive activities that yield an income stream
Fixed assets	Land, housing, cars, machinery
Intangible assets	Human and social capital

others. This definition of firm assets is informative because it provides for the inclusion of intangible assets. It is not, therefore, such a far-fetched idea to consider an augmented definition of individual assets that would also include intangible assets such as human capital and social or political capital.[7] (See box 16-1.)

While there are many motivations for migration, the goal of obtaining employment and being able to send remittances back to the home country features especially prominently in the life stories of Salvadoran migrants (Mahler 1995; Gammage and others 2005). For the recipient family, remittances are often the hoped-for product of an extremely costly investment. For the remitter the remittances represent an obligation to repay a debt, a commitment to maintain a family, or a desire to remain linked to their country of origin. Yet the choice or ability to send remittances home may vary substantially by the gender of the remitter and the individual's access to employment in the host country.

It is clear that assets are both generated and depleted through the process of migration. The average cost of undocumented entry into the United States from El Salvador hovered between U.S.$3,000 and $8,000 over the last three years, depending on the type of service offered. The extent of accompaniment and supervision from El Salvador onwards, the method of travel (by road, train, or air), and the types and numbers of documents to be obtained, falsified, or offered all vary widely and influence the final cost. To finance this investment in a future stream of remittances, individuals and households sell assets and borrow from moneylenders, family members, and "coyotes."[8]

Leveraging a trip north is something few individuals undertake alone. The journey of an individual migrant is frequently part of a household strategy to secure remittances, and any debt accumulated is borne by a collective of individuals. Social capital is also drawn upon and renovated in the process of migration. A successful migrant will cross the border and obtain work—enabling him or her to earn money, repay debts owed, and send remittances home. Success is more likely if migrants have strong social ties and a social network that will mediate access to housing and employment and help them navigate the complex waters of their new home.

An asset framework can be useful when analyzing one dimension of the costs and benefits of migration. Yet any analysis of those assets created and drawn down in the process of migration should by definition be transnational or translocal. The migrant is rarely separate from the home-country household, and the links between households at home and in the host country are maintained and nurtured over time and distance. Migration is frequently part of a household survival strategy; the product of a costly investment in a stream of income and remittances that sustains more than one household across national boundaries. Consequently, any analysis of the assets should be contextualized and seen through this translocal lens. Unfortunately, few data sets exist that span home and host communities and link remittance-sending and remittance-receiving households so as to capture the transnational and translocal nature of their decisionmaking and livelihood strategies.

Gender, Migration, and Remittances

The primary goal for most newly arrived Salvadoran immigrants in the United States is to secure a job and send remittances home. These remittances take a variety of forms and include flows of money, goods, ideas, knowledge, and financial and human capital across borders. Analysis of the 2004 EHPM reveals that approximately 22 percent of all households in El Salvador report receiving dollar remittances. This figure rises to almost 50 percent when remittances in-kind are included. Formal and informal couriers exist side by side, and migrants and their families make use of these as best fits their needs and preferences, sending clothing, medicine, food, children's toys, letters, videos, and funds.[9] Households that are separated by time and distance struggle to remain attached through telephone calls, sending gifts and letters, and making joint decisions about the use of remittances garnered in the United States. The remittance couriers and services such as Bancomercio, Gigante Express, and Western Union cement these ties, ensuring that exchanges are made between individuals and households in far-flung parts of the globe.

Migration and displacement also precipitate qualitative shifts in economic, social, and political activities, changing the role that women play as providers and caregivers and generating new identities for women in sending and receiving communities. There is a wealth of sociological and anthropological literature that emphasizes how the migration experience differs for men and women. Gender plays a dominant role in determining who migrates and when, under

Table 16-2. *Households in Receipt of Remittances, El Salvador, 2004*
Units as indicated

| | Headship | | |
Household type	Male	Female	Total
Total households	1,102,628	523,408	1,626,036
Number receiving remittances	190,811	171,378	362,189
Percent of male- or female-headed households that receive remittances	17.3	32.7	22.3
Percent of all households that receive remittances	52.7	47.3	100.0
Remittances as a percent of total income	27.6	42.4	34.1

Source: Author's calculations based on data from the EHPM 2004 (DIGESTYC 2004).

what circumstances, and with what resources (Katz 1998; Chant 1992). Gender is also likely to shape the fortunes of migrants in the host country by determining how rapidly they are incorporated into labor markets, what types of labor markets they seek out or are eligible for, the types of visas and protective status they enjoy, and whether they experience any mobility to higher-paying, higher-status employment (Gammage and Schmitt 2004; Repak 1995; Mahler 1995).

The receipt of remittances is equally likely to reflect a gender dimension. Table 16-2 reveals how distinctly gendered receipt of remittances is. In 2004 approximately 17 percent of all male-headed households in El Salvador reported receiving remittances versus 33 percent of female-headed households. Similarly, remittances made up 28 percent of total household income in male-headed households and 42 percent of income in female-headed households.

Remittances are typically not unidirectional but reciprocal; they flow across national boundaries from the north and south simultaneously. The micro–data set for greater Washington, D.C., for 2004 reveals that both men and women send a variety of goods, as well as letters and pictures, to family members and friends in El Salvador. Interestingly, the types and volume of goods sent and received are broadly similar for men and women. Clothes dominate the flow of goods sent south by men and women, and nostalgic foods and to a lesser extent medicines dominate the flow of goods sent north. Men appear to send bigger and more costly items more infrequently, while women send smaller and less costly items more frequently. Among the larger items that were sent to family members in El Salvador the preceding year were appliances, such as televisions, refrigerators, sewing machines, photocopiers, and stereo equipment. Some of these larger items were for small businesses and microenterprises—most notably the refrigerators, sewing machines, and photocopiers. Among the smaller items sent were shoes, clothes, CDs, photographs, videos, toys, perfume, medicines, and books.

The reciprocity of sending goods not only fulfils a vital connective role, but it may also ensure that family members in the north remain committed to sending remittances south. The act of remitting goods and letters, food, and greetings from El Salvador to migrants in the United States appears to perform an essential function, cementing family ties and ensuring that the exchange continues by underscoring its reciprocity.

Savings in the Home and Host Country

One asset created and potentially drawn down in the process of migration is savings. Savings rates in general are low in El Salvador. Nationally, private savings hover at about 10 percent of GDP. Clearly, savings rates and amounts vary by type of household. Data from the EHPM for 2004 report that approximately 6 percent of all remittances are saved, with urban households exhibiting a greater propensity to save (DIGESTYC 2004).

Savings rates appear to be higher for households in receipt of remittances than for those that are not. Data for 2000 from El Salvador (DIGESTYC 2000) indicate that less than 2 percent of households not receiving remittances report holding savings. In contrast, this figure rises to over 4 percent among households in receipt of remittances. Some of the households not actively saving may have accumulated significant debt, and many of these households may still be servicing that debt, repaying moneylenders, family members, and the coyote service.

Because the 2004 EHPM did not collect data on household savings, it is not possible to use this particular data set to observe how savings rates may have changed over time in El Salvador. Despite this shortcoming in the national survey, some micro–data sets have been collected that explore savings and asset acquisition as a result of migration. Studies underscore that most remittances are used for consumption—to meet the immediate needs of the recipient household.[10] Some remittances are saved, however, and a small portion of these savings may be invested in productive activities. The microdata set for Salvadorans in greater Washington and their home communities reveals that 16 percent of

Figure 16-1. *Remittance Recipients with and without Savings in El Salvador, 2004*

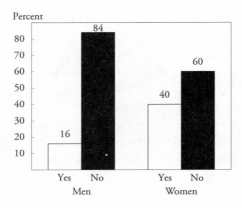

Source: Microdata set from greater Washington, D.C., survey. See Rutgers, "Destination DC: Migration and Transnational Communities" (www.rci.rutgers.edu/~migrate1 [November 2006]).

Figure 16-2. *Remittance Senders with and without Savings in El Salvador, 2004*

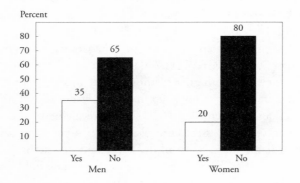

Source: See figure 16-1.

male recipients of remittances in El Salvador reported having savings compared to almost 40 percent of women recipients (see figure 16-1). Sixty-seven percent of male immigrants and 38 percent of female immigrants in this sample report holding savings. These savings can be held by the migrants in the United States or El Salvador. Approximately 35 percent of men and 20 percent of women immigrants report having been able to accumulate savings in El Salvador (see figure 16-2).

Housing in the Home and Host Country

Migration and the receipt of remittances have been strongly associated with the ability to upgrade and improve housing. The recent Human Development Report for El Salvador (UN Development Program 2005, p. 83) underscores that "remittances constitute a determining factor in the quality of the material with which housing is constructed, and moreover, in the housing conditions themselves and access to basic services such as electricity and sanitation."

Table 16-2 reinforces this assertion. Households in receipt of remittances in El Salvador have better housing stock, more rooms, are made of better quality materials, and are more likely to have access to piped water and sanitation.[11] Adding a gender dimension, female-headed households are also slightly better off with respect to the quality of the housing stock and the assets they command—a difference that is magnified when those female-headed households are also in receipt of remittances.

Data on housing for Salvadorans in the United States are not directly comparable. The market for housing and mortgages is not equivalent, nor is the housing stock itself. Figure 16-3 reports the distribution of homeownership in the United States, comparing the native-born and Salvadorans in the United States.[12] What is clear from these data is that Salvadorans have increased their homeownership significantly between 1980 and 2000, almost doubling their ownership. The equivalent data are not available for El Salvador since many people report owning their house—because they purchased the materials to build the house—without owning the land upon which the house is built. Additionally, the financial market for mortgages is not well developed in El Salvador, and few households have borrowed money through a bank to purchase a house.[13] Consequently, those who own houses and the land upon which the houses are built—especially in urban areas—have typically purchased them outright. Finally, the housing stock is not directly comparable, particularly for households in rural areas that generally occupy houses made of palm and wood, with compacted earth or concrete floors and corrugated tin roofs.

A house in the United States represents a significant financial asset. An estimated 450,000 Salvadorans in the United States owned houses in 2000; the total value of these properties was approximately U.S.$13.2 billion or approximately the equivalent of total GDP in El Salvador for that year (UN Development Program 2005).

Figure 16-4 provides a breakdown of homeownership for Salvadorans in the United States by sex and year of arrival. The respondents are the primary respondents in the PUMS 1 percent sample of the 2000 U.S. census.[14] It is clear that migrants who arrived earlier are more likely to have purchased a house:

Figure 16-3. *Homeownership, by Country of Origin, in the United States, 2000*ᵃ

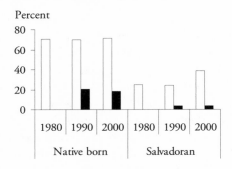

Source: Author's calculations using the PUMS 1 percent sample of the 2000 U.S. census. See Bureau of the Census, "Public-Use Microdata Samples (PUMS)" (www.census.gov/main/www/pums.html [December 2006]).

a. White bars indicate homeownership; black bars, mortgage paid.

almost 80 percent of Salvadorans who arrived in the 1950s report owning a house. This percentage declines by year of arrival, although it is clear that Salvadorans are able to obtain mortgages and purchase houses. Among those who report arriving in the 1990s, 26 percent are homeowners.

Migration, Remittances, and Social Capital

Migration both relies upon and fosters the growth of transnational social capital. But this social capital has to be renovated and maintained. Networks of migrants in the host country provide one means of securing and building social capital. These networks encompass a variety of immigrant associations, church groups and civil society organizations, political groups, and recreational groups. Some of these associations engage in activities and exchanges simultaneously in the home and host countries.

The social remittances and the political and cultural activities that occur on the periphery of these exchanges are critical for the immigrant community. In the United States, these networks and associations work to build social capital and transnational linkages by strengthening social ties and exchanging information about jobs, migration services, health care, and housing (Levitt 2001; Menjívar 2000). Likewise, the collective transfer of remittances to hometowns in the country of origin requires social capital and also helps to generate it in the process of designing and implementing projects and negotiating with home- and host-country governments and multilateral agencies. In turn, the home-

Figure 16-4. *Homeownership, by Year of Arrival in the United States, 2000*[a]

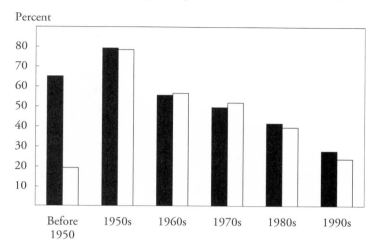

Percent

Source: See figure 16-3.
a. White bars indicate male homeownership; black bars, female.

town associations that have grown up around the collective transfer of remittances have become important campaign sites for political candidates and focal points for state actors in both host and home countries (Itzigsohn and Saucedo 2002).[15] Hometown associations provide sites for migrants to exchange information about their economic, social, and political rights in the host country. They may take on the role of advocating for the rights of the migrant community to regularize or formalize their migration status or for the receipt of state benefits such as housing, education, health care, and welfare. Similarly, these organizations and associations may also build transnational advocacy networks fostering rights awareness among immigrants and home-country affiliates.

Men and women may be incorporated into these networks differently and perform different roles in building, maintaining, and renovating transnational social capital. Although migrant women play essential roles as fundraisers, community organizers, and conveners of meetings, they may often be less prominent in decisions about how to invest the collective remittances or whether to seek counterpart funds from a development agency or governmental organization. In her study of Mexican hometown organizations, Goldring (2001) finds that women are often deprived of access to power and political capital associated with the development projects. This exclusion reflects what Pessar and Mahler (2001) term the "gendered geographies of power."

The participatory research undertaken in greater Washington among Salvadoran organizations, however, does not point to such pronounced or mutually exclusive gendered geographies of power (Gammage and others 2005). Male and female spheres of influence in the diaspora were overlapping. In the meetings that my colleagues and I attended, women were active participants and decisionmakers. Three of the four committees that we observed for over two years had women among the leadership, and their concerns and preferences clearly shaped the projects selected and the fundraising activities pursued. In the committee without women in the immediate leadership, their influence from the membership was certainly felt, and their preferences were followed in many decisionmaking forums. The distribution of tasks at fundraising events may have appeared gendered in many of the activities (Santillán 2004), with women making *pupusas* and men delivering them, or women making and serving food while men checked tickets at the door, but their spheres of influence were not mutually exclusive. In other events men shared tasks side by side with women, cleaning banana leaves, chopping potatoes, and removing chicken meat from the bones to make tamales.

From a gender perspective, while some literature suggests that hometown associations build upon and create opportunities for social capital formation for women (1998 report from the Comisión Económica para America Latina y el Caribe, cited in Mahler 1999), other literature suggests that women's participation is often limited to subordinate and supportive roles, rather than leadership and decisionmaking ones (Goldring 2001). Of the four hometown associations that participated in the greater Washington research project, however, three had women in key positions as active members of the leadership, and their role as protagonists was both apparent and meaningful.

Debt and Indebtedness

Finally, any discussion of the assets built up and drawn down in the process of migration must include an analysis of debt. Undocumented entry into the United States is costly.[16] Current estimates place the cost at between U.S.$3,000 and $8,000 depending on the type of service chosen and the extent to which the potential migrant assumes the costs of travel by air or overland through Guatemala and Mexico. A network of coyotes and travel agencies operate in El Salvador to facilitate entry into the United States.[17] The trip is time consuming, dangerous, and costly. (See Gammage and others 2005.)

> Oh, yes, there was always a *viajero* [an informal remittance courier] or a coyote who would take you to the U.S. . . . You go with who you know.

. . . My oldest sister went recently, she went without documents, she went with ____, it took several tries, she spent 3 months, but she finally got in.

—Woman, resident La Unión.

My granddaughter got there in only twenty-five days. She went with _____. She was lucky.

—Woman, resident La Unión.

My son suffered a lot. Just in crossing the border, it took him four days, and they only gave him food once. He went with a coyote from San Salvador. They were detained in Mexico, so I sent the viajero to help get him out. It costs so much. It cost us $8,000. And you suffer to pay so much money. They even have my life as a deposit!

—Woman, resident La Unión.

The cost of undocumented entry frequently indebts households and entire kinship networks. Many households sell livestock, land, and farm implements to raise the money. Frequently, the money is borrowed from local lenders and coyotes. The migrant's family usually pays half of the costs up front and owes the remainder.[18]

Yes, we gave our house and the land it is on as a guarantee, as security that we would pay. But we didn't give the papers to the coyote; no, the *prestamista* [lender] has the papers.

—Woman, resident La Unión.

Yes, you can suffer here. Especially if they [the migrants] don't find work or can't pay or forget you.

—Woman, resident La Unión.

No coyote works for free. It costs $3,000 here and the rest, $4,000 up there.

—Woman, resident La Unión.

Yes, everything is loaned. And we just go on paying bit by bit.

—Woman, resident La Unión.

Migration loans can be shared transnationally between relatives in the United States and in El Salvador. Gloria, a young woman from San Miguel who helped to pay for her brother's journey to the United States, reported that she continues to contribute to paying off the U.S.$6,500 debt that her family incurred to bring him here. Gloria's family members in the United States and in El Salvador were obligated to make debt payments on the loan and pay what was owed to the coyote over the course of two years.

A recent article in the *Washington Post* highlighting the financial costs of migrating north reported that the cost of passage to the United States in 2006 was around U.S.$6,000.[19] The same article attested to the extent of debt that households incurred in seeking to pay these high prices. The authorities, concerned that the mayor of Cara Sucia in Ahuachapán, El Salvador, was still engaged in migrant smuggling, searched his house. In so doing, they discovered the deeds to more than 200 homes that the mayor had confiscated from his clients who were unable to pay their fees.

Unfortunately, the costs of migration have not been fully researched in El Salvador. None of the national survey instruments that collect data on migration and remittances ask about the financial or other costs of migration nor the debt assumed as a result of migration. Furthermore, there is little discussion of the gendered nature of these costs. Although households frequently acquire a financial debt to leverage a journey to the United States, this debt does not represent the only cost incurred. There are the psychological and emotional costs of separation. Moreover, households typically send their best workers to the United States. The loss of young, able-bodied migrants imposes other costs upon the household and necessarily increases the responsibility of those who remain to cover household expenses, generate income, and repay debt in the absence of an immediate stream of remittances.

Further Research

Further research is required to understand how migration acts as a livelihood strategy in lower-income countries and to explore the role that migration plays in acquiring assets and transforming migrant-sending countries. Such an analysis should link households across countries and over time to uncover the multiplicity of strategies that can be deployed through risk sharing and international and intergenerational transfers. Consequently, better data sets are needed that follow households over time and attempt to track and document translocal livelihood strategies. Moreover, these data sets should be used to develop a fuller accounting of the costs and benefits of migration.

That such research should be gendered is self-evident. Men and women face different opportunities and have different entitlements and capabilities to deploy the resources they possess.[20] Any analysis of the productive use of remittances should emanate from an intimate understanding of who generates and who receives these remittances, their age, sex, labor market insertion, and ability to sustain or use this income stream.

Unfortunately, the gendered nature of savings, consumption, and asset acquisition and disposal is poorly understood at a household and intrahousehold level largely because of methodological limitations. Individuals typically live in households composed of several people who may, or may not, be related. Household members may act cooperatively or competitively in different realms of economic and social behavior. Frequently, researchers use the sex of the household head as a proxy for the gendered predisposition of an entire household to specific outcomes. Yet headship is a noisy indicator of any one household member's experience of poverty and deprivation or surplus and well-being. Not everyone in a household may be equally poor. Furthermore, not everyone in that particular household has the same set of entitlements and capabilities. Expanding a gender analysis beyond headship to include maintenance (whether more than 50 percent of the income is generated by male or female workers in a household) and the economic and demographic dependency ratio of a household can broaden understanding of the gendered nature of the constraints and opportunities a household faces as a collective.[21]

Finally, any expanded analysis of transnational asset acquisition needs to include a broader understanding of debt and indebtedness. Few survey instruments explicitly ask individuals and households about the debt they have acquired to leverage a trip north, yet indebtedness is one of the single most important challenges facing migrants today.

This snapshot of transnational asset accumulation only illustrates some of the assets that can be acquired or depleted in the process of migration. Many questions remain unanswered because of the lack of data on the costs of migration. How does time and task allocation change within the household? How has productive and reproductive work changed as a result of out-migration? Who bears the cost of debt repayment if the migrant is unsuccessful? To even begin to satisfactorily answer these and other questions will require significant additional research and analysis.

Notes

1. Assets are drawn down when their stock is depleted and the stream of benefits or income that they yield is reduced.

2. The Salvadoran National Accounts are available from the Banco Central de Reserva (www.bcr.gob.sv [December 2006]). The Public Use Microdata Sample can be obtained through the Bureau of the Census (www.census.gov/acs/www/Products/PUMS/pums 2002.htm [December 2006]).

3. This data set was developed with funding from the Ford Foundation and the Inter-American Foundation. See Rutgers, "Destination DC: Migration and Transnational Communities" (www.rci.rutgers.edu/~migrate1 [November 2006]).

4. This 2004 figure is based on estimates using U.S. census data from 2000 and the corrections made by the Mumford Center at SUNY Albany. See Lewis Mumford Center for Comparative Urban and Regional Research, "Metropolitan Racial and Ethnic Change—Census 2000" (www.albany.edu/mumford/census/index.html [November 2006]).

5. Statistics based on data from the Banco Central de Reserva.

6. Fixed assets are usually valued at cost less depreciation written off. Generally, goodwill is a rather amorphous concept embracing many features of a company's activities that could lead to superior earning power, such as company name, excellent management, an outstanding workforce, effective advertising and market penetration, and good relations with government. It is considered an asset, however, and as such is frequently valued in firm appraisals.

7. Social capital refers to the presence of extrafamilial associations and networks of civic engagement characterized by norms of reciprocity and trust that are collectively imbued with meaning and capable of capturing and facilitating a stream of political, economic, and social benefits to members or individuals accessing these resources.

8. A coyote is an intermediary contracted to facilitate undocumented entry into the United States or another host country.

9. Formal services are those that are officially registered, pay the business and income taxes applicable, and operate legally in both home and host countries. Informal services are largely unregistered and pay few or no taxes. There is likely to be a continuum between formal and informal.

10. See for example Suro (2003).

11. No attempt has been made to control for endogeneity and selection bias. It is quite possible that those households in receipt of remittances were wealthier ex ante the migration decision. Correcting for any selection bias would require panel data on households in receipt of remittances and those without remittances over time. This would enable selection of a control group with which to compare the investment decisions of remittance recipients and net out any fixed effects.

12. Households are defined by the country of birth of the primary respondent.

13. Author's calculations based on data from the 2004 EHPM (DIGESTYC 2004) reveal that less than 5 percent of households in El Salvador held a mortgage or reported that they were homeowners who were paying for the house over time.

14. Primary respondents are not necessarily household heads.

15. See Mary Beth Sheridan, "Regions' Immigrants Building a Better Life—Back Home," *Washington Post*, March 19, 2001, p. A1.

16. Documented entry into the United States is also costly but not as much as undocumented entry.

17. See note 8 for definition of "coyote."

18. A story by the *Houston Chronicle* documents the case of thirty-one Latin American men held in a motel room until payment had been made in full for their illegal passage to the United States. The men, many of whom were Central American, had paid between $1,800 and $5,000 to be smuggled to Houston. See Anne M. Kilday, "Thirty One Men Found in Motel Room," *Houston Chronicle*, November 13, 2004.

19. See Nurith C. Aizenman, "The Migrants' Mayor: Salvadoran's Path to Politics Built on Reputation for Smuggling People North," *Washington Post*, June 2, 2006, p. A13.

20. This draws on Amartya Sen's analysis of poverty in terms of a lack of entitlements and capabilities. Traditionally poverty was conceived of as a lack of access to specific resources, productive assets, and income resulting in a state of material deprivation (Sen 1999). The shift to a capabilities and entitlements analysis allows practitioners to focus on the processes that underpin or precipitate material deprivation—highlighting the causes and not just the symptoms.

21. The economic and demographic dependency ratios provide a measure of the proportion of a population or household that is composed of dependents (people who are not working and generating income or those over the age of 65 and under the age of 15).

References

Chant, Silvia, ed. 1992. *Gender and Migration in Developing Countries*. London: Belhaven Press.

DIGESTYC. 2004. *Encuesta de Hogares de Propósitos Múltiples, 2004*. San Salvador: Ministerio de Economía.

———. 2000. *Encuesta de Hogares de Propósitos Múltiples, 2000*. San Salvador: Ministerio de Economía.

Gammage, Sarah, and John Schmitt. 2004. "Los inmigrantes Mexicanos, Salvadoreños y Dominicanos en el mercado laboral Estadounidense: Las brechas de género en los años 1990 y 2000." Serie Estudios y Perspectivas 20. Distrito Federal, México: Comisión Económica para America Latina y el Caribe (June).

Gammage, Sarah, and others. 2005. "Gender, Migration and Transnational Communities." Draft report. Washington: Inter-American Foundation.

Goldring, Luin. 2001. "The Gender and Geography of Citizenship in Mexico-U.S. Transnational Spaces." *Identities* 7, no. 4: 501–37.

Hamilton, Nora, and Norma Chinchilla. 1991. "Central American Migration: A Framework for Analysis." *Latin American Research Review* 26, no. 1: 75–110.

Itzigsohn, José, and Silvia Saucedo. 2002. "Immigrant Incorporation and Sociocultural Transnationalism." *International Migration Review* 36, no. 3: 766–98.

Katz, Elizabeth. 1998. "Individual, Household and Community-Level Determinants of Migration in Ecuador: Are There Gender Differences?" Working Paper. Barnard College, Columbia University.

Landolt, Patricia. 1997. "Salvadoran Transnationalism: Towards the Redefinition of the National Community." Working Paper 18. Johns Hopkins University, Program in Comparative and International Development.

Levitt, Peggy. 2001. *The Transnational Villagers*. University of California Press.

Mahler, Sarah. 1999. "Engendering Transnational Migration: A Case Study of Salvadorans." *American Behavioral Scientist* 42, no. 4: 690–719.

Mahler, Sarah. 1995. *American Dreaming: Immigrant Life on the Margins*. Princeton University Press.

Menjívar, Cecilia. 2000. *Fragmented Ties: Salvadoran Immigrant Networks in America*. University of California Press.

Pessar, Patricia R., and Sarah Mahler. 2001. "Gender and Transnational Migration." Paper presented at the conference on Transnational Migration: Comparative Perspectives. Princeton, June 30–July 1.

Repak, Terry A. 1995. *Waiting on Washington, Central American Workers in the Nation's Capital.* Temple University Press.

Santillán, Diana. 2004. "'Service Is Like Marriage': Gender Discourse in a Salvadoran Faith-Based Organization." Destination DC Working Paper 6. George Washington University and Rutgers (December).

Sen, Amartya. 1999. *Development as Freedom.* Oxford University Press.

Suro, Roberto. 2003. "Remittance Senders and Receivers: Tracking the Transnational Channels." Grantee Report. Washington: Pew Hispanic Center.

Stanley, William. 1987. "Economic Migrants or Refugees from Violence? A Time-Series Analysis of Salvadoran Migration to the United States." *Latin American Research Review* 22, no. 1: 132–54.

UN Development Program. 2005. *Informe sobre desarrollo humano, El Salvador 2005. Una mirada al nuevo nosotros, el impacto de las migraciones.* San Salvador: Programa de Las Naciones Unidas para El Desarrollo.

World Bank. 2000. *World Development Indicators 2000.* Oxford University Press.

17

Claiming Rights:
Citizenship and the Politics of Asset Distribution

CLARE FERGUSON, CAROLINE MOSER, AND ANDY NORTON

Accepting the premise that an assets approach offers a solid basis for addressing poverty and poor people's strategies for moving out of poverty, this chapter focuses on the proposition that concepts of citizenship and rights can be used as an entry point for analyzing the political processes and power relations that constrain or enable asset accumulation and distribution. First, concepts of citizenship, rights, and power are discussed, and their links to asset accumulation are explored. It is argued that rights can be understood as a form of political capital that enables people to make claims to other types of assets. A conceptual framework is then presented for analyzing the political processes through which people contest and claim their rights. The framework builds on an exploration of how people engage with different rights regimes, from customary law through to international human rights, and with the social, administrative, and political channels through which rights are contested and implemented. Finally, the argument is made that linking assets to the concepts of citizenship and rights provides a means of understanding the institutions and

This paper builds on frameworks and analysis from "To Claim Our Rights" (Moser and Norton 2001), a paper funded by the Social Development and Livelihood Departments of the Department for International Development, London, and the Social Development Department of the World Bank, Washington, D.C.

processes that shape individual access to assets and broader asset distribution. In addition, it is argued that the internationally agreed human rights framework incorporates discourses and institutional channels that have been used to strengthen collective demand for more equitable asset distribution and can be seen as a useful source of political capital for people living in poverty.[1]

Citizenship, Power Relations, Rights, and Assets

Asset-based approaches focus on strategies that enable people living in poverty to gain access to and accumulate a range of different types of assets. This chapter draws on a classification of assets in terms of natural, physical, social, financial, and human capital that is familiar from a range of analytical work on themes of livelihoods and poverty (Moser 1998; Scoones 1998) but extends it to include political capital. Understanding the processes by which people secure these assets requires an approach that goes beyond issues of welfare and poverty reduction to address a range of concerns relating to citizenship, governance, and accountability (Moser 2006). Citizenship describes what it means to be a member of a particular political community, as well as the rights and responsibilities that identity confers. Rights resemble what Amartya Sen calls entitlements: enforceable claims on the delivery of goods, services, or protections by specific others (Sen 1981, as cited in Tilly 2002). While the terms *citizenship* and *rights* describe identities and institutions, power denotes the degree of agency that individuals or groups have to act in different societies. Unequal power relations between poor people and officials, clients and their patrons, and men and women constrain people's capacity to engage in negotiations over resources. Power relations shape the political processes of claiming rights to assets where the political is understood as "the antagonistic dimension that is inherent in human societies and which is located within the struggles of diverse social groups for power and resources" (Mouffe 1993, as cited in Hickey 2005, p. 5).

Western social and political theory traditionally emphasized structural power and the coercive capacity of the state. More recent perspectives have emphasized the ways in which "capillary" power spreads out through all aspects of everyday life, including language, bureaucratic procedures, and discourses—the structures of terms, categories, and beliefs that underpin the legitimization and control of knowledge. It is the connection between formal authority and informal relationships of power that shapes the nature of people's engagement with authorities. Governance and reform agendas generally focus on formal processes, such as decentralization and structures of representation, in the hope that this will have an impact on unequal, informal power relations (Mosse 2005). Empowerment agendas start with the individual's capabilities to engage with local institutions and have the end objective of achieving structural change.

Rights provide entry points to understanding—and potentially changing—both formal and informal power relations. Rights can be analyzed as concepts that are an important part of philosophical debates, as legally defined entities, and as entitlements that people are able to claim in their everyday lives.[2] In addition, people have locally defined ideas about rights, which may or may not be recognized by formal authorities. The progression of rights from concept or claim to legitimized entitlement is the product of struggles between different groups of people. The definition, interpretation, and implementation of rights are therefore dynamic processes that are inherently political in nature.

Rights can also be conceptualized as a form of political asset.[3] Rights, once established, create a resource that enables people to make claims to a range of other assets from specified authorities. Mobilization around rights helps to build the individual and collective political capabilities that are necessary to engage in negotiations over resources. Nijera Kori, a nongovernmental organization working in Bangladesh, aims for structural political and legal changes but takes the individual as its starting point. Many poor rural women in Bangladesh have a deep sense of powerlessness and do not know or believe that they have any rights. The organization provides women with information about their rights and helps them to reflect on what this means for their own lives. Personal change within family and community relationships is seen as a first step toward collective action for broader structural changes. Nijera Kori groups have mobilized around a range of issues from establishment of rights over local resources, including land and water reservoirs, to local government decisions that undermine the interests of the landless (Kabeer 2005).

Struggles about rights are often also about who is, or is not, a citizen and the responsibilities the state has to provide different types of resources to particular groups of people. Identification as a citizen generally strengthens individual claims to a range of assets directly from the state, such as health and education, and is also the basis of an official identity and rights in relation to labor, financial, or land and property markets. The objective of collective citizen action is often social justice and a more equitable distribution of assets among social groups. Western women's movements, for example, have unmasked the notion of supposedly universal citizenship and have challenged the differential status, rights, and political voice of women and men in relation to state, civil society, and private sector institutions (Lister 1995).

Processes of globalization and conflict have challenged understandings of the boundaries of the nation-state and, concomitantly, meanings of citizenship. In this context it has been argued that the United Nations framework of human rights, setting out states' obligations to their citizens, provides a set of international standards and an additional layer of accountability to citizen-state relations. The treaties that make up the human rights framework incorporate claims to a range of resources that, in Sen's terms, relate to human, social, and political capabilities (Sen 1997).[4] It is also possible to categorize human rights in terms of the claims to the different types of assets—human, physical, financial, social, and natural—that they represent (Moser and Norton 2001). Human rights include people's rights to health, education, social security, food, water and sanitation, labor standards, and to association and participation. All these rights can be understood as a form of political capital, as set out above, which can be used in negotiations about assets with gatekeeping authorities. The challenge for development agencies is to identify interventions that strengthen poor people's position in these contestations.

Analytical Framework for Applying a Rights Perspective to Assets

Rights can be utilized at three different levels in relation to development interventions. These levels can be categorized as normative, analytical, and operational (Moser and Norton 2001). Development organizations that have stated that they are adopting a rights-based approach have taken human rights standards and principles as their normative baseline. Reviews suggest, however, that among development agencies, principles have not been translated into operational change (Piron 2005; Uvin 2004). While the value of human rights as a set of guiding norms may seem self-evident to human rights experts, in order to engage development practitioners in this agenda and gain operational traction, it is necessary to demonstrate the analytical links between rights and poverty. Conceptualizing rights as a form of political capital helps to clarify how rights can be used by people living in poverty as a resource to negotiate access to assets and claim more equitable asset distribution. The analytical framework below provides a means of identifying entry points for interventions that support poor people's claims.

Institutional Channels and Contestation

The framework developed here addresses the political processes and power relations that constrain or enable asset accumulation. It builds on the institutional channels through which people can contest their claims and rights. These channels are represented in schematic form, looking first at the vertical connections between different legal systems, from local to international, and then examining the linkages to the political, social, and bureaucratic channels through which rights are implemented. Each of these arenas represents a channel through which people can negotiate access to assets, individually or collectively, with gatekeeping authorities.

LEGAL STRUCTURE: MULTIPLE LEVELS OF SOCIOLEGAL AUTHORITY. Legal systems are the primary structures of authority that grant legitimacy to the definition of people's rights. The meaning of "legal" in this context is derived from the social theory concept of law as "social process" rather than solely as text or formal legal structures (Harris 1996). From this perspective law is understood to encompass informal as well as formalized codes and mechanisms of dispute resolution, and to refer to the operation of a plurality of different structures of legal authority in any particular context.

Local level studies suggest that legal pluralism is a messy reality, where there are no rigid boundaries between the various legal forums and where different principles of legitimacy and ideas of the basis for claims are implemented. Each layer has associated structures of social and political authority, which may not have an explicitly legal appearance or rationale (such as kinship elders, local elites, and political leaders). In any one instance, the different operating layers of the sociolegal regime are also associated with different rights, systems for determining and interpreting those rights, and systems for making claims and resolving disputes.

This can best be illustrated by a regional example. In most southern and eastern African countries, informal, local level means of dispute settlement, including kinship mechanisms, shape social norms, practices, and processes—or the "living law." In some instances the state delegates powers to local level mechanisms or traditional authorities to adjudicate customary law, the officially recognized version of traditional legal norms. Formal state courts may also draw on customary law in certain contexts. In addition, each state has its own formalized national legal code, encompassing both statutory and common law elements.[5] Constitutional law is the highest law in a country and usually can only be changed by the legislative body. To these national and subnational systems, legal regimes operating at the global and regional levels can be added. The European Court of Human Rights, for example, increasingly imposes legal standards, derived from the globally generated agreements of the major human rights conventions, on countries within its jurisdiction.

This complex layering of different rights associated with different norms and claims can be categorized in terms of rights regimes: a system of rights that derives from a particular regulatory order or source of authority. This is depicted in table 17-1, which identifies rights regimes at different levels and links them

Table 17-1. *Rights Regimes Analysis*

Social and political contestation	Rights regime	Forms of rights and domain	Level of operation; institutional framework and authority structures	Legal and administrative implementation
↑ Livelihood and social groups seeking to make claims on assets. Capacity to make claims and influence rights regimes depends on social identity—gender, caste, class—and the authority and power that this confers. ↓	International human rights law	Human rights (economic, social, cultural, political, legal, civil, labor standards). Universal application.	International, global level. Implemented and monitored through UN intergovernmental processes.	↑ Rights regimes implemented through the operation of the legal system and the allocation of resources and administration of service. ↓
	Regional law	Human rights (as above). Applies to regional populations.	International, regional level. Increasingly with statutory powers of enforcement, for example, via European Court of Human Rights.	
	Constitutional law (for example, Bill of Rights)	National constitutional rights (mostly civil and political—starting to include economic and social through influence of human rights [South Africa]).	National level. Enforced through constitutional courts, national legal mechanisms.	
	Statutory law (civil law)	Statutory rights (conferred by the national framework of criminal, commercial, and other law).	National or local level (through devolved local government enacting bylaws). Enforced through formal legal system.	
	Religious law	Religious rights and norms (mostly operating in the domestic sphere—under some conditions considerably extended).	Religious systems of law can operate at multiple levels— global, regional, national, and local. Forms of authority and enforcement depend on relation with the state.	
	Customary law	Customary rights (mostly referring to kinship and resource rights). Not usually written down. Specific to localities and social and ethnic groups.	Local level (generally in colonial or postcolonial states only). Enforced through structures of customary authority (for example, chiefs).	
	Living law	Informal rights (mostly kinship and resource rights) and norms of behavior. Applies to localities through varying cultures (including institutional cultures).	Microlevel. No formal incorporation into national legal systems. Nonetheless, local elites may be able to co-opt elements of the state to help enforce elements of living law. Living law can also be taken as describing the norms of behavior operating within bureaucracies (governments, donor agencies).	

with associated domains or authority structures. While rights regimes operate at different levels, the content of rights may be passed from one level to another. Different levels of authority confer power on other levels—with the nation-state being by far the most powerful point of articulation, conferring authority both upward (through regional and global intergovernmental agreements) and downward (for example, on customary law systems). Each rights regime may influence outcomes at the microlevel directly. For example, the right to education—established at the international level—can lead directly to changes in the implementation of local services.

Interaction between legal systems is the product of political struggle. In many sub-Saharan African countries, the codification of customary law was one of the instruments of indirect rule by which colonial governments attempted to maintain control over rural African populations, instituting rigid inequities based on differential status and identity (Chanock 1985; Mamdani 1996). Once embedded in local social practices and authorities, these systems have proved difficult to shift. Customary law and traditional authorities remain more relevant in many sub-Saharan societies than national law and its associated institutions.

Where they are able to, those people who are disadvantaged by customary law—often rural women—draw on the values, norms, and institutions of different levels of the law to strengthen and maximize their claims within local systems (Stewart 1996). Strategies to engage with different levels are pursued by organizations, as well as individuals, seeking to establish new claims and contest existing entitlements. International law, including human rights law, and international institutions may appear remote from the lives of people living in poverty in developing countries. Nonetheless, human rights standards of equality and nondiscrimination provide a potentially useful resource in struggles around poverty because they place an emphasis on meeting the rights of the poorest first and ensuring that minimum standards of well-being are met regardless of impact upon growth.

The advocacy for homeworkers undertaken by the Self-Employed Women's Association (SEWA) of India demonstrates how local experience can feed into global rights agreements, which in turn serve to reinforce rights at the local level. SEWA was a leading actor in a global coalition of nongovernmental organizations, community groups, and sympathetic trade unions and governments that successfully lobbied the International Labour Organization to pass the Convention on Home Work in 1996. This corrected a severe form of exclusion through which homeworkers worldwide had lacked legal recognition as workers and were denied most of the rights of minimum pay, working conditions, and social protection. While only four countries have ratified the Convention so far, others have adopted the Convention's recommendation regarding the formulation of a national policy on homeworking. Even where the new global normative framework has not been codified in national law, it is helping to shape discourse and policy regarding the livelihoods of a previously marginalized group (Moser and Norton 2001).

In many countries human rights standards are incorporated into constitutions and national level legislation. The extent to which constitutional and statutory law provides opportunities for poor people to claim their rights depends on the accessibility, effectiveness, and reliability of a country's system of justice. In many developing countries, corrupt and ineffective justice systems serve to undermine, rather than uphold, the rights of poor people. In South Africa the constitution entrenches rights to housing, access to health care, sufficient food and water, social security, and education. The exceptional feature of the South African constitution, however, is the establishment of institutions that enable cases to be brought and resources to be mobilized on behalf of individuals and groups, including children, who lack the capacity to pursue a legal case for themselves. Provisions allowing public interest litigation have been used by civil society organizations to bring claims for the violation of socioeconomic rights before the South African Constitutional Court. These claims have been upheld in two landmark judgments regarding the right to housing and the right to health (Vizard 2006).

Legal action by itself is rarely enough to ensure the realization of rights, even where people who are poor are able to access the justice system, but it can provide a platform for political action. The Right to Food campaign in India began with the submission to the Indian Supreme Court in April 2001 by the People's Union for Civil Liberties, demanding that the country's food stocks should be used to protect people from starvation. This petition was based on the existence of the fundamental "right to life" enshrined in the Indian constitution. When it became clear that the legal process was not sufficient to ensure action, a range of other activities were initiated, including public hearings, media advocacy, rallies, and lobbying of politicians. The campaign now includes demands for a national "employment guarantee scheme," universal midday meals in primary schools, and implementation of nutrition-related programs for children.[6]

Rights enshrined in legislation can provide a predictability that encourages demand and local level social mobilization to make claims for assets and services. The 1977 Maharashtra Employment Guarantee Act obliges the government of Maharashtra to operate an employment guarantee scheme for the rural poor. The Maharashtra Employment Guarantee Scheme (MEGS) is a public works program implemented on a large scale throughout the state of 79 million people. It has been estimated that over the 1980s it provided an annual average of nine work days for every member of the rural workforce, with 40 to 50 percent of all MEGS employment going to women. The longevity and relative success of the scheme can be attributed to the basis of the MEGS in legislative rights. The stability offered by legislation has meant that activist organizations and workers have mobilized around the scheme to demand their rights and have, consequently, ensured that MEGS survives and continues to evolve in response to the changing needs of the rural poor (Joshi and Moore 2001).

SOCIAL, POLITICAL, AND ADMINISTRATIVE CHANNELS FOR CONTESTING CLAIMS. Rights are fulfilled—or withheld—by a range of social, administrative, and political institutions. People make individual claims on assets in everyday interactions in the household and community and also mobilize to make collective claims on services or governance institutions. People have varying degrees of power and status and, consequently, negotiating ability in these different arenas. For instance, women may have greater capacity to negotiate in local political forums in relation to bureaucrats than within the household in relation to their husbands (Petchesky and Judd 1998). Three key "moments" shaping the delivery of rights can be identified: definition, interpretation, and implementation (Fraser 1989). The best entry point for action depends on context. Research on women's land rights in Uganda, for example, suggests that in some cases it may be more effective to strengthen women's voices in the processes of implementation and administration of existing legislation than to start by trying to change the definition of women's land rights through legislative reform.[7]

Most political communities allow for formal mechanisms of participation and leverage, such as voting for legislators and joining political parties. Politicians' decisions shape the policies and legislation that determine whether the state or the market should provide particular resources, the level of state provision, and the distribution of entitlements among different groups of people. Citizens may influence these decisions through advocacy, party politics, or direct political participation. Decentralization programs, such as the *panchayat raj* reforms in India, which created a system of elected authorities down to the village level, have been seen as a key mechanism for increasing poor people's engagement in political decisions. The conditions that strengthen citizen participation in local governance include a clear legal framework setting out the institution's mandate, resources to enable people to participate, and links with other organizations and individuals both at the grassroots level and in government structures (Shankland 2006).

Even where the legislature makes a positive decision to support people's entitlements to assets, the policies, decisions, and actions of the executive will shape how those rights are fulfilled. It is often local level service providers that determine which entitlements are delivered or withheld, making the interactions between citizens and "street-level bureaucrats" central to the conversion of abstract rights into concrete reality (Lipsky 1980). In Zimbabwe concepts of reproductive rights, as defined at the international conferences in Beijing and Cairo, have been incorporated into family planning policies and programs, but local community-based distributors of contraceptives were reluctant to provide services to women who had not already given birth and were, therefore, unmarried according to Shona norms (Ferguson 1999). In the absence of clear accountability mechanisms, it is often the living law that determines how entitlements are interpreted and delivered through administrative structures.

Different mechanisms have been used to clarify the levels and standards of services to which people are entitled, to increase accountability, and to empower citizens in relation to public organizations. These include the use of benchmarks, codes of conduct or citizens' charters, and report cards for identifying service standards and monitoring their implementation.[8] Such approaches may be more effective when mechanisms for monitoring and redress are embedded in higher-level institutions.[9] For example, section 27 of the South African constitution enshrines the right of access to sufficient water. The Water Department introduced legislation that recognized this right, providing a more detailed definition in terms of people's entitlements. It quantified the minimum water supply at twenty-five liters per person per day, available within 200 meters of the dwelling and at a flow rate from the outlet of not less than ten liters per minute. The department set itself a medium-term target of supplying fifty to sixty liters of water per capita per day. By establishing concrete benchmarks, the government of South Africa aimed to facilitate implementation of the right to water, monitored by the South Africa Human Rights Commission and civil society organizations (International Human Rights Internship Program 2000).

Access to information and transparency are critical factors in ensuring that services are delivered and standards are met. Information is necessary for individuals dealing with service providers and authorities as well as for public accountability. Rights to information have been central to citizens' budget initiatives, which aim to influence and monitor the expenditure of public funds on services.[10] Fundar, a research and advocacy project organization based in Mexico City, has used budget analysis, within a human rights framework, to demonstrate how the Mexican government is failing to fulfill its obligations to meet citizens' right to health (Hofbauer, Blyberg, and Krafchik 2004). While article 4 of the Mexican constitution stipulates that every person has the right to health protection, Fundar's analysis indicates that expenditure is skewed toward "rightholders"—families that have at least one person in the formal economy, paying taxes and social security fees. A far smaller proportion of the health budget is directed to health facilities for the "open population"—the 50 percent of the population who are unemployed or informally employed, therefore including the most vulnerable members of society.

Table 17-2 presents a typology for identifying the institutional channels through which claims can be made, the types of claims that relate to each institutional domain, and the methods of citizen action that can be used to make those claims.

The following questions help identify the political processes through which bottom-up claims to assets may be contested.

Table 17-2. *Channels of Contestation: Definition, Interpretation, and Implementation of Rights*

Institutional channel	Types of claims	Method of citizen action
Political system	Processes of identifying new rights and securing changes to formally recognized freedoms and entitlements, for example, women's movement demand for reproductive rights Negotiations over how entitlements should be implemented—for example, through private or public sector provision—and distributed	Voting in formal elections and referendums (national and local) Lobbying for change through representational system Media reporting on government action and budgets Public hearings (for example, 1998 South Africa poverty hearings) Open advocacy (intermediate groups acting on behalf of people seeking to assert claims), use of media, and campaigning Informal and invisible advocacy through contacts (for example, interactions with sympathetic officials) Participation in local council meetings and committees Open struggle
Legal system	Process of interpretation and implementation of legally recognized rights, often relating to physical, natural, and financial assets (for example, land) but also to social assets, for example, regarding discrimination, marital relations, and human assets (such as education and health-related claims)	Legal action and challenge at local, national, and international levels Engagement with law enforcement agencies: disputes may be settled through local police rather than the courts Appeal to arbitration and monitoring services, such as human rights commissions, ombudspersons, industrial tribunals, and arbitration services, which monitor and regulate public services and private sector standards Engagement in formal human rights treaty monitoring processes, that is, state reports to treaty monitoring bodies
Policy channels	Negotiation over interpretation and distribution of public provision of entitlements, often most directly relating to human assets (for example, provision of public services)	Engagement in international policy processes, such as the Rio and Beijing conferences Engagement in policy and planning processes at national and local levels such as PRSPs, SWAps, and local governance planning, often about public service priorities (for example, levels and quality of health and education provision)[a] Engagement in budget processes—resource allocation for policy priorities (for example, participatory budgeting)
Administrative channels	Negotiation over interpretation and implementation of entitlements, often relating to human and social assets	Individual claims on resources and services, such as everyday interactions with health workers Collective monitoring of public services and provision through report cards, citizen service groups, benchmarking, monitoring codes of conduct, and social audits
Social channels	Negotiation over access to natural resources (such as land) and social resources (such as labor)	Informal negotiation over entitlements to resources Informal debates about gender roles and responsibilities including terms of marital contract
Private sector channels	Negotiation over interpretation and implementation of private sector related entitlements, often relating to human assets (such as labor rights) and access to financial assets	Union and civil society action over labor standards and collective bargaining for wages with employees Engagement with banks and other organizations to ensure credit provision Engagement in defining and monitoring voluntary codes of conduct Consumer action, such as boycotting products or monitoring quality of services Shareholder action

a. PRSPs, poverty reduction strategy papers; SWAps, sectorwide approaches.

WHAT IS BEING CLAIMED? To access assets, people need the capacity to make successful claims and the ability to achieve positive responses from regulatory bodies. Poor people's strategies to access assets incorporate both direct claims and broader strategies to influence policy design and implementation in favor of redistributive equity (Webster and Engberg-Pedersen 2002). Direct claims commonly include rights to manage and use common property resources, access to a market stall, permission to use a dwelling as the site for a small enterprise, access to credit, better working conditions, or access to health and education services. The institutional channels for such direct claims on assets are likely to include administrative, private sector, and social channels. Direct claims to assets are often the basis for building grassroots organizational capacity and social mobilization for broader structural change.

WHO IS MAKING THE CLAIM?   The key axes of social identity and inequality—such as gender, age, citizenship, ethnicity, class, and caste—shape people's opportunities for contestation and offer differing degrees of purchase on negotiations at different levels. The most disadvantaged are the least likely to have the political space to contest claims to assets and have the most to lose in entering into negotiations with any authority. Where those contesting their rights are not part of a political constituency, the outcomes are unlikely to be very positive. Where people from the middle classes see their interests as being linked to the reduction of poverty, there may be more possibilities for pro-poor political alliances (Moore and Putzel 1999). The idea of human rights provides a potentially powerful discourse for creating alliances because it focuses on universal rights, such as the right to education, rather than simply the rights of the poor (Archer 2005). In Peru the Department for International Development (DFID) helped strengthen the spaces for civil society engagement with political parties through support for multiparty discussions about party governance and sponsorship of party-membership events around issues of poverty and social deprivation (DFID 2005).

ON WHOM IS THE CLAIM BEING MADE, AND WHAT IS THE NATURE OF THE OBLIGATION?   The means by which poor people can assert claims depend on the type of organization on which the claim is being made, whether that organization recognizes any obligation to respond, and its position within global hierarchies of power. In many situations where claims have been successfully asserted, civil society organizations have been critical in bridging the levels of power and helping poor people to negotiate.[11]

Increasingly, the organizations with which poor people must engage include international actors: private companies, as well as governmental and nongovernmental development organizations. Many international organizations have decisionmaking structures that are neither transparent nor accessible. A key issue for development organizations is how to make their own procedures more accountable to the people they are supposed to support. This is not always straightforward, as such organizations may have conflicting duties and chains of accountability to constituencies in their home countries (Eyben and Ferguson 2004).

Conclusion

The institutions and political and power relations that shape poor people's capacity to claim entitlements to assets are context specific and complex and cannot be comprehensively explored in one chapter. The goal here has been to use a framework that analyzes institutions and relations of power and authority to identify key questions concerning how poor people can best pursue claims on rights to different types of assets. The interconnections between the operation of local, national, and international level legal structures have been emphasized as well as their linkages to the social, administrative, and political institutions through which rights are delivered. These processes and channels form important elements of the political space for the poor, determining the types and ranges of possibilities open to poor people, or their representatives, for pursuing poverty reduction (Webster and Engberg-Pedersen 2002).[12] While particular sociopolitical contexts shape people's possibilities and strategies for moving out of poverty, rights can be understood as a form of political capital that can be used in many different societies to strengthen claims to a range of assets.

The human rights framework offers a set of resources that is particularly useful for the struggles of people living in poverty because it combines a set of individual entitlements to different assets with discourses about equality and equitable asset distribution. Human rights have consequently been used as tools for empowering individuals and in the mobilization of collective action that challenges decisions about particular distributions of assets. While we do not present specfic operational recommendations from these conclusions, a number of general observations can be drawn from the use of a rights and citizen perspective on asset accumulation.

Struggles for poor people's rights often start at the local level with direct claims to assets. Such struggles form a key entry point and foundation for building poor people's capacity to make claims through a focus on the confidence, knowledge, and organizational capabilities of the individuals involved. Without this kind of foundation, it is unlikely that people will be able to develop the capacity to challenge authority structures and engage in collective action as citizens.

The analysis of institutional channels highlights the central importance of building relationships that link different kinds of organizations at all levels, from local to global. To link local action to decisionmaking structures at regional, national, and global levels requires a strategic approach to skills, staff, and structures. The example of SEWA demonstrates how a membership organization has been able to develop relationships and capabilities to influence policy processes at state, national, and global levels. For a major donor agency, the corresponding challenge is to develop the relationships at the country level that enable them to play a facilitating role in strengthening poor people's capacity to make claims as citizens. The work of DFID in Peru illustrates the central importance of building and maintaining a range of alliances (DFID 2005).

A focus on rights and citizenship reemphasizes the importance of the state not just as a competent manager of resources but as a set of arenas and spaces for political contestation. This suggests that development organizations could focus more of their support on policy mechanisms that strengthen poor people's capacity to make claims as citizens—including identity registration processes, mechanisms for increasing political representation of marginalized groups, and political literacy campaigns. It also points to the dangers of actions that diminish poor people's political space, including attempts to control policy processes by defining issues, such as the respective roles of market and state, as developmental rather than political and placing obstacles between civil society organizations and potential political partners.

Notes

1. This paper does not set out to define or evaluate the utility of rights-based approaches to development.

2. See Gunsteren (1978) for a discussion of these categorizations in relation to citizenship.

3. Hickey (2005) discusses the relative utility of concepts of political capital, political capabilities, and political space.

4. See Vizard (2006) for a review of Sen's contribution to human rights.

5. See Whitehead (2001).

6. See "Right to Food Campaign" (www.righttofoodindia.org [November 2006]).

7. Personal communication to Andy Norton from Ann Whitehead, professor of social anthropology, University of Sussex, 2001.

8. The effectiveness of these mechanisms depends upon a number of conditions including the capacity of civil society to organize and engage as well as commitment and capacity within public institutions (see Goetz and Gaventa 2001).

9. Plant (1998) makes this case in relation to the U.K.'s citizen charter initiative.

10. For an overview of citizens' budget initiatives, see Norton and Elson (2002).

11. See Hughes, Wheeler, and Eyben (2005) for a discussion of the power constraints on the capacity of development organizations to support struggles for rights.

12. Blackburn and others (2005) note that Moser and Norton's "channels of contestation" (Moser and Norton 2001) operationalize the concept of political space.

References

Archer, Robert. 2005. "What Can Be Gained and What Might Be Lost through Adopting a Rights-Based Approach to Pro-Poor Development?" Paper presented at the conference on Winners and Losers from Rights-Based Approaches to Development. University of Manchester, February 21–22.

Blackburn, James, and others. 2005. "Operationalising the Rights Agenda: Participatory Rights Assessment in Peru and Malawi." *Institute of Development Studies Bulletin* 36, no. 1: 91–99.

Chanock, Martin. 1985. *Law, Custom and Social Order.* Cambridge University Press.

DFID. 2005. *Alliances against Poverty. DFID's Experience in Peru, 2000–2005.* London.

Eyben, Rosalind, and Clare Ferguson. 2004. "Can Donors Be More Accountable to Poor People?" In *Inclusive Aid: Changing Power and Relationships in International Development*, edited by Leslie Groves and Rachel Hinton, pp.163–80. London: Earthscan.

Ferguson, Clare. 1999. "Reproductive Rights and Citizenship: Family Planning in Zimbabwe." Ph.D. dissertation, London School of Economics, Department of Anthropology.

Fraser, Nancy. 1989. *Unruly Practices: Power, Discourse and Gender in Contemporary Social Theory.* Polity Press: Cambridge.

Goetz, Anne-Marie, and John Gaventa. 2001. "Bringing Citizen Voice and Client Focus into Service Delivery." Working Paper 138. Brighton: Institute of Development Studies.

Gunsteren, Herman van. 1978. "Notes on a Theory of Citizenship." In *Democracy, Consensus and Social Contract*, edited by Pierre Birnbaum, Jack Lively, and Geraint Parry, pp. 9–36. London: Sage Publications.

Harris, Olivia, ed. 1996. *Inside and Outside the Law: Anthropological Studies of Authority and Ambiguity.* London: Routledge.

Hickey, Sam. 2005. "Capturing the Political? The Role of Political Analysis in the Multi-Disciplining of Development Studies." Paper GPRG-WPS-006. Oxford: Global Poverty Research Group.

Hofbauer, Helena, Ann Blyberg, and Warren Krafchik. 2004. *Dignity Counts. A Guide to Using Budget Analysis to Advance Human Rights.* Mexico City and Washington: Fundar, International Budget Project, and International Human Rights Internship Program.

Hughes, Alexandra, Joanna Wheeler, and Rosalind Eyben. 2005. "Rights and Power: The Challenge for International Development Agencies." *Institute of Development Studies Bulletin* 36, no 1: 63–72.

International Human Rights Internship Program. 2000. *Circle of Rights. Economic, Social and Cultural Rights Activism—A Training Resource.* Washington: Institute of International Education.

Joshi, Anuradha, and Mick Moore. 2001. "The Mobilising Potential of Anti-Poverty Programmes." Discussion Paper 374. Brighton: Institute of Development Studies.

Kabeer, Naila. 2005. "Growing Citizenship from the Grassroots: Nijera Kori and Social Mobilisation in Bangladesh." In *Inclusive Citizenship. Meanings and Expressions*, edited by Naila Kabeer, pp. 181–98. London: Zed Books.

Lipsky, Michael. 1980. *Street-Level Bureaucracy.* New York: Russell Sage.

Lister, Ruth. 1995. "Dilemmas in Engendering Citizenship." *Economy and Society* 24, no. 1: 1–40.

Mamdani, Mahmood. 1996. *Citizen and Subject.* Princeton University Press.

Moore, Mick, and James Putzel. 1999. "Thinking Strategically about Politics and Poverty." Working Paper 101. Brighton: Institute of Development Studies.

Moser, Caroline, and Andy Norton. 2001. "To Claim Our Rights: Livelihood Security, Human Rights and Sustainable Development." Concept paper. London: Overseas Development Institute.

Moser, Caroline. 1998. "The Asset Vulnerability Framework: Reassessing Urban Poverty Reduction Strategies." *World Development* 26, no. 1: 1–19.

———. 2006. "Asset-Based Approaches to Poverty Reduction in a Globalized Context." Paper presented at the Brookings Institution–Ford Foundation workshop on Asset-Based Approaches to Poverty Reduction in a Globalized Context. Washington, June 27–28.

Mosse, David. 2005. "Power Relations and Poverty Reduction." In *Power, Rights and Poverty: Concepts and Connections*, edited by R. Alsop, pp. 51–67. Washington and London: World Bank and DFID.

Mouffe, Chantal. 1993 *The Return of the Political*. London: Verso.

Norton, Andy, and Diane Elson. 2002. "What's Behind the Budget? Politics, Rights and Accountability in the Budget Process." London: Overseas Development Institute.

Petchesky, Rosalind B., and Karen Judd, eds. 1998. *Negotiating Reproductive Rights. Women's Perspectives across Countries and Cultures*. London: Zed Books.

Piron, Laure-Helene. 2005. "Rights-Based Approaches and Bilateral Aid Agencies: More than a Metaphor?" *Institute of Development Studies Bulletin* 36, no. 1: 19–30.

Plant, Raymond. 1998. "Citizenship, Rights, Welfare." In *Social Policy and Social Justice*, edited by Jane Franklin, pp. 57–72. Cambridge: Polity Press.

Scoones, Ian. 1998. "Sustainable Rural Livelihoods: A Framework for Analysis." Working Paper 72. Brighton: Institute of Development Studies.

Sen, Amartya K. 1981. *Poverty and Famines: An Essay on Entitlement and Deprivation*. Oxford: Clarendon.

———. 1997 "Editorial: Human Capital and Human Capability." *World Development* 25, no. 12: 1959–61.

Shankland, Alex. 2006. "Making Space for Citizens." *Institute of Development Studies Policy Briefing*, issue 27 (March).

Stewart, Anne. 1996. "Should Women Give Up on the State? The African Experience." In *Women and the State*, edited by Shirin M. Rai and Geraldine Livesey, pp. 23–44. London: Taylor and Francis.

Tilly, Charles. 2002 *Stories, Identities, and Political Change*. Lanham, Md.: Rowman and Littlefield.

Uvin, Peter. 2004. *Human Rights and Development*. Bloomfield, Conn.: Kumarian Press.

Vizard, Polly. 2006. *Poverty and Human Rights. Sen's "Capability Perspective" Explored*. Oxford University Press.

Webster, Neils, and Lars Engberg-Pedersen, eds. 2002. *In the Name of the Poor. Contesting Political Space for Poverty Reduction*. London: Zed Books.

Whitehead, Ann. 2001. "Policy Discourses on Women's Land Rights in Sub-Saharan Africa: The Return to 'Customary Law' and the Prospects for Achieving Gender Justice." Draft paper presented at the Association of Social Anthropologists' conference on Anthropological Perspectives on Rights, Claims and Entitlements. University of Sussex, March 30–April 2.

Contributors

Lael Brainard
Brookings Institution

Michael R. Carter
University of Wisconsin

Monique Cohen
Microfinance Opportunities

Sarah Cook
Institute of Development Studies, Sussex

Héctor Cordero-Guzmán
Baruch College, CUNY

Lilianne Fan
Oxfam

Pablo Farias
Ford Foundation

Andrew Felton
Federal Deposit Insurance Corporation

Clare Ferguson
Department for International Development
(formerly with)

Sarah Gammage
Rutgers University

Anirudh Krishna
Duke University

Amy Liu
Brookings Institution

Vijay Mahajan
BASIX, India

Caroline Moser
Brookings Institution

Paula Nimpuno-Parente
Ford Foundation, South Africa

Andy Norton
World Bank

Manuel Orozco
Inter-American Dialogue

Victoria Quiroz-Becerra
New School University

Dennis Rodgers
London School of Economics

Andrés Solimano
United Nations—ECLAC

Pamela Young
Microfinance Opportunities

Index